Ethics

Ethics

DISCOVERING RIGHT AND WRONG

Louis P. Pojman
University of Mississippi

WADSWORTH PUBLISHING COMPANY
Belmont, California
A Division of Wadsworth, Inc.

Philosophy Editor: *Ken King*
Editorial Assistant: *Michelle Palacio*
Production Editor: *Angela Mann*
Managing Designer: *Carolyn Deacy*
Designer: *Wendy Calmenson, The Book Company*
Compositor: *Karen Harding*
Cover Design: *Laurie Anderson*

The painting on the cover, The Death of Socrates *by Jacques Louis David, shows Socrates carrying out his own execution by taking the poison hemlock as described in Plato's dialogue* Crito *in 399 B.C. Socrates had been unjustly condemned to death by an Athenian court for corrupting the youth and not honoring the Athenian deities. Offered a way to escape by his friends, he reasons that it would be immoral to accept their offer. Being the first person in recorded history to put philosophy to work in the area of morals, Socrates is called the "Father of Ethics." Copyright © 1980. By the Metropolitan Museum of Art.*

Printed in the United States of America   49

1 2 3 4 5 6 7 8 9 10— 94 93 92 91 90

Library of Congress Cataloging in Publication Data

Pojman, Louis P.
    Ethics: discovering right and wrong/Louis P. Pojman.
        p.   cm.
    Includes bibliographical references.
    1. Ethics. I. Title.
BJ1012.P65   1990
170—dc20   89-16660
                                                          CIP

ISBN 0-534-12378-3

To Trudy

CONTENTS

PREFACE

In all the world and in all of life there is nothing more important to determine than what is right. Whatever the matter which lies before us calling for considera- tion, whatever the question asked us or the problem to be solved, there is some settlement of it which will meet the situation and is to be sought . . . . Wherever there is a decision to be made or any deliberation is in point, there is a right determination of the matter in hand which is to be found and adhered to, and other possible commitments which would be wrong and are to be avoided.

C. I. LEWIS, THE GROUND AND THE NATURE OF RIGHT

W HAT IS IT TO live a morally good life? Why is morality important? Are moral principles valid only as they depend on cultural approval, or are there universal moral truths? How should I live my life? Are there intrinsic values? What is the best moral theory? Can we derive moral values from facts? Why should I be moral? Is there a right answer to every problem in life? What is the relationship of religion to morality?

These sorts of questions have concerned me for several years, and I believe that they should concern all thoughtful people. Sadly, many people in our society, including university students, have conflicting ideas about morality. On the one hand, many claim in questionnaires and class conversations that they are moral relativists, which they suppose promotes tolerance. At the same time, they report that they believe in absolute religious authority or they answer no to such questions as "Is it ever morally permissible to have an abortion, except to save a mother's life?" and "Is capital punishment ever morally justified?" They often hold uncritical de-ontological, utilitarian, or egoist positions without being aware of the problems inherent in their positions. In sum, they are very far from having an articulate moral theory of their own to match their understanding of literature, science, or math, or even of basketball. Yet morality is more important than any of these subjects, for it goes to the heart of what it means to live in the right way.

I am convinced that the subject of ethics is of paramount importance to us at the end of the 20th century. With the onset of pluralism and the loss of confidence in traditional authorities, a rational approach to ethics is vital if we are to survive and flourish. Indeed, I disagree with many ethicists, including G. E. Moore in *Principia Ethica* (1903) and C. D. Broad in *Five Types of Ethical Theory* (1930), who dismiss ethics as merely theoretical.

A knowledge of ethical theory has enormous practical benefits. It can free us from prejudice and dogmatism. It sets forth comprehensive systems from which to orient our individual judgments. It carves up the moral landscape so that we can sort out the issues in order to think more clearly and confidently about moral problems. It helps us clarify in our minds just how our principles and values relate to one another, and, most of all, it gives us some guidance in how we should live.

Having taught ethical theory for ten years, I have long felt the need for a textbook that challenged the student to develop his or her own moral theory, that both emphasized the importance of the enterprise and could serve as a guide for intelligent young people. The available textbooks were too light, sweeping over important distinctions, or too heavy, getting bogged down in needless formalization, or too narrow, omitting a serious discussion of the virtues, the relationship between ethics and religion, or the nature of values.

This work is intended for undergraduates in ethics courses. I have tried to write in an interesting, conversational manner, raising key theoretical questions and analyzing them fairly closely without unnecessary jargon or technicalities. I have opened some chapters with examples of moral problems, or I have included moral problems in the discussion or at the end of each chapter, so that students can apply the theoretical discussion to real issues. This book is comprehensive, covering the major issues in contemporary moral theory, including a discussion of both classical and contemporary renditions of the problems. It has an outline similar to that of my anthology, *Ethics: Classical and Contemporary Readings* (Wadsworth, 1989), with which this book may be used as a companion and commentary. The chapters can be taught in any order. For example, many teachers, including myself at times, like to cover the relation of religion to morality, including the divine command theory, early in the course. Nothing will be lost by going directly from Chapter 1 to Chapter 10. Chapter 4 ("Value") is related to Chapter 9 ("Morality and Self-Interest"), and thus they may be read in sequence.

I have striven to be fair to both sides of every question, but whenever I offer my own solutions to problems (in a single-author text this is virtually inevitable), I do so in the spirit of openness to correction and fallibility, leaving the reader to form his or her own judgment on the matter. Philosophers will note that the title of this book reflects a fundamental disagreement with J. L. Mackie, who entitled his influential work on ethics *Ethics: Inventing Right and Wrong*. The late John Mackie was my esteemed teacher at Oxford University, and I learned much from him. I think, however, that his starting point is misleading. Ethics is more like a discovery than an invention, hence my title.

The reader will note that I raise more questions than I answer. I do this in part because what is important in philosophy is that the individual work out his or her own solutions to problems and in part because I am unsure of many of the solutions myself. Study questions and a short usable bibliography accompany each chapter. A glossary appears at the end of the book.

Michael Beaty, Bill Lawhead, Laura Purdy, and Bruce Russell were very helpful in offering me trenchant criticisms on several chapters of this book. My students in ethical theory classes at the University of Mississippi were a challenging sounding board for many of my arguments. Of special mention are John Ates, Chris Bradford, Laura Burrell, Scott Morris, and Clayton Overton. Ronald F. Duska, Rosemont College; Peter List, Oregon State University; Peter Vallentyne, Virginia Commonwealth University; and Stephen Griffith, Lycoming College, reviewed the manuscript and helped me improve the finished text. Angela Mann, production editor, Alan Titche, copy editor, and Carolyn Deacy, designer, did an excellent job of correcting and designing the manuscript to bring this work to its present form.

I owe a debt of gratitude to Ken King for encouraging me to write the work and supporting me every step of the way. Most of all, I am indebted to my wife, Trudy, for living a morally inspiring life. Without her love and devotion life would be less joyous and this book would not have been written. To her this book is dedicated.

Louis P. Pojman

A Word
to the Student:
Why Study
Moral Philosophy?

ETHICS OR MORAL PHILOSOPHY is one branch of philosophy. What is philosophy? It is an enterprise that begins with wonder at the marvels and mysteries of the world, pursues a rational investigation of those marvels and mysteries, and seeks wisdom and truth, all of which result in a life lived in passionate moral and intellectual integrity. Believing that "the unexamined life is not worth living," philosophy leaves no facet of life untouched by its inquiry. It aims at a clear, critical, comprehensive conception of reality.

The hallmark of philosophy is rational argument. Philosophers clarify concepts and analyze and test propositions and beliefs, but the major task is to analyze and construct arguments. Philosophical reasoning is closely allied with scientific reasoning in that both look for evidence and build hypotheses, which are then tested with the hope of coming closer to the truth. However, scientific experiments take place in laboratories and have procedures through which to record objective or empirically verifiable results. The laboratory of the philosopher is the domain of ideas—the mind, where imaginative thought-experiments take place; the study, where ideas are written down and examined; and wherever conversation or debate about perennial questions takes place, where thesis and counterexample and counterthesis are considered.

Let us apply this to ethics. Ethics is that branch of philosophy that deals with how we ought to live, with the idea of the Good, and with such concepts as right and wrong. As such, it is a *practical* discipline. There are two parts to this subject: the theoretical and the applied. The theoretical aspect, "Ethical Theory," deals with comprehensive theories about the good life and moral obligation. It analyzes and constructs grand systems of thought in order to explain and orient agents to the moral life. Included in this domain is a close analysis of such concepts as 'right', 'wrong', 'permissible', and the like. The applied aspect, "Applied Ethics," deals with such moral problems as the morality of abortion, premarital sex, capital punishment, euthanasia, and civil disobedience. Ethical Theory and Applied Ethics are closely related: Theory without application is sterile and useless, but action without a theoretical perspective is blind. There is an enormous difference in the quality of discussions about abortion, punishment, sexual morality, and euthanasia when those discussions are informed by ethical theory compared to when they are not. More light and less heat is the likely outcome.

With the onset of pluralism and the loss of confidence in traditional authorities, a rational approach to ethics is vital to our survival and well-being. Ethical theory may rid us of facile dogmatism and emotionalism, that is, when shouting matches replace arguments, and may also liberate us from what Bernard Williams refers to as "vulgar relativism." To repeat what I have said in the Preface, ethical theory carves up the moral landscape so that we can sort out the issues and think more clearly and confidently about moral problems. It helps us get clear in our minds just how our principles and values relate to one another, and most of all, it gives us some guidance concerning how we should conduct our lives. It is important that the educated person be able to discuss ethical situations with precision and subtlety.

But ethics is not only of instrumental value; it is valuable in its own right. It is satisfying to have knowledge of important matters for its own sake, and it is important to understand the nature and scope of moral theory for their own sake. We are rational beings who need to understand the nature of the good life and all that it implies. You may become disturbed by the variety of theories discussed in this book, many of which may seem mutually exclusive and this may produce confusion when you desire guidance. But an appreciation of the complexity of ethics is valuable in offsetting our tendency to dogmatism and provincialism. It is also a challenge to you to use your reason to endorse or produce the best ethical system or combination of sytems possible.

I have written this book in the spirit of a quest for truth and understanding, and in the hope of exciting you about the value of ethics. It is a subject that I love, for it is about how we are to live, about the best kind of life. I hope that you will share my enthusiasm for the subject and develop your own ideas in the process. Best wishes.

CHAPTER 1

Introduction: What Is Ethics?

We are discussing no small matter,
but how we ought to live.

SOCRATES IN PLATO'S REPUBLIC

A FEW YEARS AGO the nation was stunned by a report from Kew Gardens, Queens, in New York City. A young woman, Kitty Genovese, was brutally stabbed in her neighborhood while 38 respectable, law-abiding citizens watched a killer stalk and stab her in three separate attacks. Her neighbors looked on from their bedroom windows for some 35 minutes as the assailant beat her, stabbed her, left her, and returned to repeat the process two more times until she died. No one lifted a phone to call the police; no one shouted at the criminal, let alone went to Kitty's aid. Finally, a 70-year-old woman called the police. It took them two minutes to arrive, but by that time Kitty was dead. Only one other woman came out to testify before the ambulance arrived an hour later. Then the whole neighborhood poured out. Asked why they didn't do anything, the responses ranged from "I don't know" and "I was tired" to "Frankly, we were afraid."[1]

Who is my neighbor? What should these respectable citizens have done? What would you have done? What kinds of generalizations can we make from this episode about contemporary culture in America? Is it an anomaly, or is it quite indicative of a deeply disturbing trend?

What is it to be a moral person? What is the nature of morality? Why do we need morality? What function does it play? What is the Good and how will I know it? Are moral principles absolute or simply relative to social groups or cultures? Is morality, like beauty, in the eye of the

1

beholder? Is it in my interest to be moral? Is it sometimes in my best interest to act immorally? How does one justify one's moral beliefs? What is the basis of morality? Which ethical theory provides the best justification and explanation of the moral life? What is the relationship between morality and religion?

These are some of the questions that we will be looking at in this book. We want to understand the nature of morality. We want to know how we should live.

The terms 'moral' and 'ethics' come from Latin and Greek, respectively ('mores' and 'ethos'), deriving their meaning from the idea of custom. Although we sometimes use these terms interchangeably, two separate ideas may be distinguished; one is closer to the idea of custom or actual practice and the other refers to a systematic examination of those practices. I shall follow the custom of using 'morality' to refer to the principles or rules of conduct that govern a society or that ought to govern a society. That is, 'morality' refers to the principles of conduct of both actual moralities (for example, the moral code of Victorian England, of a primitive tribe, or of 20th-century corporate business) and of ideal morality (the best justified or true moral system).

'Ethics' (or 'moral philosophy', as it is sometimes called), will be used to designate the systematic endeavor to understand moral concepts and justify moral principles and theories. It undertakes to analyze such concepts as 'right', 'wrong', 'permissible', 'ought', 'good', and 'evil' in their moral contexts. Ethics seeks to establish principles of right behavior that may serve as action guides for individuals and groups. It investigates which values and virtues are paramount to the worthwhile life or to society. It builds and scrutinizes arguments in ethical theories, and it seeks to discover valid principles (for example, 'Never kill innocent human beings') and the relationship between those principles (for example, does saving a life in some situations constitute a valid reason for breaking a promise?).

Ethical theory is a practical science (using 'science' to refer to a systematic, deductively organized rational activity). Whereas much of philosophy is concerned with knowledge of what there is (for example, metaphysics, philosophy of science, philosophy of religion, and philosophy of the mind), ethics is concerned with action and practice. Whereas truth in the former areas is defined as an adequate fit (or correspondence) of propositions with facts (for example, the statement 'The snow is white' is true if and only if the snow is indeed white), in ethics the direction of the fit is just the reverse: One tries to get the facts to match the ideals or moral propositions. Here we often speak of the good rather than the true, as in the statement, 'We must try to create a gentler, more peaceful world corresponding to our ideals'. To be more precise, ethics is the study of morality, which is a practical activity aimed at effecting change in the world.

ETHICS AS COMPARED WITH OTHER NORMATIVE SUBJECTS

Ethics is concerned with values— not what is, but what ought to be. How should I live my life? What is the right thing to do in this situation? Should one always tell the truth? Do I have a duty to report a student I've seen cheating on an exam? Should I tell my friend that his spouse is having an affair? Is premarital sex morally permissible? Ought a woman ever to have an abortion? Ethics has a distinct action-guiding, or so-called normative, aspect, and, as such, belongs to the group of practical institutions that includes religion, law, and etiquette.

Ethics may be closely allied to religion, but it need not be. There are both religious and secular ethical systems. Secular, or purely philosophical, ethics is grounded in reason and common human experience. To use a spatial metaphor, secular ethics is horizontal, lacking a vertical or transcendental dimension. Religious ethics has a vertical dimension, being grounded in revelation or divine authority. These two differing orientations often generate different moral principles and standards of evaluation, but they need not do so. Some versions of religious ethics, which posit God's revelation of the moral law in nature or conscience, hold that reason can discover what is right or wrong even apart from divine revelation. We shall discuss this subject in Chapter 10.

Ethics is also closely related to law. Many laws are instituted in order to promote well-being and resolve conflicts of interest and/or issues of social harmony, just as morality does, but ethics may judge that some laws are immoral without denying that they are valid laws (for example, laws permitting slavery or discrimination against people on the basis of race). Furthermore, there are some aspects of morality that are not covered by law (for example, even though it is generally agreed that lying is usually immoral, there is no law against it). Finally, law differs from morality in that there are physical sanctions enforcing the law but only the sanctions of conscience and reputation enforcing morality.

Etiquette also differs from morality, though like ethics and unlike law, it appeals primarily to conscience, social censure, and reputation. People sometimes confuse etiquette with morality, as is the case when students condemn someone for not dressing appropriately for a social event. The two institutions have points in common but are different.

I once knew a brilliant and eccentric young scholar— call him Leo— who got carried away in conversation at a formal dinner, grabbed a four-ounce stick of butter from the table, and started gobbling it. Unfortunately, he was being considered for a research fellowship at a local college. He didn't get it. Leo often ate in public with his fingers instead of with a knife and fork, and society often showed its disapprobation. But, unless you want to condemn his grabbing the butter as greedy, Leo was not immoral in eating with his fingers. He simply violated a well-established Western custom. In India, where the custom is to eat with the fingers of one's right hand, his action may have been considered entirely acceptable.

My friend neither committed an injustice nor violated a moral principle by eating with his hands. What he did was not immoral, but rather discourteous or tasteless. He broke a rule of etiquette. Etiquette, however, does not involve actions that do serious harm. Its prescriptions have no overriding importance to the lives of reasonable people. Now it happened once that after finishing his main course, Leo in his exuberance grabbed a chicken leg from his neighbor's plate, brought it to his mouth and devoured it before the shocked faces of the dinner guests. At this point Leo's violation of etiquette became a moral violation, for he was taking what properly belonged to his neighbor. He was infringing on his neighbor's right to a chicken dinner.

Law, etiquette, and religion are all important institutions, but each has limitations. The limitation of the law is that you can't have a law against every social malady, nor can you enforce every desirable rule. The limitation of etiquette is that it doesn't get to the heart of what is of vital importance for personal and social existence. Whether or not one eats with one's fingers pales in significance when compared with the importance of being honest or trustworthy or just. Etiquette is a cultural invention, but morality is a discovery.

The limitation of the religious injunction is that it rests on authority, and we are not always sure of or in agreement about the credentials of the authority or on how the authority would rule in ambiguous or new cases. Because religion is not founded on reason but on revelation, there is no way to persuade someone who does not share your religious views that your view is the right one.

The chart on the following page characterizes the relationship between these four ways of evaluating behavior.

Ethics, as the analysis of morality, distinguishes itself from law and etiquette in going deeper into the essence of rational existence. It distinguishes itself from religion in that it seeks reasons, rather than authority, to justify its principles. Its central purpose is to secure valid principles of conduct and values that can be instrumental in guiding human actions

Subject	Normative Disjuncts	Sanctions
Ethics	Right/wrong/permissible as defined by conscience or reason	Conscience—praise and blame
Religion	Right/wrong (sin)/permissible as defined by religious authority	Conscience—hope of eternal reward and fear of punishment
Law	Legal and illegal as defined by a legislative body	Punishments executed by the judicial body
Etiquette	Proper and improper as defined by culture	Social disapprobation and approbation

and producing good character. As such it is the most important activity known to humans, for it has to do with how we are to live.

CHARACTERISTICS OF MORAL PRINCIPLES

A central feature of morality is the moral principle. We have already noted that moral principles are practical guides to action that differ from legal statutes, rules of etiquette, and even religious rules. We must say a few words about the features of moral principles. Although there is no universal agreement on which traits a moral principle must possess, the following traits have received widespread attention: (1) prescriptivity, (2) universalizability, (3) overridingness, (4) publicity, and (5) practicability.

Prescriptivity

Prescriptivity refers to the practical or action-guiding nature of morality. Moral principles are generally put forth as injunctions or imperatives (for example, 'Do not kill', 'Do no unnecessary harm', and 'Love your neighbor'). They are intended for use, to advise and to influence to action. Prescriptivity shares this trait with all normative discourse. Retroactively, this feature is used to appraise behavior, to assign praise and blame, and to produce feelings of satisfaction or guilt. We will discuss this topic further in Chapter 8.

Universalizability

Moral principles must apply to all who are in the relevantly similar situation. If one judges that act X is right for a certain person P, then it is right for anyone relevantly similar to P. This trait is exemplified in the Golden Rule, "Do unto others what you would have them do unto you (if you were in their shoes)" and in the formal Principle of Justice, "It cannot be right for A to treat B in a manner in which it would be wrong for B to treat A, merely on the ground that they are two different individuals, and without there being any difference between the natures or circumstances of the two which can be stated as a reasonable ground for difference of treatment."[2] Universalizability applies to all evaluative judgments. If I say that X is a good Y, then I am logically committed to judge that anything relevantly similar to X is a good Y. This feature is an extension of the principle of consistency: One ought to be consistent about one's value judgments, including one's moral judgments. We will look further at this trait in Chapters 6 and 8.

Overridingness

Moral principles have hegemonic authority. They are not the only principles, but they take precedence over other considerations, including aesthetic, prudential, and legal ones. Paul Gauguin may have been aesthetically justified in abandoning his family in order to devote his life to painting beautiful Pacific island pictures, but morally, or all things considered, he probably was not justified. It may be prudent to lie to save my reputation, but it probably is morally wrong to do so, in which case I should tell the truth. When the law becomes egregiously immoral, it may be my moral duty to exercise civil disobedience. There is a general moral duty to obey the law, because the law serves an overall moral purpose, and this overall purpose may give us moral reasons to obey laws that may not be moral or ideal; however, there may come a time when the injustice of a bad law is intolerable and hence calls for illegal but moral defiance (such as the antebellum laws in the South requiring citizens to return slaves to their owners). Religion is a special case, and the religious person may be morally justified in following a perceived command from God to break a normal moral rule. The Quakers' pacifist religious beliefs may cause them to renege on an obligation to fight for their country. Religious morality is morality, and ethics recognizes its legitimacy. We will say more about this in Chapter 10.

Publicity

Moral principles must be made public in order to play an action-guiding role in our lives. Because we use principles to prescribe behavior, to give advice, and to assign praise and blame, it would be self-defeating to keep them a secret. Occasionally, a utilitarian will argue that it would be better if some people did not know or try to follow the correct principles, but even they would have a higher-order principle—or some reason for this exception—subsuming this special case.

Practicability

A moral system must be workable; its rules must not lay a heavy burden on agents. The philosopher John Rawls speaks of the "strains of commitment"[3] that overly idealistic principles may cause in average moral agents. It might be desirable to have a morality enjoining more altruism, but the result of such principles could be moral despair, too much guilt, and ineffective action. Practicability may be the cause of the differences between ethical standards over time and place. For instance, there is a discrepancy in the Bible between Old Testament ethics and New Testament ethics on such topics as divorce and the treatment of one's enemy. Jesus explained the difference in the first case by saying that it was because of society's hardness of heart that God permitted divorce in pre-Christian times. In the second case he pointed toward a time when it would be a valid principle that people would love their enemies and pray for those who despitefully use them, and he enjoined his disciples to begin living by this ideal morality. Most ethical systems take human limitations into consideration.

As I said at the outset, these traits are generally held by moral philosophers as necessary to valid moral principles, but there is disagreement over them, and a full discussion would lead to a great deal of qualification. These traits should give you an idea of the general features of moral principles, however.

DOMAINS OF ETHICAL ASSESSMENT

It might seem at this point that ethics concerns itself entirely with rules of conduct based solely on an evaluation of acts. The situation is more complicated than this. There are four domains of ethical assessment:

Domain	Evaluative Terms
1. Actions, the act	Right, wrong, permissible
2. Consequences	Good, bad, indifferent
3. Character	Virtuous, vicious
4. Motive	Good will, evil will

Let us briefly illustrate these concepts.

Actions

The most common distinction concerning this concept may be the classification of right and wrong kinds of actions. Take the act of lying. It is generally seen as a wrong type of act (prohibited), whereas telling the truth is generally seen as a right kind of act (obligatory). But some acts do not seem to be either right or wrong. Whether you wash with Palmolive soap rather than Ivory or whether you write your friend a letter with a pencil or a pen seems morally neutral; either is permissible. Whether you listen to pop music or classical music is not morally significant; both are allowed. Whether you decide to marry or remain single is up to you. You are under no obligation to do either (unless you have put yourself under an obligation). Some things, such as deciding whether or not to marry , are very important but are still within the domain of permissibility, not obligation.

Within the structure of moral obligation we may define these terms as follows:

1. The 'right act' is that act which it is obligatory for one to do. One ought to do that act; it is not permissible to refrain from doing it.

2. The 'wrong act' is that act which one is forbidden to do. One ought not to do that act; it is not permissible to do it.

3. A 'permissible act' is an act which is neither right nor wrong to do. It is neither obligatory nor forbidden.

Within the range of permissible acts is the notion of "supererogatory" or highly altruistic acts. These acts are not required, but instead are challenges to go beyond what morality requires, to go "beyond the call of duty." You may have an obligation to give a donation to help people in dire need, but you are probably not obliged to sell your car, let alone become destitute, in order to help them.

Theories that place the emphasis on the nature of the act are called 'deontological' (from the Greek word for duty). The most famous of these systems is Kant's moral theory, which we will study in Chapter 6.

Consequences

We turn next to the notion of consequences. We said above that lying is generally wrong and telling the truth is generally right. But consider this situation. You are hiding in your home an innocent woman named Laura, who is fleeing gangsters. Gangland Gus knocks on your door, and when you open it, he asks if Laura is in your house. What should you do? Should you tell the truth or lie? Those who say that morality has something to do with consequences of actions would prescribe lying as the morally right thing to do. Those who deny that we should look at the consequences when considering what to do and when there is a clear and absolute rule of action will say that we should either keep silent or tell the truth. When no other rule is at stake, of course, the rule-oriented ethicist will allow the foreseeable consequences to determine a course of action. Theories that focus primarily on consequences in determining moral rightness and wrongness are called *teleological ethical theories* (from the Greek *telos*, meaning goal-directed). The most famous of these theories is utilitarianism, which we will study in Chapter 5.

Character

Some ethical theories emphasize principles of action in themselves, and some emphasize principles involving consequences of action. Other theories, such as Aristotle's ethics, emphasize character. According to Aristotle, it is most important to develop virtuous character, for if and only if we have good people can we ensure habitual right action. Although the virtues are not central to other types of moral theories, most moral theories consider the virtues important. Most of us, whatever our moral theory, would judge that the people who watched Kitty Genovese get assaulted lacked good character. Different moral systems emphasize different virtues and emphasize them to different degrees. We will study virtue (sometimes called 'aretaic ethics' after the Greek word for virtue, *arete*) in Chapter 7.

Motive

Finally, virtually all ethical systems, but especially Kant's system, accept the relevance of motive. It is important to the full assessment of any action that the intention of the agent be taken into account. Two acts may be identical, but one may be judged morally culpable and the other excusable. Consider John's pushing Joan off a ledge, causing her to break her leg. In situation A he is angry and intends to harm her, but in situation B he sees a knife flying in her direction and intends to save her life. In A what he did was clearly wrong, whereas in B he did the right thing. On the other hand, two acts may have opposite results but may be judged equally good on the basis of intention. For example, two soldiers may try to cross enemy lines to communicate with an allied force, but one gets captured through no fault of his own and the other succeeds. In a full moral description of any act, motive must be taken into consideration as a relevant factor.

WHY DO WE NEED MORALITY?
A REFLECTION ON *LORD OF THE FLIES*

Which is better— to have rules and agree, or to hunt and kill? [4]

Why exactly do we need moral codes? What function do they play in our lives and in society in general? Rather than write a discursive essay on the benefits of morality, let me draw your attention to a book every young person has, or should have read: William Golding's classic novel *Lord of the Flies*. This modern moral allegory may provide us with a clue to the nature and purpose of morality.

A group of boys between the ages of 6 and 12 from an English private school, cast adrift on an uninhabited island in the Pacific, create their own social system. For a while the constraints of civilized society prevent total chaos. All of the older boys recognize the necessity of substantive and procedural rules. Only he who has the white conch, the symbol of authority, may speak at an assembly. The leader is chosen democratically and is invested with limited powers. Even the evil Roger, while taunting little Henry by throwing stones near him, manages to keep the stones from harming the child. "Here invisible yet strong, was the taboo of the old life. Round the squatting child was the protection of parents and school and policemen and the law. Roger's arm was conditioned by a civilization that knew nothing of him and was in ruins" (p. 78).

After some initial euphoria at being liberated from the adult world of constraints into an exciting world of fun in the sun, the children come up against the usual banes of social existence: competition for power and status, neglect of social responsibility, failure of public policy, and escalating violence. Two boys, Ralph and Jack, vie for leadership, and a bitter rivalry emerges between them. As a compromise, a division of labor is established, but Jack's choirboy hunters refuse to help the others in constructing shelters. Freeloading soon becomes a common phenomenon as the majority of children leave their tasks to play on the beach. Neglect of duty results in failure to be rescued by a passing airplane. The unbridled lust for excitement leads to the great orgiastic pig-kills and finally, at its nadir, to the thirst for human blood.

Civilization's power is weak and vulnerable to atavistic, volcanic passions. The sensitive Simon, the symbol of religious consciousness (namely, Simon Peter, the first disciple of Jesus) who prophesies that Ralph will be saved and who is the first to discover and fight against the "ancient, inescapable recognition" of the beast in us, is slaughtered by the group in a wild frenzy. Only Piggy and Ralph, mere observers of the orgiastic homicide, feel vicarious pangs of guilt at this atrocity.

The incarnation of philosophy and culture—poor, fat, near-sighted Piggy, with his broken spectacles and asthma—becomes ever more pathetic as the chaos increases. The nadir of his ridiculous position is reached after the rebels led by Jack steal his spectacles in order to harness the sun's rays for starting fires. After Ralph—the symbol of not-too-bright, but morally good, civilized leadership—fails to persuade Jack to return the glasses, Piggy asserts his moral right to them:

> You're stronger than I am and you haven't got asthma. You can see. . . . But I don't ask for my glasses back, not as a favour. I don't ask you to be a sport . . . not because you're strong, but because what's right's right. Give me my glasses, . . . You got to. (p. 211).

Piggy might as well have addressed the fire itself, for in this state of moral anarchy moral discourse is a foreign tongue that only incites the worst elements to greater immorality. Roger, perched on a cliff above, responds to moral reasoning by dislodging a huge rock, which hits Piggy and flings him to his death 40 feet below.

The title *Lord of the Flies* is a translation of the Greek *Beelzebub*, which was a name for the devil. Golding shows that we need no external devil to bring about evil but that we have found the devil, and, in the words of Pogo, "he is us." Ubiquitous, ever waiting for a moment to strike out, he emerges from the depths of the subconscious whenever there is a conflict of interest or a moment of moral lassitude. As E. L. Epstein says, "The tenets of civilization, the moral and social codes, the Ego, the intelligence itself, form only a veneer over this white-hot power, this uncontrollable force, 'the fury and the mire of human veins.' "[5]

Beelzebub's ascendancy proceeds through fear, hysteria, violence, and death. A delegation starts out hunting pigs for meat. Then they find themselves enjoying the kill. In order to drown the incipient shame over bloodthirstiness, and take on a persona more compatible with their deeds, the children paint themselves with colored mud. Their lusting for the kill takes on all the powerful overtones of an orgiastic sexual ritual, so that in being liberated from their social selves they kill without remorse whoever gets in their way. The deaths of Simon and Piggy (the symbols of the religious and the philosophical, the two great fences blocking the descent to hell) and the final orgiastic hunt with the "spear sharpened at both ends" signal for Ralph the depths of evil in the human heart.

Ironically, it is the British navy that finally comes to the rescue and saves Ralph (civilization) just when all seems lost. But the symbol of the navy is a double-edged omen. On the one hand it may symbolize the fact that a military defense is, unfortunately, sometimes needed to save civilization from the barbarians (Hitler's Nazis or Jack and Roger's allies), but on the other hand it symbolizes the quest for blood and vengeance latent in contemporary civilization. The children's world is really only a stage lower than the adult world whence they come, and that shallow civilization could very well regress to tooth and claw if it were scratched too sharply. The children were saved by the adults, but who will save the adults who put so much emphasis on military enterprises and weapons systems in the euphemistic name of "defense." To quote Epstein, "The officer, having interrupted a man-hunt, prepares to take the children off the island in a cruiser which will presently be hunting its enemy in the same implacable way. And who will rescue the adult and his cruiser?" [6]

The fundamental ambiguity of human existence is seen in every section of the book, poignantly mirroring the human condition. Even Piggy's spectacles, the sole example of modern technology on the island, become a bane for the island when Jack uses them to ignite a forest fire that will smoke out their prey— Ralph—and that ends up burning down the entire forest and destroying the island's animal life. It is a symbol both of our penchant for misusing technology to vitiate the environment and of our ability to create weapons that will lead to global suicide.

THE PURPOSES OF MORALITY

What is the role of morality in human existence? What are little boys and girls and big men and women made of that requires ethical consciousness? Ralph answers these questions at the end of the tale: "And in the middle of [the children], with filthy body, matted hair, and unwiped nose, Ralph wept for the end of innocence, the darkness of man's heart, and the fall through the air of the true, wise friend called Piggy" (p. 248).

In this modern moral allegory we catch a glimpse of some of the purposes of morality. Rules formed over the ages and internalized within us hold back and, it is hoped, defeat "The Lord of the Flies" in society, whether he be inherent in us individually or an emergent property of corporate existence. The moral code restrains the Rogers of society from evil until untoward social conditions open up the sluice gates of sadism. Morality is the force that enables Piggy and Ralph to maintain a modicum of order within their dwindling society, first motivating them to compromise with Jack and then keeping things in perspective.

In Golding's allegory morality is honored more in the breach than in the observance, for we see the consequences of not having rules and principles and virtuous character.

We may say that morality has at least four related purposes:

1. To keep society from falling apart
2. To ameliorate human suffering
3. To promote human flourishing[7]
4. To resolve conflicts of interest in just ways

Morality, first of all, keeps society from falling apart, from sinking to a state of chaos in which everyone is the enemy of everyone else, in which fear and insecurity dominate the mind and prevent peace and flourishing. Thomas Hobbes (1588–1679) described this dismal condition as a "state of nature" wherein there exists a perpetual war of all against all and life is "solitary, poor, nasty, brutish, and short." The first purpose of moral rules, then, is to enable us to prevent this state of nature. As a means to prevent this condition, society must have rules of justice in order to resolve conflicts of interest in ways that are mutually agreed upon and considered just. There are scarce resources, be they positions of power and status, wealth, jobs, land, property, or whatever, and we need rules to adjudicate conflicts when different people lay claim to these goods. Unless we can satisfactorily resolve these conflicts of interest, we will not be able to reach any other goals.

But the purpose of morality is not simply negative—to prevent chaos and a state of nature. The rules also play a positive role in promoting human flourishing. They enable people to pursue their goals in peace and freedom, encouraging them to friendship and fidelity, challenging them to excellence and a worthwhile life. Deep morality, as it is ingrained in good character, is a "jewel that shines in its own light." It creates a worthwhile life for its participants and turns a potential hell into something that at its highest point (usually confined to small communities, friendships, and families) approximates a heaven on earth. In sum, it tries to promote human flourishing.

Even though these four purposes of morality are related, they are not identical, and different moral theories emphasize different purposes in different ways. Utilitarianism fastens on human flourishing and the amelioration of suffering, whereas contractual systems rooted in Hobbesian egoism emphasize the role of resolving conflicts of interest. Other systems, such as Kant's theory, place the emphasis on orderly, universal rules of justice. Virtue ethics emphasizes individual flourishing in the virtuous character. As you read this book and examine the various theories set forth, ask yourself which of these purposes the given theory emphasizes and which it neglects. Is it important for a given ethical theory to deal with all four purposes satisfactorily?

But before we go any further, we need to examine the very status of moral principles. Are they wholly relative to culture—socially approved habits—or do some of them enjoy universal validity that does not rest on whether or not societies recognize them? It is to that problem we turn next.

Notes

1. Martin Gansberg, "38 Who Saw Murder Didn't Call Police," *The New York Times*, March 27, 1964.

2. Henry Sidgwick, *The Methods of Ethics*, 7th ed. (Macmillan & Co., 1907), p. 380. Recently, some moral philosophers have denied that universalizability is a necessary condition for moral action. See, for example, Lawrence Blum, *Friendship, Altruism, and Morality* (Routledge & Kegan Paul, 1980).

3. John Rawls, *A Theory of Justice*, (Harvard University Press, 1971), pp.176, 423.

4. William Golding, *Lord of the Flies*, (G. P. Putnam's, 1959), p. 222. All references are to this work.

5. E. L. Epstein, "Notes on *Lord of the Flies*" in *"Lord of the Flies,"* p. 252.

6. E. L. Epstein, "Notes," p. 251.

7. In this work 'flourishing' means a life worth living, or happiness, leaving exactly what constitutes that state open for contemplation. I use 'flourishing' instead of 'happiness' because the latter term has come to have inordinately subjective connotations (see the discussion in Chapter 4).

For Further Reflection

1. As the illustration from William Golding's work *The Lord of the Flies* shows, we may come to understand and appreciate the need for and purposes of morality by looking at situations in which morality is absent or evil is present. Can you think of literature, social studies, or social experience where this is further illustrated?

2. Illustrate the differences between a moral principle, a legal rule, a principle of etiquette, an aesthetic judgment, and a religious principle. Are these sometimes related? Can something be so aesthetically repulsive that we conclude that it is morally wrong? For example, our laws prohibit public nudity and many people find public nudity revolting or deeply offensive, but is it necessarily morally wrong?

3. A moral dilemma is a situation in which any action you take will allow some evil to occur or one in which two accepted moral principles meaningfully conflict. Dilemmas produce most of the hard cases in applying ethical theory. Here are a few dilemmas for you to discuss.

a. In William Styron's book *Sophie's Choice,* Sophie, while a prisoner in a Nazi concentration camp, is given the task of choosing which of her two children will be executed by the Nazi commander. If she refuses to choose between them, both will be killed. If she chooses one, the other will live. What should she do?

b. You are driving a trolley down the track, when all of a sudden the brakes fail so that you cannot stop the trolley at the red light. Ahead of you are ten men working on the track, whom you will kill if you do nothing. Fortunately, there is a side spur onto which you can turn and thus spare the men. But, unfortunately, a child playing on that track will be killed if you do turn off the main track. So if you do nothing, ten men will be killed due to the brake failure; but if you voluntarily act, you will kill the child. What should you do? (The philosopher Judith Jarvis Thomson first proposed this dilemma.)

c. You have discovered that your parents have embezzled a large sum of money from the corporation for which they work. You have spoken to them about this, and they have denied it, but you know that they are lying. If you report them, they will go to jail and have their lives ruined. If you don't report them, the owners of the business will be financially ruined. How do you handle this situation?

d. You have discovered that your best friend's husband is having an affair. Should you tell your friend and risk ruining the marriage, or should you approach the husband, or should you do nothing? Do you have a moral duty at all here? Suppose you decide to talk to the husband first. You do this, and he denies the affair. You are convinced that he is lying. What should you do?

e. You and 20 friends are spelunking in a coastal cave when Fat Freddy gets caught in the mouth of the cave. The tide is rising, and soon all of you will be drowned (except Freddy, whose head is outside the cave) if Freddy isn't dislodged from the cave's mouth. Fortuitously, you just happen to have a stick of dynamite with you. Your option is to blow Freddy from his place or drown along with 19 friends. What should you do?

4. On the cover of this book is David's famous painting of Socrates bidding farewell to his disciples and friends in 399 B.C. Socrates has been

unjustly condemned to death by the citizens of Athens. While in jail awaiting execution, his friend, Crito, offers him a safe way of escape. Crito argues that Socrates has an obligation to his friends and family to accept this opportunity, but Socrates argues that it is wrong to break the law in order to save oneself. Who is right? Read Plato's dialogue *Crito* to get the details of the arguments. This is likely the first case in history in which the issue of civil disobedience is discussed. Is civil disobedience ever morally justified? If so, when and under what conditions?

5. Tom Jones, an up-and-coming young businessman, is walking to work on a bridge when he sees a small girl fall into the river below. She begins to scream for help. Tom is a good swimmer and knows that he can save the girl's life, but if he does so, he will miss an important meeting that is important to his career. In addition, the water is cold and Tom doesn't want to ruin his new suit. He doesn't want to jump in and reasons that it is not his fault that the girl has fallen into the water. Does Tom have a duty to jump in despite his objections? Why or why not? How is this case related to one in which Tom accidentally pushes the girl into the river? Or to one in which Tom purposefully pushes her into the water?

6. Think of some difficult moral issues and keep them in mind as you work through the rest of this book, asking yourself how the various theories would treat these issues.

For Further Reading

Baier, Kurt. *The Moral Point of View*. Cornell University Press, 1958. An abridged edition of this fine work is available in paperback from Random House, 1965. The work sees morality primarily in terms of social control.

Brandt, Richard. *Ethical Theory: The Problems of Normative and Critical Ethics*. Prentice-Hall, 1959. A thorough and thoughtful treatment of the ethical theory.

Frankena, William K. *Ethics*. 2nd ed. Prentice-Hall, 1973.

Gert, Bernard. *Morality: A New Justification of the Moral Rules*. 2nd ed. Oxford, 1988. A clear and comprehensive discussion of the nature of morality.

MacIntyre, Alasdair. *A Short History of Ethics*. Macmillan, 1966. A lucid, if uneven, survey of the history of Western ethics.

Mackie, J. L. *Ethics: Inventing Right and Wrong*. Penguin, 1976. This book takes a very different view of ethics from mine.

Singer, Peter. *The Expanding Circle: Ethics and Sociobiology*. Oxford University Press, 1983. A fascinating attempt to relate ethics to sociobiology.

Taylor, Paul. *Principles of Ethics*. Dickenson, 1975. This work covers many of the same topics as this book, usually from a different perspective. His discussion of the principles of universalizability (pp. 95–105) is especially useful.

Taylor, Richard. *Good and Evil*. Macmillan, 1970; Prometheus, 1984. A lively, easy-to-read work that considers the main role of morality to be the resolution of conflicts of interest.

Turnbull, Colin. *The Mountain People*. Simon & Schuster, 1972. An excellent anthropological study of a people living on the edge of morality.

Warnock, G. J. *The Object of Morality*. Methuen, 1971. A clearly written, well-argued analysis of the nature of morality.

CHAPTER 2

Ethical Relativism: Who's to Judge What's Right or Wrong?

Ethical relativism is the doctrine that the moral rightness and wrongness of actions varies from society to society and that there are no absolute universal moral standards binding on all men at all times. Accordingly, it holds that whether or not it is right for an individual to act in a certain way depends on or is relative to the society to which he belongs.

JOHN LADD, ETHICAL RELATIVISM

IN THE 19TH CENTURY Christian missionaries sometimes used coercion to change the customs of pagan tribal people in parts of Africa and some Pacific islands. Appalled by the customs of public nakedness, polygamy, working on the Sabbath, and infanticide, they paternalistically went about reforming the "poor pagans." They clothed them, separated wives from their husbands in order to create monogamous households, made the Sabbath a day of rest, and ended infanticide. In the process they sometimes created social malaise, causing the estranged women to despair and their children to be orphaned. The natives often did not understand the new religion but accepted it in deference to the white man's power. The white people had guns and medicine.

Since the 19th century we've made progress in understanding cultural diversity, and we realize that the social dissonance caused by do-

18

gooders was a bad thing. In the last century or so anthropologists have exposed our penchant for prejudicial views in which all of reality is interpreted through the eyes of our cultural beliefs and values. We have come to see the enormous variety in social practices throughout the world.

Eskimos allow their elderly to die by starvation, whereas we believe that this practice is morally wrong. The Spartans of ancient Greece believed, and Dobu of New Guinea believe today, that stealing is morally right, but we believe that it is wrong. The Nuer of East Africa throw deformed infants to the hippopotamus, but we abhor infanticide. Ruth Benedict describes a tribe in Melanesia that views cooperation and kindness as vices, and Colin Turnbull has documented that the Ik in Northern Uganda have no sense of duty toward their children or parents. Some societies make it a duty for children to kill (sometimes strangle) their aging parents. Eskimos sometimes abandon their elderly as they move on to new locations. Sexual practices vary over time and clime. Some cultures permit homosexual behavior, whereas others condemn it. Some cultures practice polygamy, whereas others view it as immoral. Some cultures accept cannibalism, whereas we detest it. **Cultural relativism** is well documented, and custom seems "king o'er all."

Today we condemn ethnocentrism, the uncritical belief in the inherent superiority of one's own culture, as a variety of prejudice tantamount to racism and sexism. What is right in one culture may be wrong in another; what is good east of the river may be bad west of the same river; what is a virtue in one nation may be seen as a vice in another. Thus it behooves us not to judge others but to be tolerant of diversity.

This rejection of ethnocentrism in the West has contributed to a general shift in public opinion about morality, so that for a growing number of Westerners, heightened consciousness about the validity of other ways of life has led to a gradual erosion of belief in moral **objectivism**, the view that there are universal moral principles that are valid for all people at all times and in all places. For example, in polls taken in my ethics and introduction to philosophy classes over the past several years (in three different universities in three areas of the country), students affirmed (by a 2 to 1 ratio) a version of **ethical relativism** over **moral absolutism**; barely 3 percent held views between these two polar opposites. Of course, I'm not suggesting that all of these students had a clear understanding of what relativism entails, for many of those who claim that they are ethical relativists also believe that "abortion except to save the mother's life is always wrong," that "capital punishment is always morally wrong," or that "suicide is never morally permissible." These apparent contradictions signal some confusion on the matter.

In this chapter we will examine the central notions of ethical relativism and the implications that seem to follow from it. After this we will explore the outlines of a very modest objectivism, which holds to the objective validity of moral principles but takes into account many of the insights of relativism.

AN ANALYSIS OF RELATIVISM

The theory of ethical relativism holds that there are no universally valid moral principles, but rather that all moral principles are valid relative to culture or individual choice. It is to be distinguished from moral skepticism—the view that there are no valid moral principles at all (or at least we cannot know whether there are any)—and from all forms of moral objectivism or absolutism. Consider again John Ladd's apt characterization of the theory:

> Ethical relativism is the doctrine that the moral rightness and wrongness of actions varies from society to society and that there are no absolute universal moral standards binding on all men at all times. Accordingly, it holds that whether or not it is right for an individual to act in a certain way depends on or is relative to the society to which he belongs.[1]

If we analyze this passage, we derive the following argument:

1. **What is considered morally right and wrong varies from society to society so that there are no universal moral standards held by all societies.**
2. **Whether or not it is right for an individual to act in a certain way depends on or is relative to the society to which he or she belongs.**
3. **Therefore, there are no absolute or objective moral standards that apply to all people everywhere and at all times.**

The Diversity Thesis

The first thesis, which may be called the *diversity thesis* and is identified with *cultural relativism*, is simply an anthropological thesis that acknowledges the fact that moral rules differ from society to society. As we noted earlier in this chapter, there is enormous variety in what may be considered a moral principle in a given society. The human condition is malleable in the extreme, allowing any number of folkways or moral codes. As Ruth Benedict has written:

The cultural pattern of any civilization makes use of a certain segment of the great arc of potential human purposes and motivations, just as we have seen . . . that any culture makes use of certain selected material techniques or cultural traits. The great arc along which all the possible human behaviors are distributed is far too immense and too full of contradictions for any one culture to utilize even any considerable portion of it. Selection is the first requirement.[2]

It may or may not be the case that any single moral principle is held in common by every society, but if there are any, they seem to be few at best. Certainly, it would be very difficult to derive one single "true" morality on the basis of observations of various societies' moral standards.

The Dependency Thesis

The second thesis, the *dependency thesis*, asserts that individual acts are right or wrong depending on the nature of the society in which they occur. Morality does not occur in a vacuum; rather, what is considered morally right or wrong must be seen in a context that depends on the goals, wants, beliefs, history, and environment of the society in question. As William Graham Sumner says, "We learn the [morals] as unconsciously as we learn to walk and hear and breathe, and [we] never know any reason why the [morals] are what they are. The justification of them is that when we wake to consciousness of life we find them facts which already hold us in the bonds of tradition, custom, and habit."[3] Trying to judge morality from an independent, noncultural point of view would be like taking out our eyes in order to examine their colors, contours, and qualities. We are simply culturally determined beings.

We could, of course, distinguish between weak and strong theses of dependency. The nonrelativist can accept a certain relativity in the way moral principles are *applied* in various cultures, depending on the cultures' beliefs, histories, and environments. For example, Orientals show respect by covering the head and uncovering the feet, whereas Occidentals do the opposite. Still, both adhere to a principle of respect for deserving people; they just apply the principle of respect differently. But the ethical relativist must maintain a stronger thesis, one that insists that the very validity of the principles is a product of the culture and that different cultures invent different valid principles. The ethical relativist maintains that, even beyond the environmental factors and differences in beliefs, there are fundamental disagreements among societies.

In a sense, we all live in radically different worlds. Each person has a different set of beliefs and experiences, a particular perspective that colors all of his or her perceptions. For example, when a farmer, a real estate agent, and an artist within the same society look at the same spatiotemporal field, each sees something different; their orientations, values, and expectations govern their perceptions. Even as our individual values arise from personal experience, so are our social values grounded in the peculiar history of the community. Morality, then, is just the set of common rules, habits, and customs that have won social approval over time; thus they seem to be part of the nature of things, to be facts. There is nothing mysterious or transcendent about these codes of behavior. They are the outcomes of our social history.

There is something conventional about *any* morality, so that every morality really depends on a level of social acceptance. Not only do various societies adhere to different moral systems, but the very same society can (and often does) change its moral views over time and place. For example, in the southern United States slavery is now viewed as immoral, whereas just over 100 years ago it was not. We have greatly altered our views on abortion, divorce, and sexuality as well.

The conclusion—that there are no absolute or objective moral standards binding on all people—follows from the first two propositions. Cultural relativism (the diversity thesis) plus the dependency thesis yields ethical relativism in its classic form. If there are different moral principles from culture to culture and if all morality is rooted in culture, then it follows that there are no universal moral principles that are valid for all cultures and people at all times.

SUBJECTIVE ETHICAL RELATIVISM (SUBJECTIVISM)

Some people think that even this conclusion is too tame. They maintain that morality is not dependent on the society but on the individual himself or herself. As students sometimes maintain, "Morality is in the eye of the beholder." This form of moral subjectivism has the sorry consequence that it makes morality a useless concept, for, on its premises, little or no interpersonal criticism or judgment is logically possible. The only basis for judging John wrong would be if John failed to live up to his own principles; but, of course, one of John's principles could be that hypocrisy is morally permissible (for him at least), so that it would be impossible for John to do wrong. For John hypocrisy and nonhypocrisy are both morally permissible. On the basis of subjectivism it could very easily turn out that Adolf Hitler was as moral as Gandhi, so long as each believed he was living by his chosen principles. Notions of moral good and bad, right and wrong cease to have interpersonal evaluative meaning. You may not like it when your teacher gives you an F on your test paper, when she gives your neighbor an A for one that is very similar, but there is no way to criticize her for injustice because justice is not one of her elected principles.[4]

Absurd consequences follow from subjective ethical relativism. If it is correct, then morality reduces to aesthetic tastes over which there can be neither argument nor interpersonal judgment. Although many students say that they hold this position, there seems to be a conflict between it and others of their moral views (for example, that Hitler was really morally bad or capital punishment is always wrong). There seems to be a contradiction between subjectivism and the very concept of morality that it is supposed to characterize, for morality has to do with *proper* resolution of interpersonal conflict and the amelioration of the human predicament. Whatever else it does, morality has the minimal aim of preventing a state of chaos in which life, as Hobbes described it, is "solitary, poor, nasty, brutish, and short." But if so, subjectivism is no help at all in doing this, for it doesn't rest on social *agreement* of principle (as the conventionalist maintains) or on an objectively independent set of norms that bind together all people for the common good.

Subjectivism treats individuals as billiard balls on a societal pool table: They meet only in radical collisions, each headed for its own goal and going there to knock others before they are themselves knocked. This atomistic view of personality is belied by the facts that we develop in families and mutually dependent communities in which we share a common language, common institutions, and similar habits, and that we often feel each other's joys and sorrows. As John Donne said, "No man is an island, entire of itself; every man is a piece of the continent."

Radical individualistic relativism seems incoherent. If so, it follows that the only plausible view of ethical relativism must be one that grounds morality in the group or culture. This form of relativism is called "conventionalism," and to it we now turn.

CONVENTIONAL ETHICAL RELATIVISM (CONVENTIONALISM)

Conventional ethical relativism—the view that there are no objective moral principles but rather that all valid moral principles are justified by virtue of their cultural acceptance—recognizes the social nature of morality.[5] That is precisely its power and virtue. It does not seem subject to the same absurd consequences that plague subjectivism. Because they recognize the importance of social environment in generating customs and beliefs, many people suppose that ethical relativism is the correct ethical theory. Furthermore, they are drawn to it for its liberal philosophical stance. It seems to be an enlightened response to the sin of ethnocentricity, and it seems to entail or strongly imply an attitude of tolerance toward other cultures. As Benedict says, in recognizing ethical relativity "we shall arrive at a more realistic social faith, accepting as grounds of hope and as new bases for tolerance the coexisting and equally valid patterns of life which mankind has created for itself from the raw materials of existence."[6] The most famous of those holding this position is the anthropologist Melville Herskovits, who argues even more explicitly than Benedict that ethical relativism entails intercultural tolerance:

1. **Morality is relative to its culture.**
2. **There is no independent basis for criticizing the morality of any other culture.**
3. **Therefore, we ought to be tolerant of the moralities of other cultures.**[7]

Tolerance is certainly a virtue, but is this a good argument for it? I think not. If morality is simply relative to each culture, then if the culture does not have a principle of tolerance, its members have no obligation to be tolerant. Herskovits seems to be treating the principle of tolerance as the one exception to his relativism. But from a relativistic point of view there is no more reason to be tolerant than to be intolerant, and neither stance is objectively morally better than the other.

Not only do relativists fail to offer a basis for criticizing those who are intolerant, but they cannot rationally criticize anyone who espouses what they might regard as a heinous principle. If, as seems to be the case, valid criticism supposes an objective or impartial standard, then relativists cannot morally criticize anyone outside their own culture. Adolf Hitler's genocidal actions, so long as they were culturally accepted, would be as morally legitimate as Mother Teresa's works of mercy. If conventional relativism is accepted, then racism, genocide of unpopular minorities, oppression of the poor, slavery, and even advocacy of war for its own sake are as equally moral as their opposites. And if a subculture decided that starting a nuclear war was somehow morally acceptable, we could not morally criticize these people, for any actual morality, whatever its content, is as valid as every other and more valid than ideal moralities because the latter aren't adhered to by any culture.

There are other disturbing consequences of ethical relativism. It seems to suggest that reformers are always (morally) wrong because they go against the tide of cultural standards. In the 18th century William Wilberforce was thus wrong to oppose slavery, and the British were immoral in opposing suttee (the burning of widows, which is now illegal) in India. The early Christians were wrong in refusing to serve in the Roman army or to bow down to Caesar because the majority in the Roman Empire believed that these two acts were moral duties. In fact, Jesus himself was immoral in advocating the beatitudes and the principles of the Sermon on the Mount, for it is clear that few in his time (or in ours) accepted them.

Yet we normally feel just the opposite, that the reformer is the courageous innovator who is right, who has the truth, in the face of the mindless majority. Sometimes the individual must stand alone with the truth, risking social censure and persecution. As Dr. Stockman says in Ibsen's *Enemy of the People*, after he loses the battle to declare his town's profitable, polluted tourist spa unsanitary, "The most dangerous enemy of the truth and freedom among us—is the compact majority. Yes, the damned, compact and liberal majority. The majority has *might*—unfortunately—but *right* it is not. Right—are I and a few others." Yet if relativism is correct, the opposite is necessarily the case: Truth is with the crowd and error with the individual.

Similarly, conventional ethical relativism entails disturbing judgments about the law. Our normal view is that we have a prima facie duty to obey the law because law, in general, promotes the human good. According to most objective systems, this obligation is not absolute but relative to the particular law's relation to a wider moral order. Civil disobedience is warranted in some cases in which the law seems to be in serious conflict with morality. However, if moral relativism is true, then neither law nor civil disobedience has a firm foundation. On the one hand—from the side of the society at large—civil disobedience will be morally wrong so long as the culture agrees with the law in question. On the other hand—to those who belong to the relevant subculture that doesn't recognize the particular law in question—disobedience will be morally mandated. The Ku Klux Klan, which believes that Jews, Catholics, and Blacks are evil or undeserving of their status, is, given conventionalism, morally permitted or required to break the laws that protect these endangered groups. Why should I obey a law that my group doesn't recognize as valid?

To sum up, unless we have an independent moral basis for law, it is difficult to see why we have any general duty to obey it; and unless we recognize the priority of a universal moral law, we have no firm basis to justify our acts of civil disobedience against "unjust laws." Both the validity of law and morally motivated disobedience of unjust laws are annulled in favor of a power struggle.

There is an even more basic problem with the notion that morality is dependent on cultural acceptance for its validity. The problem is that the notion of a culture or society is notoriously difficult to define, especially in a pluralistic society like our own in which the notion seems to be vague. One person may belong to several societies (subcultures) with different emphases on values and arrangements of principles. Another person may belong to the nation (as a single society) that has certain values of patriotism, honor, courage, and laws (including some that are controversial but have majority acceptance, such as the law on abortion). But he or she may also belong to a church that opposes some of the laws of the state. He or she may also be an integral member of a socially mixed community in which different principles hold sway, and he or she may also belong to clubs and a family that adhere to still other rules. Relativism would seem to tell us that when people are members of societies with conflicting moralities, they must be judged both wrong and not wrong whatever they do.

For example, if Mary is a U.S. citizen and a member of the Roman Catholic Church, she is wrong (qua Catholic) if she chooses to have an abortion and not wrong (qua citizen of the United States) if she acts against the teaching of the Church on abortion. As a member of a racist university fraternity, John has no obligation to treat Black students as equals; but as a member of the university community itself (in which the principle of equal rights is accepted), he does have the obligation. As a member of the surrounding community (which may reject the principle of equal rights), John again has no such obligation; but as a member of the nation at large (which accepts the principle), he is obligated to treat others with respect. What are the morally right things for Mary and John to do? The question no longer makes much sense in this moral Babel; morality has lost its action-guiding function.

Perhaps the relativist would adhere to a principle that says that in such cases the individual may choose which group to consider primary. If Mary chooses to have an abortion, she is choosing to belong to the general society relative to that principle. And John must likewise choose among groups. The trouble with this option is that it seems to lead back to counterintuitive results. If Mafia Mike feels like killing Bank President Ortcutt and wants to feel good about it, he identifies with Mafia society rather than the general public morality. Does this justify the killing? In fact, couldn't one justify anything simply by forming a small subculture that approved of it? Charles Manson would be morally pure in killing innocents simply by virtue of forming a little coterie. How large must the group be in order to be a legitimate subculture or society? Does it need 10 or 15 people? How about just 3? Come to think about it, why can't my partner in crime and I found our own society with a morality of its own? Of course, if my partner dies, I could still claim that I was acting from an original social set of norms. But why can't I dispense with the interpersonal agreements altogether and invent my own morality? After all, morality, in this view, is only an invention anyway. Conventionalist-relativism seems to reduce to subjectivism. And subjectivism leads, as we have seen, to the demise of morality altogether.

Should anyone object that this is an instance of the **slippery slope fallacy**, let them give an alternative analysis of what constitutes a viable social basis for generating valid moral principles. Perhaps we might agree (for the sake of argument, at least) that the very nature of morality entails two people making an agreement. This agreement saves the conventionalist from moral solipsism, but it still permits almost any principle at all to count as moral. And what's more, those principles can be thrown out and their contraries substituted for them as the need arises. If two or three people decide that they will make cheating morally acceptable for them at their university, qua "Cheaters Anonymous," then cheating is moral. Why not?

However, although we may fear the demise of morality as we have known it, this in itself may not be a good reason for rejecting relativism (that is, for judging it false). Alas, truth may not always be edifying. But the consequences of this position are sufficiently alarming to prompt us to look carefully for weaknesses in the relativist's argument. So let's reexamine the premises and conclusion listed earlier as the three theses of relativism:

1. **Moral rightness and wrongness of actions vary from society to society so that there are no universal moral standards held by all societies.**

2. **Whether or not it is right for an individual to act in a certain way depends on or is relative to the society to which he or she belongs.**

3. **Therefore, there are no absolute or objective moral standards that apply to all people everywhere and at all times.**

Does any one of these seem problematic? Let's consider the first thesis, the diversity thesis, which we have also called cultural relativism. Perhaps there is not as much diversity as anthropologists like Sumner and Benedict suppose. One can also see great similarities between the moral codes of various cultures. E. O. Wilson has identified over a score of common features,[8] and before him, Clyde Kluckhohn has noted some significant common ground:

Every culture has a concept of murder, distinguishing this from execution, killing in war, and other "justifiable homicides." The notions of incest and other regulations upon sexual behavior, the prohibitions upon untruth under defined circumstances, of restitution and reciprocity, of mutual obligations between parents and children—these and many other moral concepts are altogether universal.[9]

And Colin Turnbull, whose description of the sadistic, semidisplaced Ik in Northern Uganda was seen as evidence of a people without principles of kindness and cooperation, has produced evidence that underneath the surface of that dying society there is a deeper moral code from a time when the tribe flourished that occasionally surfaces and shows its nobler face.[10]

On the other hand, there is enormous cultural diversity, and many societies have radically different moral codes. Cultural relativism seems to be a fact; but even if it is, it does not by itself establish the truth of ethical relativism. Cultural diversity in itself is neutral among theories: The objectivist could concede complete cultural relativism but still defend a form of universalism, for he or she could argue that some cultures simply lack correct moral principles.

Still, a denial of complete cultural relativism (that is, an admission of some universal principles) does not disprove ethical relativism. For even if we did find one or more universal principles, this would not prove that they had any objective status. We could still *imagine* a culture that was an exception to the rule and be unable to criticize it. So the first premise doesn't by itself imply ethical relativism, and its denial doesn't disprove ethical relativism.

We turn to the crucial second thesis, the dependency thesis. Morality does not occur in a vacuum, but rather what is considered morally right or wrong must be seen in a context that depends on the goals, wants, beliefs, history, and environment of the society in question. We distinguished between a weak and a strong thesis of dependency. The weak thesis says that the application of principles depends on the particular cultural predicament, whereas the strong thesis affirms that the principles themselves depend on that predicament. The nonrelativist can accept a certain relativity in the way moral principles are *applied* in various cultures, depending on beliefs, history, and environment. For example, a harsh environment with scarce natural resources may justify the Eskimos' brand of euthanasia to the objectivist, who in another evironment would consistently reject that practice. The Nuer in Sudan throw their deformed children into the river because of their belief that such infants belong to the hippopotamus, the god of the river. We believe that they have a false belief about this, but the point is that the same principles of respect for property and respect for human life are operative in these contrary practices. The Nuer differ with us only in belief, not in substantive moral principle. This is an illustration of how nonmoral beliefs (for example, that deformed children belong to the hippopotamus) when applied to common moral principles (for example, give to each his or her due) generate different actions in different cultures. In our own culture the difference in the nonmoral belief about the status of a fetus generates opposite moral prescriptions. So the fact that moral principles are weakly dependent doesn't show that ethical relativism is valid. In spite of this weak dependency on nonmoral factors, there could still be a set of general moral norms, applicable to all cultures and even recognized in most, that are disregarded at a culture's own expense.

What the relativist needs is a strong thesis of dependency—that somehow all principles are essentially cultural inventions. But why should we choose to view morality this way? Is there anything to recommend the strong thesis over the weak thesis of dependency? The relativist may argue that in fact we don't have an obvious impartial standard from which to judge: "Who's to say which culture is right and which is wrong?" But this argument seems dubious. We can reason and perform thought-experiments in order to make a case for one system over another. We may not be able to *know* with certainty that our moral beliefs are closer to the truth than those of another culture or those of others within our own culture, but we may be *justified in believing* that they are. If we can be closer to the truth regarding factual or scientific matters, why can't we be closer to the truth on moral matters? Why can't a culture simply be confused or wrong about its moral perceptions? Why can't we say that a society like that of the Ik, which sees nothing wrong with enjoying watching its own children fall into fires, is less moral in that regard than the culture that cherishes children and grants them protection and equal rights? To take such a stand does not commit the fallacy of ethnocentrism, for in doing so we are seeking to derive principles through critical reason, not simply through uncritical acceptance of one's own mores.

THE CASE FOR
MORAL OBJECTIVISM

If nonrelativists are to make their case, they must offer a better explanation of cultural diversity and of why we should nevertheless adhere to moral objectivism. One way of doing this is to appeal to a divine law and to human sin, which causes deviation from that law. Although I think that human greed, selfishness, pride, self-deception, and other maladies have a great deal to do with moral differences and that religion may lend great support to morality (see the discussion in Chapter 10), I don't think that a religious justification is necessary for the validity of moral principles. In any case, in this section I shall outline a modest nonreligious objectivism, first by appealing to our intuitions and then by giving a naturalist account of morality that transcends individual cultures.

First, I must make it clear that I am distinguishing moral *absolutism* from moral *objectivism*. The absolutist believes that there are nonoverridable moral principles that ought never to be violated. Kant's system (see Chapter 6) is a good example of this: One ought never break a promise, no matter what. Act utilitarianism also seems absolutist, for the principle 'Do that act that has the most promise of yielding the most utility' is nonoverridable. An objectivist need not posit any nonoverridable principles, at least not in unqualified general form, and so need not be an absolutist. As Renford Bambrough put it,

> To suggest that there is a *right* answer to a moral problem is at once to be accused of or credited with a belief in moral absolutes. But it is no more necessary to believe in moral absolutes in order to believe in moral objectivity than it is to believe in the existence of absolute space or absolute time in order to believe in the objectivity of temporal and spatial relations and of judgements about them.[11]

In the objectivist's account moral principles are what William Ross refers to as "prima facie principles"[12]—valid rules of action that should generally be adhered to, but that may be overridden by another moral principle in cases of moral conflict. For example, even though a principle of justice may generally outweigh a principle of benevolence, there are times when enormous good could be done by sacrificing a small amount of justice; thus an objectivist would be inclined to act according to the principle of benevolence. There may be some absolute or nonoverridable principles, but there need not be many (or even any) for objectivism to be true.[13]

If we can establish or show that it is reasonable to believe that there is at least one objective moral principle that is binding on all people everywhere in some ideal sense, we will have shown that relativism is probably false and that a limited objectivism is true. Actually, I believe that there are many qualified general ethical principles that are binding on all rational beings, but one will suffice to refute relativism. The principle I've chosen is the following:

A. It is morally wrong to torture people for the fun of it.

I claim that this principle is binding on all rational agents, so that if some agent, S, rejects A, we should not let that affect our intuition that A is a true principle; rather, we should try to explain S's behavior as perverse, ignorant, or irrational instead. For example, suppose Adolf Hitler doesn't accept A. Should that affect our confidence in the truth of A? Is it not more reasonable to infer that Hitler is morally deficient, morally blind, ignorant, or irrational than it is to suppose that his noncompliance is evidence against the truth of A?

Suppose further that there is a tribe of "Hitlerites" somewhere who enjoy torturing people. The whole culture accepts torturing others for the fun of it. Suppose that Mother Teresa or Gandhi tries unsuccessfully to convince them that they should stop torturing people altogether, and they respond by torturing them. Should this affect our confidence in A? Would it not be more reasonable to look for some explanation of "Hitlerite" behavior? For example, we might hypothesize that this tribe lacked a developed sense of sympathetic imagination that is necessary for the moral life. Or we might theorize that this tribe was on a lower evolutionary level than most *Homo sapiens*. Or we might simply conclude that the tribe was closer to a Hobbesian state of nature than are most societies, and as such probably would not survive. But we need not know the correct reason why the tribe was in such bad shape in order to maintain our confidence in A as a moral principle. If A is a basic or core belief for us, we will be more likely to doubt the tribe members' sanity or ability to think morally than we are to doubt the validity of A.

We can perhaps produce other candidates for membership in our minimally basic, objective moral set. For example:

B. Do not kill innocent people.

C. Do not cause pain or suffering except when a higher duty prescribes it.

D. Do not commit rape.

E. Keep your promises and contracts.

F. Do not deprive another person of his or her freedom.

G. Do justice, treating equals equally.

H. Tell the truth.

Fortunately, it isn't as though A through H were arbitrary principles, for we can give reasons why we believe that these rules will be necessary to any satisfactory social order. Principles like the Golden Rule, not killing innocent people, treating equals equally, telling the truth, keeping promises, and the like are central to the fluid progression of social interaction and the resolution of conflicts of which ethics are about (at least minimal morality is, even though there may be more to morality than simply these kinds of concerns). For example, language itself depends on a general and implicit commitment to the principle of truth-telling, for accuracy of expression is a primitive form of truthfulness. Hence, every time we use words correctly we are telling the truth. Without this behavior, language wouldn't be possible. Likewise, without the recognition of a rule of promise-keeping, contracts are of no avail and cooperation is less likely to occur. And without the protection of life and liberty, we could not secure our other goals.

A morality would be adequate if it contained a requisite set of these objective principles (call them the stable core morality), but there could be more than one adequate morality that contained different rankings of these principles and other principles that are consistent with core morality. That is, there may be a certain relativity to secondary principles (for example, whether to opt for monogamy rather than polygamy, whether to include a principle of high altruism in the set of moral duties, whether to allow for limited euthanasia, and so forth), but in every morality a certain core will remain, even though it may be applied somewhat differently because of differences in environment, belief, tradition, and the like.

The core moral rules are analogous to the set of nutrients necessary for a healthy diet. We need an adequate amount of each nutrient—some people need more of one than of another—but in prescribing a nutritional diet we don't have to specify recipes, specific foods, place settings, or culinary habits. Gourmets will meet the requirements differently than will ascetics and vegetarians, but the basic nutrients may be had by all without rigid regimentation or an absolute set of recipes.

Stated more positively, an objectivist who bases his or her moral system on a common human nature with common needs and desires might argue for objectivism somewhat in this manner:

1. Human nature is relatively similar in essential respects in that it has a common set of needs and interests.
2. Moral principles are functions of human needs and interests, instituted by reason in order to promote the most significant interests and needs of rational beings (and perhaps others).

3. Some moral principles promote human interests and meet human needs better than others.

4. Those principles that meet essential needs and promote the most significant interests of humans in optimal ways can be said to be objectively valid moral principles.

5. Therefore, because there is a common human nature, there is an objectively valid set of moral principles, applicable to all humanity.

If we leave out any reference to a common human nature, the argument would be even simpler:

1. Objectively valid moral principles are those, adherence to which meets the needs and promotes the most significant interests of persons.

2. Some principles are such that adherence to them meets the needs and promotes the most significant interests of persons.

3. Therefore, there are some objectively valid moral principles.

Either argument would satisfy objectivism, but the former makes it clearer that it is our common human nature that generates the common principles.[14]

If this argument succeeds, then there are ideal moralities (and not simply adequate ones). Of course, there could still be more than one ideal morality that an ideal observer would presumably choose under optimal conditions. The ideal observer may conclude that, out of an infinite set of moralities, two, three, or more combinations would tie for first place. One would expect that these moralities would be similar, but there is every reason to believe that all of them would contain the set of core principles.

Of course, we don't know what an ideal observer would choose, but we can imagine that the conditions under which such an observer would choose would be conditions of impartiality and maximal knowledge about the consequences of action-types, second-order qualities that ensure that agents have the best chance of making the best decisions. If this is so, then the more we learn to judge impartially and the more we know about possible forms of life, the better chance we have to approximate an ideal moral system. And if there is the possibility of approximating ideal moral systems with an objective core and other objective components, then ethical relativism is certainly false, and we can confidently dismiss it as an aberration and get on with the job of working out better moral systems.

Let me appeal to your intuitions in another way to make the same point. Imagine that you have been mysteriously transported to the dark kingdom of hell, and there you get a glimpse of the sufferings of the damned. What is their punishment? Well, they have eternal back itches that ebb and flow continuously. But they cannot scratch their backs, for their arms are paralyzed in front of them, and so they writhe with itchiness through eternity. But just as you are beginning to feel the itch in your own back, you are miraculously transported to heaven. What do you see in the kingdom of the blessed? Well, you see people with eternal back itches who cannot scratch their own backs, but they are all smiling instead of writhing. Why? Because everyone has his or her arms stretched out to scratch someone else's back, and, with their arrangement in one big circle, a hell of agony is turned into a heaven of ecstasy.

If we can imagine some states of affairs or cultures that are better than others in a way that depends on human action, we can ask what are those character traits that make them so. In our story the people in heaven, but not those in hell, cooperate for the amelioration of suffering and the production of pleasure. These are very primitive goods; they are not sufficient for a full-blown morality, but they give us a hint about the objectivity of morality. Moral goodness has something to do with the ameliorating of suffering, the resolution of conflict, and the promotion of human flourishing. If our heaven is really better than the eternal itchiness of hell, then whatever makes it so is constitutively related to moral rightness.

AN EXPLANATION OF THE ATTRACTION OF ETHICAL RELATIVISM

Why, then, is there such a strong inclination toward ethical relativism? I think that there are five reasons, which haven't been emphasized. One is the fact that absolutism and relativism are usually presented as though they were the only alternatives, so conventional ethical relativism wins out against an implausible competitor. My student questionnaire reads as follows: "Are there any ethical absolutes, moral duties binding on all persons at all times, or are moral duties relative to culture? Is there any alternative to these two positions?" Less than 5 percent suggest a third position, and very few of them identify objectivism. Granted, it takes a little philosophical sophistication to make the crucial distinctions, and it is precisely because of the lack of this sophistication or reflection that relativism has attained its enormous prestige. But, as Ross and others have shown and as I have argued in this chapter, one can have an objective morality without being absolutist.

The second reason for an inclination toward ethical relativism is similar to the first. Some philosophers and thoughtful people confuse objectivism with realism—the view that moral truths make up an independent reality, just as scientific truths do. Plato is perhaps the classic realist; he believed in a separate and transcendental sphere of reality ("the really real") wherein existed ideal forms that all the things in our world more or less copied. Moral ideals and principles would have their existence in this sphere of reality. Most contemporary moral realists hold less extravagant views, but they believe, nevertheless, in an independent status for moral truths. But moral objectivists need not be realists. They may only affirm the validity of moral principles on the basis of common human nature and intersubjective agreement among people in favorable conditions.

In his attack on moral objectivism, a leading relativist, J. L. Mackie, admits that there is a great deal of intersubjectivity in ethics: "There could be agreement in valuing even if valuing is just something people do, even if this activity is not further validated. Subjective agreement would give intersubjective values, but intersubjectivity is not objectivity."[15] But Mackie fails to note that there are two kinds of intersubjectivity and that one of them provides all that the objectivist wants for a moral theory. Consider the following situations of intersubjective agreement:

A1. All the children in first grade at school S would agree that playing in the mud is preferable to learning arithmetic.

A2. All the youth in the district would rather take drugs than go to school.

A3. All the people in Jonestown, British Guiana, agreed that Rev. Jones was a prophet from God and loved him dearly.

A4. Almost all the people in community C voted for George Bush.

B1. All thirsty people desire water to quench their thirst.

B2. All humans (and animals) prefer pleasure to pain.

B3. Almost all people agree that living in society is more satisfying than living as hermits.

The naturalist contrasts these two sets of intersubjective agreements and says that the first set is accidental—not part of what it means to be a person—whereas the agreements in the second set are basic to being a person, basic to our nature. Agreement on the essence of morality, on the core set, is the kind of intersubjective agreement that is more like the second set, not the first. It is part of the essence of a human in a community, part of what it means to flourish as a person, to agree and adhere to the moral code.

The third reason for an inclination toward ethical relativism is that our recent sensitivity to cultural relativism and to the evils of ethnocentrism, which have plagued the relations of Europeans and Americans with those of other cultures, has made us conscious of the frailty of many aspects of our moral repertoire, so that there is a tendency to wonder "Who's to judge what's really right or wrong?" However, the move from a reasonable cultural relativism, which rightly causes us to rethink our moral systems, to an ethical relativism, which causes us to give up the heart of morality altogether, is an instance of the fallacy of confusing factual or descriptive statements with normative ones. Cultural relativism doesn't entail ethical relativism. The very reason that we are against ethnocentrism constitutes the same basis for our being for an objective moral system: Impartial reason draws us to it.

We may well agree that cultures differ and that we ought to be cautious in condemning what we don't understand, but this in no way need imply that there are not better and worse ways of living. We can understand and excuse, to some degree at least, those who differ from our best notions of morality without abdicating the notion that cultures without principles of justice or promise-keeping or protection of the innocent are morally poorer for these omissions.

A fourth reason, which has driven some to moral nihilism and others to relativism, is the decline of religion in western society. As one of Dostoevsky's characters said, "If God is dead, all things are permitted." The person who has lost religious faith feels a deep vacuum and understandably confuses it with a moral vacuum, or he or she finally resigns himself or herself to a form of secular conventionalism. Such people reason that if there is no God to guarantee the validity of the moral order, then there must not be a universal moral order; there is only radical cultural diversity and death at the end. I have tried to argue that even without God objective moral principles are valid. The relationship of religion to morality will be discussed at length in Chapter 10.

The fifth reason, which is influential with philosophers who are overly impressed with **metaethics**, is that many philosophers believe that it is important to begin to study ethics with a morally neutral definition. *Webster's Ninth New Collegiate Dictionary* defines 'ethics' as "the principles of conduct governing an individual or a group." No judgment is made from the outset about the content of those principles, and because the diversity thesis is plausible, one can be led to think that a certain relativism follows.

Although this definition may be a fair one for sociology or anthropology, it is inadequate for philosophy. There is a narrower definition of the term that has to do with the Good, with human (and probably nonhuman sentient creatures') flourishing. And this flourishing involves the amelioration of suffering, the promotion of happiness, and the resolution of conflicts of interest. Given this content-laden conception of morality, we can explain why we are loath to call Hitler's actions or torturing little children morally right, regardless of whether a majority approves of them.

So who's to judge what's right or wrong? We are. We are to do so on the basis of the best reasoning we can bring forth and with sympathy and understanding.

Notes

1. John Ladd, ed., *Ethical Relativism* (Wadsworth, 1973), p. 1.

2. Ruth Benedict, *Patterns of Culture* (New American Library, 1934), p. 257.

3. W. G. Sumner, *Folkways* (Ginn & Co., 1906), section 80., p. 76. Ruth Benedict indicates the depth of our cultural conditioning this way: "The very eyes with which we see the problem are conditioned by the long traditional habits of our own society." ["Anthropology and the Abnormal," *The Journal of General Psychology* (1934): 59–82.]

4. The following quote from Ernest Hemingway is an example of subjective relativism: "So far, about morals, I know only that what is moral is what you feel good after and what is immoral is what you feel bad after and judged by these moral standards, which I do not defend, the bullfight is very moral to me because I feel very fine while it is going on and have a feeling of life and death and mortality and immortality, and after it is over I feel very sad but very fine" [*Death in the Afternoon* (Scribner's, 1932), p. 4.]

5. Part of this section has been influenced by Fred Feldman's treatment of the same topic in *Introductory Ethics* (Prentice-Hall, 1978).

6. Ruth Benedict, *Patterns of Culture* (New American Library, 1934), p. 257.

7. Melville Herskovits, *Cultural Relativism* (Random House, 1972).

8. E. O. Wilson, *On Human Nature* (Bantam Books, 1979), p. 22f.

9. Clyde Kluckhorn, "Ethical Relativity: Sic et Non," *Journal of Philosophy* (1955): LII.

10. Colin Turnbull, *The Mountain People* (Simon & Schuster, 1972).

11. Renford Bambrough, *Moral Skepticism and Moral Knowledge* (Routledge & Kegan Paul, 1979), p. 33.

12. William Ross, *The Right and the Good* (Oxford University Press, 1932), p. 18ff.

13. See Marcus Singer's "The Idea of a Rational Morality" (*Proceedings of the American Philosophical Association*, 1986): in which he argues that such principles as 'It is always wrong to lie for lying's sake' are absolutely wrong. "Given any moral rule to the effect that some kind of action is generally wrong, it follows that it is always wrong to do an act of that kind just for the sake of doing it" (p. 28). An unqualified general principle would be of the form 'Always do X' or 'In general do X', but a qualified general principle would be in the form 'In general do X except in condition C' or 'Except under condition C, always do X'. Suitably conditioned objective principles might turn out to be qualified absolutes. I'm sympathetic to this approach and suspect that there are some absolutes that are valid. Most valid moral principles seem to be merely objective, however.

14. I owe the reformulation of this argument to Bruce Russell, who offered valuable criticisms of an earlier version of this chapter.

15. J. L. Mackie, *Ethics: Inventing Right and Wrong* (Penguin, 1977), p. 22.

For Further Reflection

1. After reading this chapter, how would you respond to the question, "Are there any moral absolutes, or is morality completely relative?" Can we separate the descriptive aspect of anthropological study from the prescriptive aspect of evaluating cultures? Are there some independent criteria by which we can say that some cultures are better than others? Can you think how this project of evaluating cultures might be begun?

2. Ruth Benedict has written that our culture is "but one entry in a long series of possible adjustments" and that "the very eyes with which we see the problem are conditioned by the long traditional habits of our own society." What are the implications of these statements? Is she correct? How would an objectivist respond to these claims?

3. In an ancient writing, the Greek historian Herodotus (485–430) relates that the Persian King Darius once called into his presence some Greeks and asked them "what he should pay them to eat the bodies of their fathers when they died." They replied that no sum of money would tempt them to do such a terrible deed, whereupon Darius sent for certain people of the Callatian tribe, who eat their fathers, and asked them in the presence of the Greeks "what he should give them to burn the bodies of their fathers at their decease [as the Greeks do]." The Callatians were horrified at the thought and bid him desist in such terrible talk. So, Herodotus concludes, "Culture is King o'er all." Is this a good illustration of the truth of ethical relativism? Why or why not?

For Further Reading

Brink, David. *Moral Realism and the Foundation of Ethics*. Cambridge University Press, 1989.

Fishkin, James. *Beyond Subjective Morality*. Yale University Press, 1984.

Gilbert Harman. "Moral Relativism Defended," *Philosophical Review* 84, 1975.

Ladd, John, ed. *Ethical Relativism*. Wadsworth , 1973. A good collection of basic readings.

Mackie, J. L. *Ethics: Inventing Right and Wrong*. Penguin, 1976.

Stace, W. T. *The Concept of Morals*. Macmillan, 1937.

Taylor, Paul. *Principles of Ethics*. Dickenson, 1975, Chapter 2.

Wellman, Carl. "The Ethical Implications of Cultural Relativity," *Journal of Philosophy* LX, 1963.

Westermarck, Edward. *Ethical Relativity*. Humanities Press, 1960.

Williams, Bernard. *Morality*. Harper Torchbooks, 1972.

Williams, Bernard. *Ethics and the Limits of Philosophy*. Harvard University Press, 1985.

Wong, David. *Moral Relativity*. University of California Press, 1985.

CHAPTER 3

Egoism
and Ethics

Evaluate this statement (S): "Everyone is an egoist, for everyone always tries to do what will bring one satisfaction." I first encountered this statement in a student paper. Is it true or false?

WHAT IS THE PLACE of self-interest in morality? Is everything we do really done out of the motive of self-interest, so that morality is necessarily egoistic? Is some form of egoism the best moral theory? Or is egoism really diametrically opposed to true morality? What is the relationship of egoism to morality? These are the questions that we shall discuss in this chapter, but before we can consider them we need to make some careful distinctions and define our terms. First of all, there are at least four different types of egoism: psychological egoism, personal egoism, individual ethical egoism, and universal ethical egoism. These may be roughly defined in the following way:

1. Psychological egoism is the doctrine that everyone always does that act that one perceives to be in one's best self-interest. Accordingly, we have no choice but to be selfish; we cannot be motivated by anything other than what we believe will promote our interests. I always try to promote my self-interest and you always try to promote your self-interest.

2. Personal egoism is the state of being selfish by choice. I simply always choose to serve my own best interests, regardless of what happens to anyone else. This is not a reflective judgment about what is right or wrong or what ought to be the case; as such it is

not an ethical theory at all, but a phenomenal state of exclusive self-love. We might call this form of egoism "phenomenal *egotism*" or just plain selfishness.

3. Individual ethical egoism is the view that everyone *ought* to serve *my* best interest. Unlike personal egoism or phenomenal egotism, this doctrine prescribes that others serve me (the speaker). This claims to be a moral theory that obligates others to look after my interests before everything else. It also is a version of selfishness, a version that claims moral authority.

4. Universal ethical egoism is the view that everyone *ought* to do those acts that will best serve his or her best self-interest, even when it conflicts with the interests of others.

We turn now to an examination of each of these views, beginning with psychological egoism.

PSYCHOLOGICAL EGOISM

Mr. Lincoln once remarked to a fellow-passenger on an old-time mud-coach that all men were prompted by selfishness in doing good. His fellow-passenger was antagonizing this position when they were passing over a corduroy bridge that spanned a slough. As they crossed this bridge they espied an old razorbacked sow on the bank making a terrible noise because her pigs had got into the slough and were in danger of drowning. As the old coach began to climb the hill, Mr. Lincoln called out, "Driver, can't you stop just a moment?" Then Mr. Lincoln jumped out, ran back and lifted the little pigs out of the mud and water and placed them on the bank. When he returned, his companion remarked: "Now Abe, where does selfishness come in on this little episode?" "Why, bless your soul Ed, that was the very essence of selfishness. I should have had no peace of mind all day had I gone on and left that suffering old sow worrying over those pigs. I did it to get peace of mind, don't you see?" [Quoted from the *Springfield Monitor* by F. C. Sharp in *Ethics* (Appleton-Century, 1928), p. 28.]

Psychological egoism (PE) purports to be a *description* of human nature. It claims that we cannot do other than act from self-interested motivation, so that **altruism**—the theory that we can and should sometimes act in favor of others' interests—is simply invalid because it is impossible. Because 'ought' implies 'can' (that is, we can never be under an obligation to do what is impossible), it follows that we cannot do anything but act in our own interests. Psychological egoism is not itself an ethical theory. It is a psychological theory about human nature or the nature of motivation, but as such it seems to imply ethical egoism—the doctrine that it is morally right always to seek one's own self-interest. The argument might be set down like this:

1. Everyone always seeks to maximize one's own self-interest. (PE)
2. If one cannot do an act, one has no obligation to do that act.
3. Altruistic acts involve putting other peoples' interests ahead of our own
4. But **altruism** contradicts human nature (PE or premise 1) and so is impossible.
5. Therefore, (by premises 2 and 4) altruistic acts are never morally obligatory. We have no duty to put another's interests ahead of our own.

It follows from this that the only obligations we can be said to have are those that maximize our own self-interest, as ethical egoism prescribes.

Let us begin our analysis by examining the statement at the beginning of this chapter as an illustration of psychological egoism: (S) "Everyone is an egoist, for everyone always tries to do what will bring one satisfaction." Is (S) true? What can be said in its favor? Well, at first sight it seems ambiguous. On the one hand, it may mean that

(S1) For any act A, everyone does A *in order* to obtain satisfaction.

Satisfaction is the goal. From this interpretation it may be inferred that everyone always acts in such a way as to maximize one's self-interest (PE), which is interpreted in terms of satisfaction of wants. But (S) may conceivably mean that

(S2) Everyone does the act one most wants to do and *as a consequence* is satisfied by the success of carrying out the act.

The first interpretation implies psychological egoism, but the second does not.

Consider the first interpretation, which might be enlarged to read: "We all want to be happy—to find satisfaction in life—and everything we do we consciously do toward that end." Abe Lincoln (in the story quoted at the beginning of this section) claimed to help the piglets out of the slough to relieve his conscience, sheerly out of selfish motivation. As he says of his rescue of the piglets, "Why, bless your soul Ed, that was the very essence of selfishness. I should have had no peace of mind all day had I gone on and left the suffering old sow worrying over those pigs. I did it to get peace of mind. . . ."

Lincoln argued that there is no such thing as disinterested or altruistic action. Is he correct about this? Is everything we do done out of selfish motivation? Consider a variation on the Lincoln story. The situation is the same, only it is Ed who asks the driver to halt and spontaneously jumps out to save the piglets. He returns from the ordeal, pleased. Lincoln now greets him with these words, "Ed, you know that what you did was the very essence of selfishness. You couldn't have lived with yourself had you not tried to help those piglets."

But Ed replies, "Abe, I wasn't aware of seeking my own happiness in trying to help those piglets. I did it because I believe that suffering should be alleviated. Of course I feel satisfaction for having succeeded, but satisfaction is an automatic accompaniment of any successful action. Even if I had failed to help them, I would have felt a measure of satisfaction in that I succeeded in *trying* to help them."

Lincoln seems wrong and Ed seems right in his assessment of the relation of motivation to success. We do not always consciously seek our own satisfaction or happiness when we act. In fact, some people seem to seek their own unhappiness, as masochists and self-destructive people do, and we all sometimes seem to act spontaneously without consciously considering our happiness.

Ed's position approximates the second interpretation of the motivation statement (S):

(S2) Everyone does the act that one most wants to do and *as a consequence* is satisfied by the success of carrying out the act.

Actually, (S2) doesn't seem quite right, for it is doubtful whether we always do what we most want to do. When I am on a diet, I most want to refrain from eating delicious chocolate cakes and rich ice cream, but I sometimes find myself yielding to the temptation. Alcoholics and other addicts have even more poignant experiences of doing what they don't want to do. Such experiences of weakness of will count heavily against (S2). Let us therefore attempt one more interpretation of (S):

(S3) Everyone always tries to do what one most wants to do and as a consequence of success in carrying out the act experiences satisfaction.

(S3) takes weakness of will into account and so seems closer to the truth. It also seems better for the following reason: We usually are not conscious of any concern for satisfaction when we seek some goal, but satisfaction seems to follow naturally on accomplishing any task. Suppose I were told by some super psychologist who could reliably predict outcomes that two courses of action were open to me: I could (a) commit a perfect robbery, kill Bank President Ortcutt, and flee to Switzerland to live a happy life or (b) live as a low-paid college teacher. Suppose further that this psychologist convinced me that (a) would actually yield 1,000 units of happiness or satisfaction (call these units "hedons"), whereas (b) would only yield 100 hedons. I would choose (b) without a moment's deliberation; wouldn't you? This seems to show that we act out of our overall value schemas and find satisfaction in achieving our goals, but that satisfaction is not itself the only goal. This is what John Stuart Mill meant when he said, "Better to be Socrates dissatisfied, than a fool satisfied."[1] Seeking satisfaction for its own sake and nothing else seems to merit Mill's pejorative "Pig Philosophy." We all want to be happy, but we don't want happiness at any price or to the exclusion of certain other values.

Moreover, happiness itself seems a peculiar kind of goal. As the **paradox of hedonism** asserts, the best way to get happiness is to forget about it. That is, you'll have a higher probability of attaining happiness if you aim at accomplishing worthy goals that will indirectly bring about happiness:

> I sought the bird of bliss, she flew away.
> I sought my neighbor's good, she flew my way.

Happiness seems to be an elusive goal so long as we desire it alone and for its own sake. It is in the process of reaching other intrinsically worthy goals that happiness comes into being. Joel Feinberg puts the paradox of hedonism this way. Imagine a person, Jones,

> who is, first of all, devoid of intellectual curiosity. He has no desire to acquire any kind of knowledge for its own sake, and thus is utterly indifferent to questions of science, mathematics, and philosophy. Imagine further that the beauties of nature leave Jones cold: he is unimpressed by the autumn foliage, the snow-capped mountains, and the rolling oceans. Long walks in the country on spring mornings and skiing forays in the winter are to him equally a bore. Moreover, let us suppose that Jones can find no appeal in art. Novels are dull, poetry a pain, paintings nonsense and music just noise. Suppose further that Jones has neither the participant's nor the spectator's passion for baseball, football, tennis, or any other sport. Swimming to him is a cruel aquatic form of calisthenics, the sun only a cause of sunburn. Dancing is coeducational

idiocy, conversation a waste of time, the other sex an unappealing mystery. Politics is a fraud, religion mere superstition; and the misery of millions of underprivileged human beings is nothing to be concerned with or excited about. Suppose finally that Jones has no talent for any kind of handicraft, industry, or commerce, and that he does not regret that fact.

What then is Jones interested in? He must desire something. To be sure, he does. Jones has an overwhelming passion for, a complete preoccupation with, his own happiness. The one exclusive desire of his life is to be happy. It takes little imagination at this point to see that Jones's one desire is bound to be frustrated.[2]

The paradox of hedonism seems to suggest that psychological egoism has severe problems.

But suppose that the psychological egoist alters the interpretation of (S) to include subconscious motivation. The thesis now states that sometimes we are self-deceived about our motivation, but whenever we overcome self-deception and really look deeply into our motivational schemes, we find an essential selfishness.

Is the self-deception argument sound? One problem with it is that it seems to be an unfalsifiable dogma, for what evidence could ever count against it? Suppose that you look within your motivational structure and do not find a predominant egoistic motive. What does the egoist say to this? The egoist responds that you just haven't looked deep enough! But how, you may wonder, do I know when I have looked deep enough? The egoist contends it is when you discover the selfish motive.

Perhaps the self-deception argument is simply an outcome of dubious psychological theories. Or perhaps it is built on the doctrine of original sin or the Calvinist notion of the total depravity of human nature, in which case it is a theological doctrine, not a truth discoverable by empirical investigation. For example, if Lincoln's friend Ed introspects his motivational scheme in pulling the piglets out of the slough and fails to find a selfish motive, Abe might respond, "Ed, I don't mean that the selfishness is always conscious. Self-deception is very deep in humans, so you just haven't looked deep enough."

This contention may show that we can never disprove psychological egoism, but it doesn't offer support to the egoist thesis. Quite the contrary. If we look as deep as we can and still don't come up with a selfish motive, then we're justified in believing that not all action is motivated by agent-utility considerations. The burden of proof is on the egoist to convince us that we are still self-deceived. The egoist seems to be guilty of committing the fallacy of unwarranted generalization: Just because we are sometimes self-deceived about our motives, the egoist reasons, we must always be. But this doesn't follow at all.

Suppose it is the case that humans are predominantly psychological egoists—that we are very often motivated by self-regarding motives. This does not imply that we are entirely egoists, nor does it mean that we are necessarily selfish. *Webster's Collegiate Dictionary* defines 'selfish' as "regarding one's own comfort, advantage, etc. in disregard of, or at the expense of that of others." But we may find that our values are such that we incorporate the good of others as part of our happiness. A friend's or lover's happiness is so bound up with the good of the other that the two cannot be separated. So if psychological egoism is interpreted as selfishness, it is surely false. If it is simply a statement of how we are motivated, then it probably still is false. Something like it—predominant psychological egoism—may be true, but this does not rule out the possibility of disinterested action. We will examine the implications of predominant psychological egoism shortly.

Let us now return to our original argument against the possibility of altruism, the view that we are able at times to act on other-regarding motives.

1. Everyone always seeks to maximize one's own self-interest. (PE)
2. If one cannot do an act, one has no obligation to do that act.
3. Altruistic acts involve putting other peoples' interests ahead of our own.
4. But altruism contradicts human nature (PE or premise 1) and so is impossible.
5. Therefore, (by premises 2 and 4) altruistic acts are never morally obligatory. We have no duty to put another's interests ahead of our own.

We see that the first premise, if interpreted as selfishness, is false, for sometimes we do put other people's interests ahead of our own; thus the argument is unsound and does not show that altruism is impossible. Whether or not altruism is a moral duty is another question, which we'll examine in the next two sections. We turn now to other forms of egoism.

ETHICAL EGOISM

In this section we will consider three other forms of egoism: personal egoism, individual ethical egoism, and universal ethical egoism. Personal egoism does not claim to be an ethical theory, though some people live by it. Individual ethical egoism and universal ethical egoism claim to be ethical theories.

Personal egoism is not a description of human nature, but merely a description of a type of personality. It does not imply any of the other theories and is neutral between egoist and nonegoist ethical theories. Although psychological egoism is false, there seem to be many personal egoists. Personal egoism may be equated with selfishness, and it comes closest to *egotism*, the behavioral pattern in which one constantly draws attention to oneself. Egoists need not be egotists, but may be more subtle about their self-interestedness.

Individual ethical egoism is the view that everyone ought to serve *my* self-interest. That is, moral rightness is defined solely in terms of what is good for me, whether or not it is good for anyone else. Of course, everyone of us may put his own name in the place of "me." Say, for example, that Aunt Ruth is a personal egoist. So all moral rightness defines itself in terms of what is good for Aunt Ruth. It would then follow that whether or not a mother in India loves her child is morally irrelevant, for it has no effect on Aunt Ruth. Once Aunt Ruth is dead, morality is dead, for it has no object. Interestingly enough, although individual ethical egoism seems implausible, it may be the central position of many religious people who define ethics as "that which serves God's interests and pleases him." Be that as it may, as far as mere mortals are concerned, individual ethical egoism seems a partial and absurd theory. What makes *you* so special that all of us have an obligation to grant your interests as our primary concern?

Universal ethical egoism is the theory that everyone ought to serve his or her own self-interest. That is, everyone ought to do what will maximize one's own expected utility or bring about one's own happiness, even when it means harming others. This theory has all the earmarks of a legitimate ethical theory. It is a universal theory, which individualist egoism is not. It is not egotistical, but rather it is prudential and favors long-term interests over short-term ones. In its most sophisticated form it urges everyone to *try* to win in the game of life, and it recognizes that in order to do this, some compromises are necessary. Indeed, the universal egoist will admit that to some extent we must all give up a certain amount of freedom and cooperate with others to achieve our ends.

Are there any arguments that support an adequate moral theory based on egoism? There are three that we should consider: (1) The Economist Argument, (2) The Ayn Rand Argument for the Virtue of Selfishness, and (3) The Hobbesian Argument. Let's examine each of them in turn.

The Economist Argument

Economists in the mold of Adam Smith often argue that individual self-interest in a competitive marketplace produces a state of optimal goodness for society at large because the peculiar nature of self-interested competition causes each individual to produce a better product and sell it at a lower price than competitors. Thus enlightened self-interest leads, as by an invisible hand, to the best overall situation.

The Ayn Rand Argument for the Virtue of Selfishness

In her book *The Virtue of Selfishness*, Ayn Rand argues that selfishness is a virtue and altruism is a vice, a totally destructive idea that ultimately undermines individual worth: "If a man accepts the ethics of altruism, his first concern is not how to live his life, but how to sacrifice it. . . . Altruism erodes men's capacity to grasp the value of an individual life; it reveals a mind from which the reality of a human being has been wiped out."[3] Altruism calls on one to sacrifice his or her life, not to find happiness, which is the highest goal of life.

Her argument seems to go something like this:

1. The perfection of one's abilities in a state of happiness is the highest goal for humans. We have a moral duty to attempt to reach this goal.
2. The ethics of altruism prescribes that we sacrifice our interests and lives for the good of others.
3. Therefore, the ethics of altruism is incompatible with the goal of happiness.
4. Ethical egoism prescribes that we seek our own happiness exclusively, and as such it is consistent with the happiness goal.
5. Therefore, ethical egoism is the correct moral theory.

The Hobbesian Argument

According to Hobbes we are predominantly psychological egoists by nature, and we might as well recognize that as a given. It is permissible to live self-interested lives because we cannot do otherwise without unreasonable effort. However, enlightened common sense tells us that we should aim at fulfilling our long-term versus our short-term interests, and so we need to refrain from immediate gratification of our senses—from doing those things that would break down the social conditions that enable us to reach our goals. We should even, perhaps, generally obey the Golden Rule, "Do unto others as you would have them do unto you," for doing good unto others will help ensure that they do good unto us. However, sometimes we should cheat when our doing so will maximize agent utility, and sometimes we should harm others when it is in our overall self-interest to do so.

Sometimes this version of egoism is based on the notion of agent-relative values. The theory is that all values are essentially owned by an agent and that each of us has our own hierarchy and specific set of values, so that each of us has different reasons for acting. There are no agent-neutral values (material conception of values) that are identical in all persons. Naturally, we will have to cooperate with others in the pursuit of our projects, but ultimately we are alone in the world, the only ones who know exactly what the values are. Sometimes we may have to harm others in order to realize our projects.[4]

A CRITIQUE OF ETHICAL EGOISM

Essentialy the Economist Argument is not an argument for ethical egoism. It is really an argument for utilitarianism (see Chapter 5), which makes use of self-interest to attain (paradoxically) the good of all. The goal of this argument is social utility, but it places its faith in an invisible hand inherent in the free enterprise system that guides enlightened self-interest to reach that goal. We might say that it is a two-tiered system: On its higher level it is utilitarian, but on the lower level of day-to-day action it is practical egoism.

Tier 2   General Goal: Social Utility
Tier 1   Individual Motivation: Egoistic

It suggests that we not worry about the social good but only our own good, for in that way we will attain the highest social good possible.

There may be some truth in such a two-tiered system, but in the first place, it is unclear (at best) whether you can transpose the principles of economics (which are debatable) into the realm of personal relations. Personal relations may have a different logic than economic relations. The best way to maximize utility in an ethical sense may be to give one's life for others, rather than to kill another person, as an egoist may enjoin. Secondly, it is not clear whether classical laissez-faire capitalism works. Since the 1929 depression, most economists have altered their faith in classical capitalism, and most western nations have supplemented capitalism with some governmental intervention. Likewise, although self-interest may often lead to greater social utility, it may get out of hand and need to be supplemented by a concern for others. Just as classical capitalism has been altered to allow governmental intervention—resulting in a welfare system for the worst-off people, public education, social security, and medicare— an adequate moral system may need to draw attention to the needs of others and direct us to meeting those needs even when we do not consider it to be in our immediate self-interest.

The Ayn Rand Argument for the Virtues of Selfishness appears to be flawed by the fallacy of a false dilemma: It simplistically assumes that absolute altruism or absolute egoism are the only alternatives. But this is an extreme view of the matter. There are plenty of options between these two positions. Even a predominant egoist would admit that (analogous to the paradox of hedonism) sometimes the best way to reach self-fulfillment is for us to forget about ourselves and strive to live for goals, causes, or other persons. Even if altruism is not required (as a duty), it may be permissible in many cases. Furthermore, self-interest may not be incompatible with other-regarding motivation. Even the Second Great Commandment set forth by Moses and Jesus states not that you must always sacrifice yourself for the other person, but that you ought to love your neighbor *as* yourself (Lev. 19:18; Matt. 22:39). Self-interest and self-love are morally good things, but not at the expense of other people's legitimate interests. When there is a moral conflict of interests, a fair process of adjudication needs to take place.

With respect to the Hobbesian Argument, which is the most plausible of the three arguments for ethical egoism, we can say that it seems to rest too heavily on psychological egoism. It assumes that we cannot do any better than be egoists, so we should be as enlightened about our egoism as possible. But if, as we have argued above, psychological egoism is false, then there is no reason to rule out the possibility of nonegoistic behavior. If Hobbesians qualify their position to embrace predominant psychological egoism—the theory that human nature causes us to be heavily biased toward our own self-interest over that of others' interest—then we need not of necessity become ethical egoists. However, the modified Hobbesian argument may make ethical egoism plausible.

Next we'll turn our attention to attempts to refute egoism in order to assess just how plausible it is as an ethical theory.

ATTEMPTED REFUTATIONS OF EGOISM

The Inconsistent Outcomes Argument

Brian Medlin argues that ethical egoism cannot be true because it fails to meet a necessary condition of morality—that of being a guide to action. He claims that ethical egoism is like advising people to do inconsistent things based on incompatible desires.[5]

Medlin's argument goes like this:

1. **Moral principles must be universal and categorical.**

2. I must universalize my egoist desire to come out on top over Tom, Dick, and Harry.

3. But I must also prescribe Tom's egoist desire to come out on top over Dick, Harry, and me (and so on).

4. Therefore, I have prescribed incompatible outcomes and have not provided a way of adjudicating conflicts of desire. In effect, I have said nothing.

The proper response to this is that of Jesse Kalin, who argued that we can separate our beliefs about ethical situations from our desires.[6] He likens the situation to a competitive sporting event, in which you believe that your opponent has a right to try to win as much as you, but you desire that you (and not he) will in fact win. An even better example is that of a chess game in which you recognize that your opponent ought to move her bishop to prepare for checkmate on your king, but you hope she won't see it. The belief that A ought to do y does not commit you to wanting A to do y!

The Publicity Argument

On the one hand, in order for something to be a moral theory it seems necessary that its moral principles be publicized. Unless principles are put forth as universal prescriptions that are accessible to the public, they cannot serve as guides to action or as aids in resolving conflicts of interest. But on the other hand, it is not in the egoist's self-interest to publicize his or her moral principles. Egoists would rather that the rest of us be altruists (Why did Friedrich Nietzsche and Ayn Rand write books announcing their positions? Were the royalties obtained by announcing ethical egoism worth the price of "letting the cat out of the bag?")

Thus it would be a bad thing for the egoist to argue for his position and even worse that he should convince others of it! But it is perfectly possible to have a private morality that does not resolve conflicts of interest (for that purpose the egoist publicizes standard principles of traditional morality). So, if you're willing to pay the price, you can accept the solipsistic-directed norms of egoism.

If the egoist is prepared to pay the price, egoism could be a consistent system that has some limitations. Although the egoist can cooperate with others in limited ways and perhaps even have friends—so long as their interests don't conflict with his—he has to be very careful about preserving his isolation. The egoist can't give advice or argue about his position—not sincerely at least. He must act alone, atomistically or solipsistically in moral isolation, for to announce one's adherence to the principle of egoism would be dangerous to one's purposes. He can't teach his children or justify himself to others or forgive others.

The Paradox of Egoism

The situation may be even worse than the sophisticated, self-conscious egoist supposes. Could the egoist have friends? And if limited friendship is possible, could he or she ever be in love or experience deep friendship? Suppose the egoist discovers that in the pursuit of the goal of happiness, deep friendship is in his best interest. Can he become a friend? What is necessary in deep friendship? A true friend is one who is not always preoccupied about his own interest in the relationship—one who forgets about himself altogether, at least sometimes, in order to serve or enhance the other person's interest. "Love seeketh not its own." A true friend must have an altruistic disposition, the very opposite of egoism. So the paradox of egoism is that in order to reach the goal of egoism, one must give up egoism and become (to some extent) an altruist, the very antithesis of egoism.

The Argument from Counterintuitive Consequences

The final argument against ethical egoism is that it is an absolute ethic that not only permits egoistic behavior, but demands it. Helping others at one's own expense is not only not required, it is morally wrong. Whenever I do not have good evidence that my helping you will end up to my advantage, I must refrain from helping you. If I can save the whole of Europe and Africa from destruction by pressing a little button, then so long as there is nothing for me to gain by it, it is wrong for me to press that button. The Good Samaritan was, by this logic, morally wrong in helping the injured victim and not collecting on it. It is certainly difficult to see why the egoist should be concerned about environmental matters if he or she is profiting from polluting the environment (for example, if the egoist gains 40 hedons in producing P, which produces pollution that in turn causes others 1,000 dolors—units of suffering—but he only suffers 10 of those dolors himself, then by an agent maximizing calculus he or she is morally obligated to produce P). Neither is there any obligation to preserve scarce natural resources for future generations. "Why should I do anything for posterity?" the egoist asks, "What has posterity ever done for me?"[7]

In conclusion, we see that ethical egoism has a number of serious problems. It cannot consistently publicize itself, nor often argue its case. It tends toward solipsism and the exclusion of many of the deepest human values, such as love and deep friendship. It violates the principle of fairness, and most of all, it entails an absolute prohibition on altruistic behavior, which we intuitively sense as morally required (or at least permissible).

Ethical egoism begins with a valid assumption of the importance of calm self-love. In a sense it is often the opposite of psychological egoism, which says that everyone is always selfish. It recognizes that the very opposite is often true. Many people do not love themselves, but rather hate themselves and are ridden with irrational guilt and masochism. It seeks to awaken us to legitimate self-love, but in doing so it may err.

Martin Luther once said that humanity is like a man who, when mounting a horse, always falls off on the opposite side, especially when he tries to overcompensate for his previous exaggerations. So it is with ethical egoism. Trying to compensate for an irrational, guilt-ridden, self-hating altruism, it falls off the horse on the other side, embracing a solipsistic preoccupation with self-interest that robs the self of the deepest joys in life. Only the person who mounts properly, avoiding both extremes, is likely to ride the horse of happiness to its goal.

=====================

Notes

1. John Stuart Mill, *Utilitarianism*, 1863. p.165.

2. Joel Feinberg, "Psychological Egoism,"*Reason and Responsibility* (Wadsworth,1985), p. 484.

3. Ayn Rand, *The Virtues of Selfishness* (New American Library, 1964), pp. 27–32, 80ff.

4. See Jesse Kalin, "In Defense of Egoism," *Ethical Theory*, edited by Louis Pojman (Wadsworth, 1989), p. 92f.

5. Brian Medlin "Ultimate Principles and Ethical Egoism," *Australasian Journal of Philosophy* (1957), pp. 111–118; reprinted in Louis Pojman, *Ethical Theory*, pp. 81–85.

6. Kalin,"In Defence of Egoism," pp. 86–96.

7. There is one other argument against egoism that you may want to consider: the relevant difference argument. This argument, based on a concept of universalizability and developed by James Rachels, goes like this: All differences of treatment among people must be justified by some relevant difference in the description of the people or their acts. For example, I am justified in paying Mary twice as much as John because she is working twice as long and producing twice as many widgets, but I am not justified in paying Mary twice as much as Sam simply because Mary is Black and Sam is Asian; race is an irrelevant difference. Racism, sexism, and fanatical nationalism are all prejudices that violate the relevant difference principle. But this principle applies to egoism as well, for the question is, "What makes you so different from everyone else that you will allow your preferences to count for more than those of other rational beings?" It seems unjust.

Of course, the egoist will reject the relevant difference principle in his or her behavior and so allow racism and sexism and other forms of discrimination, but can he do so without sliding into individual egoism? Isn't his principle unacceptably arbitrary? See James Rachels, *The Elements of Moral Philosophy* (Random House, 1986), Chapter 6.

For Further Reflection

1. Distinguish between psychological and ethical egoism. Is either position plausible? Explain your answer.

2. In Chapter 1 we began with the story of the murder of Kitty Genovese. Review that story and discuss how an ethical egoist would respond to her plight. Would egoists admit that there is a duty to come to the aid of such a victim?

3. Does the egoist have a point in believing that most moral systems fail to adequately recognize that morality should be in our own best interests? Seen in this light, ethical egoism could be seen as an attempt to compensate for the inadequacies of other ethical views that emphasize doing duty for duty's sake or for the sake of others. We will discuss this point at length in Chapter 9, but you may want to work out your initial response now.

4. Some philosophers, beginning with Plato, have argued that ethical egoism is irrational because it precludes psychological health. In an article entitled "Ethical Egoism and Psychological Dispositions," *(American Philosophical Quarterly* 17(1), 1980) Laurence Thomas sets forth the following argument:

> "P1 A true friend could never, as a matter of course, be disposed to harm or to exploit anyone with whom he is a friend (definition of a friend).
>
> P2 An egoist could never be a true friend to anyone (for the egoist must be ready to exploit others whenever it is in his or her interest).
>
> P3 Only someone with an unhealthy personality could never be a true friend to anyone (definition of a healthy personality).
>
> P4 Ethical egoism requires that we have a kind of disposition which is incompatible with our having a healthy personality (from P1–P3).
>
> Conclusion: Therefore, from the standpoint of our psychological makeup, ethical egoism is unacceptable as a moral theory."

Do you agree with Thomas? How might the ethical egoist respond?

For Further Reading

Baier, Kurt. *The Moral Point of View.* Cornell University Press, 1958.

Brandt, Richard. "Rationality, Egoism, and Morality," *The Journal of Philosophy* 69, 1972.

Falk, W. D. "Morality, Self, and Others," in *Ethics*, eds. J. J. Thomson and G. Dworkin. Harper and Row, 1968.

Gauthier, David, ed. *Morality and Rational Self-Interest*. Prentice-Hall, 1970.

Gauthier, David. *Morality by Agreement*. Clarendon Press, 1986.

MacIntyre, Alasdair, "Egoism and Altruism," in *The Encyclopedia of Philosophy*, ed. Paul Edwards. MacMillan, 1967.

Nagel, Thomas. *The Possibility of Altruism*. Clarendon Press, 1970.

Pojman, Louis, ed. *Ethical Theory: Classical and Contemporary Readings*. Wadsworth, 1989. Contains essays by Feinberg, Medlin, Kalin, and Singer.

Rachels, James. *The Elements of Moral Philosophy*. Random House, 1986. Chapters 5 and 6.

Sidgwick, Henry. *The Methods of Ethics*. 7th ed. Hackett, 1981.

Singer, Peter. *The Expanding Circle: Ethics and Sociobiology*. Oxford University, 1983. A good discussion of egoism in the light of sociobiology.

Slote, Michael. "An Empirical Basis for Psychological Egoism," *Journal of Philosophy* 61, 1964.

Thomas, Laurence. "Ethical Egoism and Psychological Dispositions," *American Philosophical Quarterly* 17(1), 1980.

CHAPTER 4

Value

Socrates (S): Tell me, do you think there is a kind of good which we welcome not because we desire its consequences but for its own sake: joy, for example, and all the harmless pleasures which have no further consequences beyond the joy which one finds in them?

Glaucon (G): Certainly, I think there is such a good.

S: Further, there is the good which we welcome for its own sake and also for its consequences, knowledge for example and sight and health. Such things we somehow welcome on both account.

G: Yes.

S: Are you also aware of a third kind such as physical training, being treated when ill, the practice of medicine, and other ways of making money? We should say that these are wearisome but beneficial to us; we should not want them for their own sake, but because of the rewards and other benefits which result from them.

PLATO'S REPUBLIC

THE TERM 'VALUE' (from the Latin *valere,* meaning "to be of worth") is highly elastic. Sometimes it is used narrowly as a synonym for 'good' or 'valuable', and sometimes it is used broadly for the whole scope of evaluative terms, ranging from the highest good through the indifferent to the worst evil. In the narrow sense the opposite of 'value' is 'evil' or 'disvalue', but in the broader sense its opposite is 'fact', which suggests that values are not recognized in the same way as empirical facts are. In a comprehensive value theory (sometimes referred to as "axiology"), the broader meaning of the word is used. In this chapter we shall generally refer to negative value as 'disvalue', use 'value' to signify what is good or valuable, and use 'axiology' to refer to the whole range of positive and negative values. The range may be illustrated by the following axiology chart:

-10	Evil	0	Good	+10
	Negative Value	Indifference	Positive Value	
Worst Evil	Disvalue	Value – Neutral		Highest Good

The central questions in value theory are these:

1. What are the different types of values and how are they related to each other?
2. What things or activities are valuable or good?
3. Are values objective or subjective? That is, do we desire the Good because it is Good or is the Good good because we desire it?
4. What is the relation of value to morality?
5. What is the good life?

We'll examine each of these questions. But before you read any further you should make a list of your values: What things do you consider good or desirable? You might reflect a moment on why you chose the things you did and how they relate to one another.

WHAT IS THE GOOD?

1. What Types of Value Are There?

The question "What things are good or valuable?" is ambiguous. We need first to separate the kinds of values or goods there are. At the outset of this chapter we quoted from the second book of the *Republic,* in which Socrates distinguishes among three kinds of goods: (1) purely intrinsic good (of which simple joys are an example); (2) purely instrumental good (of which the practice of medicine and making money are examples); and (3) combination goods (such as knowledge, sight, and health), which are both good in themselves and good as a means to further goods.

If you made a list of things you value examine it now in order to decide whether you can distinguish among the three kinds of goods mentioned by Socrates. The essential difference is between intrinsic goods and instrumental goods. We consider some things good or worthy of desire (desirable) in themselves (intrinsic goods) and other things good or desirable only because of their consequences (instrumental goods). Instrumental goods are worthy of desire because they are effective means of attaining our intrinsic goods.

We may further distinguish an *instrumental good* from a *good instrument*. If something is an instrumental good, it is a means to attaining something that is intrinsically good; a good instrument is simply an effective means to any goal, whether good or bad. For example, poison is a good instrument for murdering someone, but murder is not an instrinsically good thing. Thus poison, in this instance at least, is not an instrumental good.

Your list of values probably contains many things that are instrumental values. In our selection from the *Republic*, Socrates mentions two instrumental values: medicine and money. Medicine is an instrumental good in that it can hardly be valued for its own sake. We can ask, "What is medicine for?" The answer is, "It is to promote health." But is health an intrinsic value or an instrumental one? We can ask, "What is health for?" Some will agree with Socrates that health is good for itself and for other things as well (for example, happiness or creative activity). Others will dispute Socrates' contention and judge health to be wholly an instrumental good. We will look at this more closely later in the this chapter.

Money is also an instrumental value, for few, if any, of us really value money for its own sake, but almost all of us value it for what it can buy. When we ask, "What is money for?", we arrive at such goods as food and clothing, shelter and automobiles, entertainment and education. But are any of these in fact intrinsic goods, or are they all instrumental goods? When we ask, for example, "What is entertainment for?", what answer do we come up with? Most of us would mention enjoyment or pleasure—Socrates' example of an intrinsic good. We can further ask, "What is enjoyment or pleasure for?" We will examine this question soon, but before we do we need to ask whether the notion of intrinsic values makes any sense.

Are there any intrinsic values? Are there any entities whose values are not derived from anything else—that are sought for their own sake, that are simply good in themselves? Or are all values relative to desirers—instrumental to goals that are the creation of choosers? Those who espouse the notion of intrinsic value usually argue that pleasure is an example of an intrinsic value and that pain is an example of an intrinsic disvalue; it is good to experience pleasure and bad to experience pain. These philosophers will admit that individual experiences of pleasure can be bad (because they result in some other disvalue, like a hangover after a drinking spree) and that individual painful experiences can be valuable (for example, having a painful operation to save one's life). The intrinsicalist affirms that pleasure is just better than pain. But we can see this straight off; we don't need any arguments to convince us that pleasure is good or that meaningless pain is intrinsically bad. If we asked someone to stop torturing a child and he replied, "I agree that the child is experiencing great pain, but why should I stop torturing her?" we would suspect some mental aberration on his part.[1]

The nonintrinsicalist denies that the above arguments have any force. The notion that the experience itself has any value is unclear. It is only by our choosing pleasure over pain that the notion of value begins to have meaning, and thus in a sense all value is extrinsic or a product of choosing. Many existentialists, most notably Jean-Paul Sartre, believe that we invent our values by arbitrary choice. The freedom to create our values and so define ourselves is godlike and, at the same time, deeply frightening, for we have no one to blame for our failures but ourselves. "We are condemned to freedom."[2]

The response of the intrinsicalist is that we do not choose to desire pleasure and eschew pain. These are *givens*, existing in themselves or in the nature of things. Pleasure or enjoyment is just desirable and pain is just undesirable.

2. What Things Are Good?

Philosophers divide into two broad camps: hedonists and nonhedonists. The hedonist (derived from *hedon*, the Greek word for 'pleasure') asserts that all pleasure is good, that pleasure is the only thing good in itself, and that all other goodness is derived from this value. An experience is good in itself if and only if it provides some pleasure and to the extent that it provides pleasure. Sometimes this definition is widened to include the amelioration of pain, for pain is seen as the only thing bad in itself. For simplicity's sake we will use the former definition, realizing that it may need to be supplemented by reference to pain.

Hedonists subdivide into (a) sensualists, who equate all pleasure with sensual titillation and (b) satisfactionists, who equate all pleasure with satisfaction or enjoyment (which may not involve sensuality). Satisfaction is a pleasurable state of consciousness, such as one we experience after accomplishing a successful venture or receiving a gift. The opposite of (a), sensual enjoyment, is pain; the opposite of (b), satisfaction, is displeasure or dissatisfaction.

The Greek philosopher Aristippus (ca. 435–356 B.C.) and his school, the Cyrenaics, espoused the sensualist position: that the only (or primary) good was sensual pleasure and that this goodness was defined in terms of its intensity. Most hedonists since the third century B.C. follow Epicurus (342–270 B.C.), who had a broader view of pleasure:

> It is not continuous drinkings and revellings, nor the satisfaction of lusts, nor the enjoyment of fish and other luxuries of the wealthy table, which produce a happy life, but sober reasoning, searching out the motives for all choice and avoidance, and banishing mere opinions, to which are due the greatest disturbance of the spirit.[3]

The distinction between pleasure as satisfaction and sensation is important, and failure to recognize it results in confusion and paradox. One example of this is the paradox of masochism. How can it be that the masochist enjoys (that is, takes pleasure in) pain, which is the opposite of pleasure? "Well," the hedonist responds, "because of certain psychological aberrations the masochist enjoys (qua satisfaction) what is painful (qua sensation). He or she does not enjoy (qua sensation) what is painful (qua sensation)." It could also be the case that there is a two-level analysis available to explain the masochist's behavior: On a lower or basic level he is experiencing either pain or dissatisfaction, but on a higher level he approves and finds satisfaction in that pain or dissatisfaction.

Nonhedonists divide into two camps. Monist nonhedonists assert that there is a single intrinsic value but that it is not pleasure. Perhaps it is a transcendent value, 'The Good', which we do not fully comprehend but which is the basis of all our other values. This seems to be Plato's view. Pluralist nonhedonists generally admit that pleasure or enjoyment is an intrinsic good but add that there are other intrinsic goods as well, such as knowledge, friendship, freedom, love, conscientiousness, and life itself.

A hedonist like Jeremy Bentham (1748–1832; see Chapter 5) argues that even though these qualities are good, their goodness is *derived* from the fact that they bring pleasure or satisfaction. Such hedonists as Bentham will ask what each of the above-mentioned values are for. What is knowledge for? If it gave no one any satisfaction or enjoyment, would it really be good? Why do we feel there is a significant difference between knowing how many stairs there are in San Francisco and whether or not there is life after death? We do not normally value knowledge of the first kind, but knowledge of the second kind is relevant to our enjoyment.

What are friendship and love for? the hedonist asks. If we were made differently and did not get any satisfaction out of love and friendship, would they still be valuable? Are they not highly valuable, significant instrumental goods because they bring enormous satisfaction?

Even moral commitment or conscientiousness is not good in itself, avers the hedonist. Morality is not intrinsically valuable, but is meant to serve human need, which in turn has to do with bringing about satisfaction.

And life certainly is not intrinsically good. It is quality that counts. An amoeba or a permanently comatose patient has life, but no intrinsic value. Only when consciousness is present does the possibility for value exist. Consciousness is a necessary but not a sufficient condition for satisfaction, for value.

The nonhedonist responds that this is counterintuitive. Consider, for example, the possibility of living in a Pleasure Machine. We have invented a complex machine into which people may enter in order to find pure and constant pleasure. Attached to their brains are electrodes that send currents to the limbic area of the cerebral cortex and to other parts of the brain, producing very powerful sensations of pleasure. If you get into the machine, you will experience these wonderful feelings. Would you enter the machine?

If all you want is pleasure or satisfaction, then the Pleasure Machine seems the right choice. You're guaranteed to have all the pleasure you've ever dreamt of—without frustration or competition from other people! But if you want to *do* something and *be* something (for example, have good character or a certain quality of personality) or experience reality (for example, friendship and competition), then you might think twice about this choice. Is not the Pleasure Machine just another addiction, like alcohol, cocaine, or "crack"? Once in the machine, would we become forever addicted to it?

Or suppose that there were two worlds with the same number of people and the same amount of total pleasure, but in World 1 the people were selfish and even evil, whereas in World 2 the people were deeply moral. Wouldn't it seem that World 2 was intrinsically better than World 1?

Or imagine two lives, those of Suzy and Izzy. Suzy possesses 100 hedons (units of pleasure), even though she is severely retarded and physically handicapped, whereas Izzy enjoys great mental acumen and physical prowess but only possesses 99 hedons. Isn't it obvious that Izzy has the better life? But hedonists are committed to saying that Suzy's life is better, which seems implausible.

It was these sorts of cases that led John Stuart Mill (1806–1873) to modify the hedonic doctrine, admitting that "it is better to be a human dissatisfied than a pig satisfied; better to be Socrates dissatisfied than a fool satisfied."[4] He suggested that there were different qualities of pleasure and that those who had experienced them could distinguish among them. Whether the notion of 'quality of pleasure' can save hedonism is a controversial matter, but many of us feel uneasy with the idea that pleasure alone is good. Some broader notion, such as *happiness* or *object of desire,* seem more adequate candidates for what we mean by value. We will discuss these criteria in questions 3 and 5. We proceed now to our third question.

3. Are Values Objective or Subjective?

Put another way, this question asks whether we desire the Good because it is good or whether the Good is good because we desire it. The objectivist holds that values are worthy of desire whether or not anyone actually desires them; they are somehow independent of us. The subjectivist holds, to the contrary, that values are dependent on desirers, are relative to desirers.

The classic objectivist view on values (the absolutist version) was given by Plato (428–348 B.C.), who taught that the Good was the highest form, was ineffable, godlike, independent, and knowable only after a protracted education in philosophy. We desire the Good because it is good. Philosophers in the Platonic tradition, like G. E. Moore (see Chapter 8), hold to the independent existence of values apart from human or rational interest. Moore claims that the Good is a simple, unanalyzable quality like the color yellow, but one that must be known through the intuitions. Moore asks us to "imagine one world exceedingly beautiful. Imagine it as beautiful as you can . . . and then imagine the ugliest world you can possibly conceive. Imagine it simply one heap of filth."[5] He further asks us, even if there were no conscious being who might derive pleasure or pain in either world, wouldn't we want the first world to exist rather than the second? Moore believes that a world with beauty is more valuable than one that is a garbage dump, regardless of whether or not there are conscious beings in those worlds.

Other, weaker objectivist versions treat values as *emergent* properties or qualities in the nature of things. That is, just as the wetness of water is not in the H_2O molecules but in the interaction of our nervous systems with millions of these molecules, and just as a table's smoothness is not in the table but in the relationship between the electrical charges of the sub-atomic particles of which the table is made and my nervous system, so values (or good qualities) emerge in the relationship between conscious beings and physical and social existence. For example, if we were not beings with desires, we would not be in a position to appreciate values; but once there are such beings, certain things (for example, pleasure, knowledge, health) will be valuable and others not so valuble, depending on objective factors. Perhaps this should be called a mixed view, for it recognizes both a subjective and an objective aspect to value.

Subjectivism treats values as merely products of conscious desire. In his interest theory of values, R. B. Perry (1876–1957) states that a value is simply the object of interest: "A thing—any thing—has value, or is valuable, in the original and generic sense when it is the object of an interest—any interest. Or, whatever is an object of interest is ipso facto valuable."[6] Values are created by desires, and they are valuable just to that degree to which they are desired; the stronger the desire, the greater the value. The difference between the subjectivist and the weak objectivist position (or mixed view) is simply that the subjectivist makes no normative claims about "proper desiring," judging instead all desires to be equal. Anything one happens to desire is, by definition, a value, a good.

The objectivist responds that we can separate the Good from what one desires. We can say, for example, that Joan desires more than anything else to get into the Pleasure Machine, but it is not good; or John desires more than anything else to join the Ku Klux Klan, but it's not good (not even for John). There is something just plain bad about the Pleasure Machine and the Klan even if Joan and John never experience any dissatisfaction on account of them.

On the other hand, suppose that Joan does not want to have any friends and that John does not want to know any history or science (beyond that which is necessary for his needs as a mud wrestler). The objectivist would reply that it really would be an objectively good thing if Joan did have friends and if John knew something about history and science.

Perhaps a way to adjudicate the disagreement between the subjectivist and the objectivist is to imagine an Ideal Desirer—a person who is impartial and has maximal knowledge of the consequences of all actions. What the Ideal Desirer chose would be by definition the 'good' and what he or she disdained would be the 'bad'. There are problems with this way of putting the matter, but if they can be met, we would have a resolution to our problem in a way that does justice to both sides of the issue. For the subjective side is met, in that the values are outcomes of actually desiring; and the objective side is satisfied, in that the values are not the outcomes of capricious choice but of an ideal situation for an ideal person. If there is a God, then he might well play this role.

4. What Is the Relation of Value to Morality?

Typically, value theory is at the heart of moral theory. The question, however, is whether moral right and wrong are themselves intrinsic values (as Kant stated, the moral law is a jewel that shines in its own light) or whether rightness and wrongness are defined by their ability to further nonmoral values, such as pleasure, happiness, health, and political harmony. In order to begin to understand this question and to get a panoramic view of the workings of morality (at the cost of oversimplifying and biasing the discussion), let me offer a schema of the moral process (see

Figure 1) that may help in locating the role of values in moral theory and may thereby provide a bridge to the discussions of various moral theories that follow in the next two chapters.

The location of values in Figure 1 (box 3) indicate that values are central to the domain of morality. Examples of values are life, loving relationships, freedom, privacy, happiness, creative activity, knowledge, health, integrity, and rationality. From our values we derive principles (box 4), which we may call action-guiding value "instantiators" or "exemplifiers" (because they make clear the action-guiding or prescriptive force latent in values). From the value 'life' we derive the principles 'Promote and protect life' and/or 'Thou shalt not kill'. From the value 'freedom' we derive the principle 'Thou shalt not deprive another of his or her freedom'. From the value 'privacy' we may derive the principle 'Respect every person's privacy'. From the value 'happiness' we may derive the principle 'Promote human happiness', and so forth with all the other values.

This schema makes no judgment on whether values are objective or subjective, intrinsic or instrumental. Neither does it take a stand on whether values or principles are absolute; they need not be absolute. Most systems allow that all or most values and principles are 'prima facie' or overridable; that is, they are considerations that direct our actions, and whenever they clash, an adjudication must take place in order to decide which principle overrides the other in the present circumstances.

We often find ourselves in moral situations in which one or more principles apply. We speak of making a judgment as to which principle applies to our situation or which principle wins out in the competition when two or more principles apply. (See box 5 in Figure 1.) The correct principle defines our duty. For example, we have the opportunity to cheat on a test and immediately we judge that the principle of honesty (derived from the value of integrity) applies to our situation.

After we judge which principle applies, we are not finished with the moral process. We must still make a *decision* to do the morally right act, and finally, we must actually do the right act.

Note the possibilities for failure all along the way. We may fail to apply the right principle to the situation (the arrow between boxes 4 and 5). For example, we may simply fail to bring to mind the principle against cheating, which is a failure of application. But even after we make the correct judgment, we may still fail to make the right choice, deciding instead to cheat anyway. In this case we have a perverse will (the arrow between boxes 5 and 6). Finally, we may make the correct choice but fail to carry out our decision (the arrow between boxes 6 and 7). We call this 'weakness of will': We mean to do the right act but simply are too weak morally to accomplish it. We mean to refrain from cheating but can't control ourselves.

Figure 1 The Moral Process

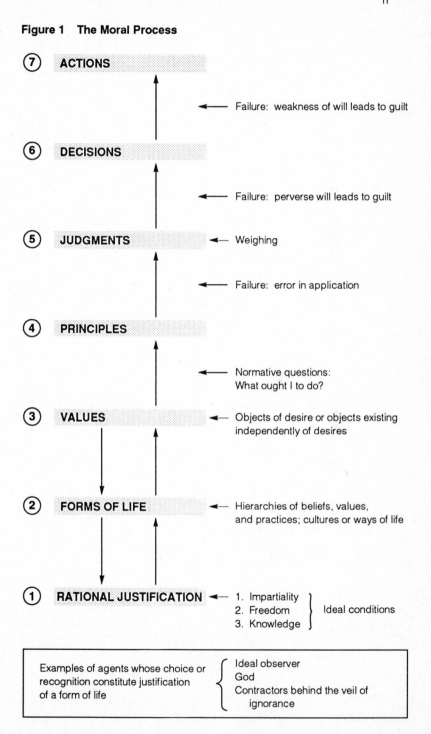

A more controversial matter concerns the deep structure in which values are rooted. Some theories deny that there is any deep value structure and assert instead that values simply exist in their own right—independently, as it were. More often, however, values are seen as rooted in whole forms of life (box 2) that can be actual or ideal, such as Plato's hierarchical society or Aristotle's aristocracy or the Judeo-Christian notion of the kingdom of God (the ideal synagogue or church). Ways of life or cultures are holistic (usually hierarchical) combinations of beliefs, values, and practices.

The deepest question about morality is whether and how these forms of life are justified (box 1). Are some forms of life better or more justified than others? If so, how does one justify a form of life? Candidates for justification are such ideas as God's will, human happiness, the flourishing of all creation, the canons of impartiality and knowledge, a deeply rational social contract (Hobbes and Rawls), and the like. For example, a theist might argue that the ideal system of morality (that is, the ideal form of life) is justified by being commanded by God. A naturalist or humanist might argue that the ideal system is justified because it best meets human need or by being be the one that would be chosen by ideally rational persons. Some ethicists would deny that there is any ideal justification at all and would contend that each moral system is simply correct by being chosen by the culture or individual. In Chapter 2 we called the latter type of ethicists 'ethical relativists'.

The main point of the schema, however, is not to decide on the exact deep structure of morality but rather to indicate that values are rooted in cultural constructs and are the foundation for moral principles upon which moral reasoning is based. We could also devise a similar schema for the relationship between values and the virtues (to be discussed in Chapter 7); each virtue is based on a value and each vice on a disvalue.

5. What Is the Good Life?

Finally, we want to ask what kind of life is most worth living. Aristotle wrote long ago that what all people seek is happiness:

> There is very general agreement; for both the general run of men and people of superior refinement say that it is happiness [they seek], and identify living well and doing well with being happy; but with regard to what happiness is they differ, and the many do not give the same account as the wise. For the former think it is some plain and obvious thing, like pleasure, wealth or honor." [7]

What is happiness? Again, objectivists, subjectivists, and combination theorists disagree. The objectivists, who follow Plato and Aristotle (384–322

B.C.), distinguish happiness from pleasure and speak of a single ideal for human nature; if we do not reach the ideal, we have failed. Happiness (*eudaimonia*, well-being or flourishing) is not merely a subjective state of pleasure or contentment but the kind of life that we would all want to live if we understood our essential nature. Just as knives have functions, so do species, even the human species. Our function (sometimes called our 'essence') is to live according to reason and thereby become a certain sort of highly rational, disciplined being. When we fulfill the ideal of living the virtuous life, we are happy. Naturally, we will no doubt know that we are happy and feel good about ourselves, but the subjective feeling does not define happiness, for people who fail to attain human excellence may also feel happy through self-deception or ignorance.

The subjectivist version of happiness states that happiness is in the eyes of the beholder: You are just as happy as you think you are—no more, no less. The concept is not a descriptive one, but a first-person evaluation. I am the only one who decides or knows whether I am happy. If I feel happy, I am that, even though everyone else despises my life-style. Logically, happiness has nothing to do with virtue; still, it usually turns out that because of our social nature we will feel better about ourselves if we are virtuous.

The combinational view incorporates aspects of both of these views. One version of this view is John Rawls's "Plan of Life" conception of happiness, which states that there are a plurality of life plans open to each person; what is important is that the plan be a freely chosen, integrated whole and that the person be successful in realizing his or her goals. This view is predominantly subjective in that it recognizes the person as the autonomous chooser of goals and a plan. Even if a person should choose a life-plan "whose only pleasure is to count blades of grass in various geometrically shaped areas such as park squares and well-trimmed lawns, . . . our definition of the good forces us to admit that the good for this man is indeed counting blades of grass."[8] However, Rawls recognizes an objective element in an otherwise subjective schema. There are primary goods that are necessary to any worthwhile life-plan: "rights and liberties, powers and opportunities, income and wealth . . . self-respect . . . health and vigor, intelligence and imagination."[9] The primary goods function as the core (or hub of a wheel) from which any number of possible life-plans (the spokes) may be derived. But unless these primary goods (or most of them) are present, the life-plan is not an authentic manifestation of an individual's autonomous choice of his own selfhood. So it is perfectly possible that people believe themselves to be happy when they really are not. Although subjectivist and plan-of-life views dominate the literature today, there is some movement back to an essentialist or Aristotelian view of happiness as a life directed toward worthwhile goals. Some life-styles are more worthy than others, and some may be worthless. The philosopher Richard Kraut asks us to imagine a man whose idea of happiness is the state of being loved, admired, or respected by his friends; he would hate to have his "friends" only pretend to care for him. Suppose that his "friends" really do hate him but "orchestrate an elaborate deception, giving him every reason to believe that they love and admire him, though in fact they don't. And he is taken in by the illusion."[10] Can we really call this man happy? Does this thought-experiment not indicate that our happiness depends, at least to some extent, on reality and not simply on our own evaluation?

Or suppose that we improve on our Pleasure Machine, turning it into a Happiness Machine. Now you get into the machine, have the electrodes attached to many more parts of your brain, and work with the technician to program all the "happy experiences" that you have ever wanted to have. Suppose that you always wanted to be a movie star, have the adulation of the masses and the passionate love of the most beautiful people in the world, and tour the world. Well, all these marvelous adventures would be simulated and you would really believe that you were experiencing them.

Would you enter the Happiness Machine? What if I told you that, once you were unplugged, you would be given the choice of staying out or going in for another round, but that no one who had entered the machine ever left it of their own accord because their sense of happiness was so overwhelming that reality couldn't match it. Would you enter the Happiness Machine? If so, why? If not, are you not voting against making the subjectivist view (or even the plan-of-life view) the sole meaning of happiness?

The objective and subjective views of happiness assess life from different perspectives; the objectivist assumes that there is some kind of independent standard of assessment, and the subjectivist denies it. Even though there seems to be an immense variety of life-styles that could be considered intrinsically worthwhile or happy and even though some subjective approval or satisfaction seems necessary before we are willing to attribute the adjective 'happy' to a life, there do seem to be limiting conditions on what may count as happy. We have a notion of fittingness for humans or for a good life that would normally exclude severely retarded humans, slaves, and drug addicts (no matter how satisfied they are) and that would include deeply fulfilled, autonomous, healthy people. It is better to be Socrates dissatisfied than the pig satisfied, but only the satisfied Socrates is happy.

This moderate objectivism is set forth by John Stuart Mill. "Happiness," according to Mill, is "not a life of rapture; but moments of such, in an existence made up of few and transitory pains, many and various pleasures, with a decided predominance of the active over the passive, and having as the foundation of the whole, not to expect more from life than it is capable of bestowing."[11] This conception of happiness is worth pondering. It includes an 'activity' component that excludes being satisfied by the passive experience of being in the Happiness Machine and supposes (the context tells us this) that some pleasing experiences are better than others, but whether it finally passes the test of careful examination is another matter; you may judge that for yourself.

Although Mill's view of happiness can be judged independently of his view of ethics, Mill himself considered his description of happiness to play a substantial role in his view of utilitarianism. If he is right about utilitarianism, we will have significant reason to accept his view of happiness. So let's turn next to utilitarianism.

Notes

1. Sometimes this judgment (that pain is bad and pleasure is good) is called, following Kant, a synthetic a priori judgment, for it is neither an analytic truth (like 'all bachelors are males') nor something we can or need to prove. It is self-evident on reflection (analogous to our notions of time or causality) and forms a foundational thought from which other judgments are derived.

2. Jean-Paul Sartre, *Existentialism and Human Emotions*, trans. Bernard Frechtman (Philosophical Library, 1957), pp. 23, 48f. "Value is nothing else but the meaning that you choose . . . . One may choose anything if it is on the grounds of free involvement."

3. Epicurus, "Letter to Manoeceus," trans. C. Bailey, in W. J. Oates, ed., *The Stoics and Epicurean Philosophers* (Random House, 1940), p. 32.

4. John Stuart Mill, *Utilitarianism* (1863), reprinted in Louis Pojman, ed., *Ethical Theory* (Wadsworth, 1989), p. 165.

5. G. E. Moore, *Principia Ethica* (Cambridge University Press, 1903), pp. 83 ff.

6. R. B. Perry, *Realms of Value* (Cambridge University Press, 1954), pp. 3, 107. Rodger Beehler similarly states that "value is the shadow cast by human affection or desire" [*The Moral Life* (Rowman, 1978), p. 143].

7. Aristotle, *Nicomachean Ethics*, trans. W. D. Ross (Oxford University Press, 1925), I, pp. 4, 1095.

8. John Rawls, *Theory of Justice* (Harvard University Press, 1971), p. 432. See Paul Taylor's discussion in *Principles of Ethics*,(Wadsworth, 1975, Chapter 6.

9. Rawls, *Theory of Justice*, p. 62

10. Richard Kraut, "Two Concepts of Happiness," *Philosophical Review* (1979): 167–197, reprinted in Pojman, *Ethical Theory*, pp. 136–146.

11. Mill, *Utilitarianism*, Chapter II, reprinted in Pojman, *Ethical Theory*, pp. 166–167.

For Further Reflection

1. Reflect on the five questions mentioned at the beginning of this chapter and try to give your own considered response to each one:

a. What things or activities are valuable or good?

b. What are the different types of values and how are they related to each other?

c. Are values objective or subjective? That is, do we desire the Good because it is good or is the Good good because we desire it?

d. What is the relation of value to morality?

e. What is the good life? Which view of happiness seem the closest to the truth to you?

2. Review the diagram of the moral process; then take a moral dispute and illustrate how opponents would form a chain of reason-action with regard to that issue. You might choose the problem of abortion: Certain pro-choice people might make their overriding value the mother's right to privacy or autonomy (as in the the 1973 *Roe v. Wade* decision), whereas the right-to-life advocate would likely insist that the basic value is the sanctity of human life. Work out the process each person would go through in reaching action.

3. Is life itself an intrinsic value? Or is the value in the quality of life? If life itself is intrinsically good, how good is it in itself? Remember that the definition of life includes more than humans and animals (life is "an organismic state characterized by capacity for metabolism, growth, reaction to stimuli, and reproduction," according to *Webster's Ninth New Collegiate Dictionary*).

4. In *Brave New World* Aldous Huxley portrays a society living according to a hedonistic worldview. People have been liberated from disease, violence, and crime through immunization, genetic engineering, and behavior modification. They are protected from depression and unhappiness by a drug, *soma*, that offers them euphoric sensations. Mustapha Mond, the brilliant manager of the society, defends this hedonistic utopia against one of the few remaining malcontents, the "Savage." We enter the dialogue with the Savage complaining that there is something missing in Utopia.

> SAVAGE: Yes, that's just like you. Getting rid of everything unpleasant instead of learning to put up with it. Whether 'tis better in the mind to suffer the slings and arrows of outrageous fortune, or to take arms against a sea of troubles and by opposing end them. . . . But you don't do either. Neither suffer nor oppose. You just abolish

the slings and arrows. It's too easy. . . . Isn't there something in living dangerously?

MUSTAPHA MOND: There's a great deal in it. . . . Men and women must have their adrenals stimulated from time to time. . . . It's one of the conditions of perfect health. That's why we've made the V.P.S. treatment compulsory.

SAVAGE: V.P.S.?

MOND: Violent Passion Surrogate. Regularly once a month. We flood the whole system with adrenin. It's the complete physiological equivalent of fear and rage . . . without any of the inconvenience.

SAVAGE: But I like the inconveniences.

MOND: In fact you're claiming the right to be unhappy. . . . Not to mention the right to grow old and ugly and impotent; the right to have syphilis and cancer; the right to have too little to eat; the right to live in constant apprehension of what may happen tomorrow; the right to be tortured by unspeakable pains of every kind.

SAVAGE (after a long silence) : I claim them all.

MOND (shrugging his shoulders): You're welcome. [adapted from Aldous Huxley, *Brave New World* (Harper and Row, 1932), p. 286f]

In your opinion, what, if anything, is missing in the Brave New World? Would you exchange our world of disease, violence, and crime for this benign hedonistic utopia? Why or why not?

For Further Reading

Alston, William. "Pleasure," in *Encyclopedia of Philosophy*, ed. Paul Edwards. Macmillan, 1969. An excellent discussion of various theories of pleasure.

Aristotle. *Nicomachean Ethics*. Books I and X. There are several good translations, including those of T. E. Irwin, Martin Ostwald, W. D. Ross, and J. A. K. Thomson.

Bond, E. J. *Reason and Value*. Cambridge University Press, 1983. A thoughtful defense of objectivism in values.

Brandt, Richard B. "Happiness," in *Encyclopedia of Philosophy*, ed. Paul Edwards. Macmillan, 1969.

Brandt, Richard B. *A Theory of the Good and the Right*. Oxford University Press, 1979. Advanced, but important for anyone who wishes to go deeply into the subject.

Hospers, John. *Human Conduct: Problem of Ethics*. Harcourt Brace Jovanovich, 1972, Chapters 2–8. An accessible introduction.

Nagel, Thomas. *The View from Nowhere*. Oxford University Press, 1986.

Nietzsche, Friedrich. *Beyond Good and Evil*, tr. Walter Kaufmann. Random House, 1966.

Perry, Ralph B. *Realms of Value*. Harvard University Press, 1954.

Pojman, Louis, ed. *Ethical Theory: Classical and Contemporary Readings*. Wadsworth, 1989. See especially Part IV. Contains several important selections on the nature of value and happiness.

Rescher, Nicholas. *Introduction to Value Theory*. Prentice-Hall, 1982.

Rorty, Amelie Oksenberg, ed. *Essays on Aristotle's Ethics*. University of California Press, 1980. Contains important articles on *eudaimonia* and other subjects.

Ross, W. D. *The Right and the Good*. Oxford University Press, 1930. See Chapters III–VII for a seminal discussion of the nature of Good.

Taylor, Paul. *Principles of Ethics*. Dickenson, 1975, Chapter 6.

Taylor, Richard. *Good and Evil*. Macmillan, 1970; Prometheus, 1984.

Von Wright, G. H. *The Varieties of Goodness*. Routledge & Kegan Paul, 1963.

CHAPTER 5

Utilitarianism

The Greatest Happiness for the Greatest Number.
FRANCIS HUTCHESON, AN INQUIRING CONCERNING MORAL GOOD AND EVIL

TRADITIONALLY, TWO MAJOR TYPES of ethical systems have dominated the field: one in which the locus of value is the act or kind of act, the other in which the locus of value is the outcome or consequences of the act. The former type of theory is called **deontological** (from the Greek *deon*, which means 'duty'), and the latter is called **teleological** (from the Greek *telos*, which means 'end' or 'goal'). Whereas teleological systems consider the ultimate criterion of morality to lie in some nonmoral value that results from acts, deontological systems consider certain features in the act itself to have intrinsic value. Thus a teleologist would judge whether lying was morally right or wrong by the consequences it produced, but a deontologist would see something intrinsically wrong in the very act of lying. In this chapter we will consider versions of the dominant type of teleological ethical theory—utilitarianism— and in Chapter 6 we will study deontological theories.

In order to get to the heart of this type of theory, let's begin with a couple of examples. Suppose that you are on an island with a dying millionaire. As he lies dying, he asks you for one final favor. He entreats you, "I've dedicated my whole life to baseball and have gotten endless pleasure (and some pain) rooting for the New York Yankees for 50 years. Now that I am dying, I want to give all of my assets, $2 million, to the Yankees. Would you take this money (he indicates a box containing the money in large bills) back to New York and give it to the Yankees' owner, George Steinbrenner?" You agree to carry out his wish, at which point a huge smile of relief and gratitude breaks out on his face as he expires in your arms. Now on traveling to New York you see a newspaper advertisement placed by the World Hunger Relief Organization (whose integrity

73

you do not doubt), pleading for $2 million to be used to save 100,000 people dying of starvation in East Africa. Not only will the $2 million save their lives, but it will also enable the purchase of certain kinds of technology and the kinds of fertilizers necessary to build a sustainable economy. You begin to reconsider your promise to the dying Yankees fan in the light of this advertisement. What should you do with the money?

Or suppose there is a raft floating on the Pacific Ocean. On the raft are two men who are starving to death. One day they discover some food in an inner compartment of a box on the raft. They have reason to believe that the food will be sufficient to keep one of them alive until the raft reaches a certain island where help is available but that if they share the food both of them will most likely die. Now one of these men is a brilliant scientist who has in his mind the cure for cancer. The other man is undistinguished. Otherwise there is no relevant difference between the two men. What is the morally right thing to do? Share the food and hope against the odds for a miracle? Flip a coin in order to see which man gets the food? Give the food to the scientist?

If you voted to give the money to the Yankees in the first example and to flip a coin or share the food in the second example, you sided with the deontologists; but if you voted to give the money to the World Hunger Relief Organization in the first example or the food to the scientist in the second example, then you sided with the teleologists, the utilitarians, who would calculate that there would be greater good accomplished as a result of the scientist getting the food and living than in any of the other likely outcomes.

What is a 'teleologist'? As we mentioned earlier, a teleologist is a person whose ethical decision-making aims solely at maximizing nonmoral goods, such as pleasure, happiness, welfare, and the amelioration of suffering. That is, the standard of right or wrong action for the teleologist is the comparative consequences of the available actions: That act is right which produces the best consequences. Whereas the deontologist is concerned only with the rightness of the act itself, the teleologist asserts that there is no such thing as an act having intrinsic worth. Whereas for the deontologists there is something intrinsically bad about lying, for the teleologist the only thing wrong with lying is the bad consequences it produces. If you can reasonably calculate that a lie will do even slightly more good than telling the truth, then you have an obligation to lie.

We have already noticed one type of teleological ethics—ethical egoism, the view that that act which produces the most amount of good for the agent is the right act. Egoism is teleological ethics narrowed to the agent himself or herself. Utilitarianism, on the other hand, is a universal teleological system that calls for the maximization of goodness in society— for the greatest goodness for the greatest number.[1]

AN ANALYSIS OF UTILITARIANISM

There are two main features of **utilitarianism** as such: (1) the consequentialist principle (its teleological aspect) and (2) the utility principle (its hedonic aspect). The consequentialist principle states that the rightness or wrongness of an act is determined by the the goodness or badness of the results that flow from it. It is the end, not the means, that counts. The utility principle states that the only thing that is good in itself is some specific type of state (for example, pleasure, happiness, or welfare). Hedonistic utilitarianism views pleasure as the sole good and pain as the only evil. To quote the English philosopher Jeremy Bentham (1748–1832), the first to systematize classical utilitarianism, "Nature has placed mankind under the governance of two sovereign masters, pain and pleasure. It is for them alone to point out what we ought to do, as well as what we shall do."[2] An act is right if it promotes more pleasure than pain or prevents pain, and an act is wrong if brings about more pain than pleasure or prevents pleasure from occurring.

Bentham invented a scheme for measuring pleasure and pain that he called the 'hedonic calculus'. The quantitative score for any experience is obtained by summing the amounts of pleasure or pain for seven aspects of the experience. The seven aspects of a pleasurable or painful experience are its intensity, duration, certainty, nearness, fruitfulness, purity, and extent. By adding up the amounts of pleasure and pain for each possible act and comparing them, we would be able to decide which act to perform. With regard to our example of deciding between giving the dying man's money to the Yankees or to the East African famine victims, we would add up the likely pleasures to all involved in terms of these seven qualities. Suppose we find that by giving the money to the famine victims we will cause at least 2 million hedons (units of happiness), but by giving the money to the Yankees we will probably cause less than 1 million hedons. Then we would have an obligation to give the money to the famine victims.

Bentham's philosophy has often been criticized for being too simplistic. Even though there might be some plausibility in estimating general overall good with regard to the above example, the calculus seems overly complicated, encumbered as it is with too many variables and with problems in giving scores to the variables. What score does one give a cool drink on a hot day or a warm shower on a cool day? Furthermore, as we saw in the previous chapter, the concept 'pleasure' seems either too sensuous or too ambiguous a notion to use in many calculations. In fact, in his own day Bentham's version was referred to as the "pig-philosophy" because a pig enjoying its life would constitute a higher moral state than a slightly dissatisfied Socrates.

It was to meet these sorts of objections and save utilitarianism from the charge of being a pig-philosophy that John Stuart Mill (1806–1873) sought to distinguish happiness from mere sensual pleasure. His version of utilitarianism, eudaimonistic (from the Greek word for 'happiness') utilitarianism, defines happiness in terms of certain types of higher-order pleasures or satisfactions, such as intellectual, aesthetic, and social enjoyments, as well as in terms of minimal suffering. That is, there are two types of pleasures: lower (elementary) pleasures and higher pleasures.

Elementary pleasures—eating, drinking, sexuality, and resting —have four properties in common: (1) they involve bodily sensation; (2) they are virtually universally enjoyed (at least to the extent that failure to enjoy them is ordinarily conceived as a basic constitutional abnormality that is in need of explanation); (3) they require little or no effort in terms of any particular training or of acquiring a taste for them; and (4) they are more intensely gratifying than more elevated or spiritual satisfaction, and the pain resulting from deprivation of these pleasures is also proportionately more intense. (This intensity is very closely linked to the short duration of the pleasure or the pain of deprivation.) The spiritual or achieved pleasures tend to be more protracted, continuous, and gradual than the elementary pleasures.[3]

Mill argues that the higher or more refined pleasures are superior to the lower ones: "A being of higher faculties requires more to make him happy, is capable probably of more acute suffering, and certainly accessible to it at more points, than one of an inferior type," but still he is qualitatively better off than the person without these higher faculties. "It is better to be a human being dissatisfied than a pig satisfied; better to be Socrates dissatisfied than a fool satisfied."[4]

Humans are the kind of creatures who require more to be truly happy. They want the lower pleasures, but they also want deep friendship, intellectual ability, culture, and the ability to create and appreciate art, knowledge, and wisdom.

But, it may be rejoined, how do we know that it really is better to have these higher pleasures? Here Mill imagines a panel of experts, and he says that of those who have had wide experience with pleasures of both kinds, almost all give a decided preference to the higher type. What else could he say? It's an empiricists' empirical answer: Look and see!

Mill has been criticized for not giving a better reply—for being an elitist and for unduly favoring the intellectual over the sensual. What do you think? Even if it is difficult to prove, doesn't Mill have a point? Don't we generally agree that if we have experienced both the lower and the higher types of pleasure, then even though a full life would include both, a life with only the former is inadequate for human beings? Isn't it better to be Socrates dissatisfied than the pig satisfied?

The point is not merely that humans would not be satisfied with what satisfies a pig, but that somehow the quality of these higher pleasures is *better*. But what does it mean to speak of better pleasure? Isn't Mill assuming some nonhedonic notion of intrinsic value to make this distinction? That is, knowledge, intelligence, freedom, friendship, love, health, and so forth are good things in their own rights. It is because Socrates, even though dissatisfied, can enjoy these experiences that he is better off than the pig that is satisfied.

The formula Mill comes up with, finally, is the following: "Happiness ... [is] not a life of rapture; but moments of such, in an existence made up of few and transitory pains, many and various pleasures, with a decided predominance of the active over the passive, and having as the foundation of the whole, not to expect more from life than it is capable of bestowing."[5] It does seem that intellectual activity, autonomous activity, and other nonhedonic qualities supplement the notion of pleasure.

TWO TYPES OF UTILITARIANISM

There are two classical types of utilitarianism: 'act' and 'rule' utilitarianism. In applying the principle of utility, act-utilitarians, including Bentham, say that we ought ideally to apply the principle to all of the alternatives open to us at any given moment. We may define act-utilitarianism in this way:

Act-Utilitarianism: An act is right if and only if it results in as much good as any available alternative.

Of course, we cannot do the necessary calculations to determine which act is the correct one in each case, for often we must act spontaneously and quickly. So rules of thumb (for example, in general don't lie, generally keep your promises) are of practical importance. However, the right act is still that alternative that results in the most utility.

The obvious criticism of act-utility is that it seems to fly in the face of fundamental intuitions about minimally correct behavior. Consider Richard Brandt's criticism of act-utilitarianism:

It implies that if you have employed a boy to mow your lawn and he has finished the job and asks for his pay, you should pay him what you promised only if you cannot find a better use for your money. It implies that when you bring home your monthly paycheck you should use it to support your family and yourself only if it cannot be used more effectively to supply the needs of others. It implies that if your father is ill and has no prospect of good in his life, and maintaining him is a drain on the energy and enjoyments of others, then, if you can end his life without provoking any public scandal or setting a bad example, it is your positive duty to take matters into your own hands and bring his life to a close.[6]

Rule-utilitarians like Brandt attempt to offer a more credible version of the theory. They state that an act is right if it conforms to a valid rule within a system of rules, which, if followed, will result in the best possible state of affairs (or the least-bad state of affairs, if it is a question of all the alternatives being bad). We may define rule-utilitarianism this way:

> **Rule-Utilitarianism: An act is right if and only if it is required by a rule that is itself a member of a set of rules, the acceptance of which would lead to greater utility for society than any available alternative.**

An oft-debated question in ethics is whether or not rule-utilitarianism is a consistent version of utilitarianism. Briefly, the argument that rule-utilitarianism is an inconsistent version that must either become a deontological system or transform itself into act-utilitarianism goes like this: Imagine that following the set of general rules of a rule-utilitarian system yields 100 hedons (positive utility units). We could always find a case in which breaking the general rule would result in additional hedons without decreasing the sum of the whole. So, for example, we could imagine a situation in which breaking the general rule 'Never lie' in order to spare someone's feelings would create more utility (for example, 102 hedons) than keeping the rule would. It would seem that we could always improve on any version of rule-utilitarianism by breaking the set of rules whenever we judge that by so doing we could produce even more utility than we would by following the set.

One way of resolving the difference between act- and rule-utilitarians is to appeal to the notion of *levels of rules*. Three levels of rules guide sophisticated utilitarians in their actions. On the lowest level is a set of utility-maximizing rules of thumb that should always be followed unless there is a conflict between them, in which case a second-order set of conflict-resolving rules should be consulted. At the top of the hierarchy is the remainder rule of act-utilitarianism—when no other rule applies, simply do what your best judgment deems to be the act that will maximize utility.

An illustration of this might be the following: Two of our lower-order rules might be 'Keep your promises' and 'Help those in need when you are not seriously inconvenienced in doing so'. Suppose you have made a promise to meet your teacher at 3 P.M. in his office. As you are on your way to his office you come upon an accident victim, who has been left stranded by the wayside. She desperately needs help. It doesn't take you long to decide to break your appointment with your teacher, for it seems obvious that the second-order rule prescribing that the first-order rule of helping people in need when you are not seriously inconvenienced in doing so overrides the rule to keep promises. However, there may be some situation in which no obvious rule of thumb applies. Say you have $50 you don't really need. How should you use this money? Put it into your savings account? Give it to your favorite charity? Use it to throw a party? Here and only here—on the third level—does the general act utility principle apply, for there is no other primary rule in force. Thus you should do what in your best judgment will do the most good.

It is a subject of keen debate whether John Stuart Mill was a rule- or an act-utilitarian. He doesn't seem to have noticed the difference, and there seem to be aspects of both theories in his work. Philosophers like J. J. C. Smart and Kai Nielsen hold views that are clearer examples of act-utilitarianism.[7] Nielsen attacks what he calls 'moral conservatism'—any "normative ethical theory which maintains that there is a privileged moral principle or cluster of moral principles, prescribing determinate actions, with which it would always be wrong not to act in accordance no matter what the consequences." For Nielsen, no rules are sacrosanct; but different situations call for different actions, and potentially any rule could be overridden (though in fact we may need to treat some rules as absolutes for the good of society).

Nielsen's argument in favor of utilitarianism makes strong use of the notion of negative responsibility; that is, we are not only responsible for the consequences of our actions, but we are also responsible for the consequences of our nonactions. Suppose that you are the driver of a trolley car and you suddenly discover that your brakes have failed. You are just about to run over five workmen on the track ahead of you. However, if you act quickly, you can turn the trolley car onto a side track on which only one man is working. What should you do? One who makes a strong distinction between active and passive evil (*allowing* versus *doing* evil) would argue that you should do nothing and merely allow the trolley car to kill the five men, but one who denies that this is an absolute distinction would prescribe that you do something positive in order to minimize evil. Negative responsibility means that you are going to be responsible for someone's death in either case. Doing the right thing, the utilitarian urges us, means minimizing the amount of evil. So we should actively cause the one to die in order to save the five.[8]

Critics of utilitarianism contend either that negative responsibility is not a strict duty or that it can be worked into systems other than utilitarianism.

THE STRENGTHS AND
WEAKNESSES OF UTILITARIANISM

Whatever the answers to these questions are, utilitarianism does have two very positive features. It also has several problems. Its first attraction or strength is that it is a single-principle, absolute system with a potential answer for every situation: Do what will promote the most utility! It's good to have a simple, action-guiding principle that is applicable for every occasion—even if it may be difficult to apply (for life's not simple). Its second strength is that utilitarianism seems to get to the substance of morality. It is not merely a formal system (that is, a system that sets forth broad guidelines for choosing principles but offers no principles; such a guideline would be 'Do whatever you can universalize'), but rather it has a material core: promoting human (and possibly animal) flourishing and ameliorating suffering. The first virtue gives us a clear procedure for arriving at our answer about what to do. The second virtue appeals to our sense that morality is made for humans (and other animals?) and that morality is not so much about rules as about helping people and alleviating the suffering in the world.

Utilitarianism seems commonsensical; it gives us clear and reasonable guidance in dealing with the Kitty Genovese case (Chapter 1). We should call the police or do what is necessary to help her (so long as helping her does not create more disutility than would leaving her alone). And in the case of deciding what to do with the dead millionaire's $2 million, something in us says that it is absurd to keep a promise to a dead man when it means allowing hundreds of thousands of famine victims to die (how would we like it if we were in their shoes?). Far more good can be accomplished by helping the needy than by giving the money to the New York Yankees!

But there are problems with utilitarianism that need to be addressed before one can give it a "philosophically clean bill of health."

Problems in Formulating Utilitarianism

The first set of problems occurs in the very formulation of utilitarianism: "the greatest happiness for the greatest number." Notice that we have two superlatives mentioned in the formula, two 'greatest' things: happiness and number. Whenever one has two variables one invites problems of incommensurability—of not being able to decide which of the variables to rank first when they seem to conflict. In order to see this point, consider the following example: Suppose I offer a $1,000 prize to the person who runs the longest distance in the shortest time. Three people participate: Joe runs five miles in 31 minutes, John runs seven miles in 50 minutes, and Jack runs one mile in 6 minutes. Who should get the prize? John has fulfilled one part of the requirement (run the longest distance), but Jack has fulfilled the other requirement (run the shortest amount of time).

This is precisely the problem with utilitarianism: Should we concern ourselves with spreading happiness around so that the greatest number obtain it—in which case we should get busy and procreate a larger population—or should we be concerned that the greatest possible amount of happiness obtains in society—in which case, we might be tempted to allow some people to become far happier than others, so long as their increase offsets the losers' diminished happiness? Should we worry about total happiness or the highest average happiness? How do we weight the many possible distributions of happiness? And just whose happiness are we talking about anyway—all sentient beings or all human beings or all rational beings (which might exclude some human beings and include some higher animals)? Finally, how do we measure happiness and make interpersonal comparisons between the amounts of happiness of different people?

Utilitarians struggle to resolve these problems. Because some of their questions take us into metaphysics (for example, what is a person and to what degree is a person continuous with himself or herself over time?) and economics (what is the best way to distribute goods over a society?), we cannot provide answers here.

The Problem of Knowing the Comparative Consequences of Actions

Sometimes utilitarians are accused of playing God. They seem to hold to an ethical theory that demands god-like powers, particularly knowledge of the future. Of course, we normally cannot know the long-term consequences of our actions, for life is too complex and the "long term" stretches into the indefinite future. One action causes one state of affairs, which in turn causes another state of affairs indefinitely, so that calculation becomes impossible. Recall the nursery rhyme:

For want of a nail
The shoe was lost;
For want of a shoe
The horse was lost;
For want of a horse
The rider was lost;
For want of a rider
The battle was lost;

For want of a battle
The kingdom was lost;
And all for the want
Of a horseshoe nail.

Poor, unfortunate blacksmith! What utilitarian guilt he must have borne all the rest of his days!

But it is ridiculous to blame the loss of a kingdom on the poor, unsuccessful blacksmith, and utilitarians are not so foolish as to hold him responsible for the bad situation. Instead, following C. I. Lewis, they distinguish among three different kinds of consequences: (1) actual consequences of an act, (2) consequences that could reasonably have been expected to occur, and (3) intended consequences.[9] An act is *absolutely* right if it has the best actual consequences. An act is *objectively* right if it is reasonable to expect that it will have the best consequences. An act is *subjectively* right if its agent intends or actually expects it to have the best consequences. It is the second kind of rightness, that based on reasonable expectations, that is central here, for only the subsequent observer of the consequences is in a position to determine the actual results. The most that the agent can do is use the best information available and do that which a reasonable person would expect would produce the best overall results. Suppose, for example, that while Hitler's grandmother was carrying little Adolf up the steps to her home, she slipped and had to choose between dropping infant Adolf and allowing him to be fatally injured, and breaking her arm. According to the formula just given, it would have been *absolutely* right for her to let him be killed (because history would have turned out better), but it would not have been within her power to know that. She did what any reasonable person would do—save the baby's life at the risk of some injury to oneself. She did what was objectively right. The utilitarian theory holds that by generally doing what our reason judges to be the best act based on likely consequences, we will in general actually promote the best consequences.[10]

EXTERNAL CRITICISMS OF UTILITARIANISM

There are several other objections that opponents raise against utilitarianism. We'll touch on four of them: (1) the no-rest objection, (2) the integrity objection, (3) the justice objection, and (4) the publicity objection. I will first go through all of the objections and then offer a utilitarian response to each of them.

The No-Rest Objection

According to utilitarianism, one should always do that act that promises to promote the most utility. But there are usually an infinite set of possible acts to choose from, and even if I can be excused from considering all of them, I can be fairly sure that there is often some preferable act that I could be doing. For example, when I am about to go to the cinema with a friend, I should ask myself whether helping the homeless in my community wouldn't promote more utility. When I am about to go to sleep, I should ask myself whether I could at this moment be doing something to help save the ozone layer. And why not simply give all my assets (beyond what is absolutely necessary to keep me alive) to the poor in order to promote utility?

The Integrity Objection

Bernard Williams argues that utilitarianism violates personal integrity by commanding that we violate those principles that are central and deepest in our lives. He illustrates this with the following example:

> Jim finds himself in the central square of a small South American town. Tied up against the wall are a row of twenty Indians, most terrified, a few defiant, in front of them several armed men in uniform. A heavy man in a sweat-stained khaki shirt turns out to be the captain in charge and, after a good deal of questioning of Jim which establishes that he got there by accident while on a botanical expedition, explains that the Indians are a random group of inhabitants who, after recent acts of protest against the government, are just about to be killed to remind other possible protestors of the advantages of not protesting. However, since Jim is an honored visitor from another land, the captain is happy to offer him a guest's privilege of killing one of the Indians himself. If Jim accepts, then as a special mark of the occasion, the other Indians will be let off. Of course, if Jim refuses, then there is no special occasion, and Pedro here will do what he was about to do when Jim arrived, and kill them all. Jim, with some desperate recollection of schoolboy fiction, wonders whether if he got hold of a gun, he could hold the captain, Pedro and the rest of the soldiers to threat, but it is quite clear from the set-up that nothing of that kind is going to work: any attempt of that sort of thing will mean that all the Indians will be killed, and himself. The men against the wall, and the other villagers, understand the situation, and are obviously begging him to accept. What should he do?[11]

Williams asks rhetorically, "How can a man, as a utilitarian agent, come to regard as one satisfaction among others, and a dispensable one, a project or attitude round which he has built his life, just because someone else's projects have so structured the causal scene that that is how the utilitarian sum comes out?" Williams's conclusion is that utilitarianism leads to personal alienation, and so is deeply flawed.

The Justice Objection

Suppose that in a racially volatile community a rape and murder is committed. You are the sheriff and you've spent a lifetime working for racial harmony. Now, just when your goal is about to be realized, this incident occurs. The crime is thought to be racially motivated and a riot that will very likely result in the death of several people and create long-lasting racial antagonisms is about to break out. You are able to frame a tramp for the crime so that he will be found guilty in a trial and executed. There is every reason to believe that a speedy trial and execution will head off the riot and save the community. Only you (and the real criminal, who will keep quiet about it) will know that an innocent man has been tried and executed. What is the morally right thing to do? The utilitarian seems committed to framing the tramp, but many would find this appalling. Justice, they would insist, overrides the social good in cases like this one. The fact that the utilitarian would even countenance such a misuse of the court system counts heavily against it, they allege.

The Publicity Objection

It is usually thought that moral principles must be known to all, so that all may freely obey the principles. But utilitarians usually hesitate to recommend that everyone act as a utilitarian, especially as an act-utilitarian, for it takes a great deal of deliberation to work out the likely consequences of alternative courses of action. It would be better if most people acted simply as deontologists.[12] So utilitarianism seems to contradict our notion of publicity.

These objections are weighty and too complicated to attempt to refute here, but perhaps we can allow the utilitarian to make an initial defense. What sorts of responses are open to utilitariarians? Well, it seems to me that a sophisticated version of utilitarianism can offset at least some of the force of these criticisms. To the no-rest objection the rule-utilitarian can respond that a rule prescribing rest and entertainment is actually the kind of rule that would have a place in a utility-maximizing set of rules. The agent should aim at maximizing his or her own happiness as well as other people's happiness.

With regard to Williams's argument from integrity, the utilitarian can argue that some alienation may be necessary for the moral life, but the utilitarian (even the act-utilitarian) can take this into account in devising strategies of action. That is, integrity is not an absolute that must be adhered to at all costs. Even as it may be required that we sacrifice our lives or limit our freedom for others at various times, we may have to limit or sacrifice something of what Williams calls our integrity. We may have to do the "lesser of evils" in many cases. If the utilitarian doctrine of negative responsibility is correct, then we need to realize that we are responsible for the evil that we knowingly allow, as well as the evil we commit.[13]

But, as Peter Railton further argues, a utilitarian may realize that there are important social benefits in having people who are squeamish about committing acts of violence, even when preliminary utility calculations seem to prescribe them. It may be that becoming certain kinds of people (the kinds endorsed by utilitarianism) may rule out being able to commit certain kinds of horrors—like Jim's killing an innocent Indian. That is, utilitarianism recognizes the utility of good character and conscience, which may militate against certain apparent utility-maximizing acts.

The same sort of strategies mentioned above may be used to offset the claim that utilitarianism permits injustice, as seen in the example of the sheriff framing the innocent derelict. The utilitarian counters that justice is not an absolute—mercy and benevolence and the good of the whole society sometimes should override it; but, the sophisticated utilitarian insists, it makes good utilitarian sense to have a principle of justice that is generally adhered to. It is not clear what the sheriff should do in the racially torn community. More needs to be said, but it may turn out that it is the right thing to sacrifice one person for the good of the whole. Wouldn't we all agree, the utilitarian continues, that it would be right to sacrifice one innocent person to stop a war or save the human race from destruction? We seem to proceed on this assumption in wartime—in every bombing raid, especially in the dropping of the A-bomb on Hiroshima and Nagasaki.

On the other hand, the sophisticated utilitarian may argue that in this instance justice should not be overridden by current utility concerns, for human rights themselves are outcomes of utility considerations and should not be violated lightly. That is, because we tend subconsciously to favor our own interests and biases, we institute the principle of rights to protect ourselves and others from capricious and biased acts that would have great disutility in the long run. So we must not undermine institutional rights too easily—but neither should we worship rights! They are to be taken seriously but not given ultimate authority.

Finally, with regard to the publicity objection, the utilitarians have two responses. First, they can counter that the objection only works against act-utilitarianism. Rule-utilitarianism can allow for greater publicity, for it is not the individual act that is important, but rather the set of rules that are likely to bring about the most good. But then the act-utilitarian may respond that this objection only shows a bias toward publicity (or even democracy). It may well be the case that publicity is only a rule of thumb to be overridden whenever there is good reason to believe that we can obtain more utility by not publicizing act-utilitarian ideas. I leave the plausability of this response for your consideration.

CONCLUSION

We see then that sophisticated, multileveled utilitarianism has responses to all of the criticisms directed toward it. Whether they are adequate is another story, one that you need to think about and settle for yourself. Many feel that utilitarianism simply is inadequate because it violates our rights in favor of some possible greater good. Others feel that it is a workable theory. Perhaps it would be better to hold off making a final judgment until after you read the next two chapters, wherein two other types of ethical theory will be discussed.

Notes

1. One of the earliest examples of utilitarian reasoning is recorded in the New Testament, when Caiaphas, the High Priest, counseled the council to deliver Jesus to the Romans for execution: "You know nothing at all; you do not understand that it is expedient that one man should die for the people, and that the whole nation should not perish" (John 11:50). Similarly, in Mark 2:27 Jesus is recorded as breaking the Sabbath laws in order to do good, saying that "the Sabbath was made for man, not man for the Sabbath."

2. Jeremy Bentham, *An Introduction to the Principles of Morals and Legislation* (1789), reprinted in Louis Pojman, ed., *Ethical Theory* (Wadsworth, 1989) pp. 111–114.

3. This analysis is dependent on that of Anthony Quinton in his *Utilitarian Ethics* (Macmillan, 1973), p. 41ff.

4. John Stuart Mill, *Utilitarianism* (1863), reprinted in Louis Pojman, ed., *Ethical Theory* (Wadsworth, 1989) p. 165.

5. Mill, *Utilitarianism*, in Louis Pojman, ed., *Ethical Theory*, pp. 166–167.

6. Richard Brandt, "Towards a Credible Form of Utilitarianism," in H. Castaneda and G. Nakhnikian, eds., *Morality and the Language of Conduct* (Wayne State University Press, 1963), pp. 109–110.

7. Kai Nielsen, "Against Moral Conservatism," *Ethics* (1972): 113–124, reprinted in Pojman, *Ethical Theory*, pp. 181–188. Nielsen no longer holds the position espoused in this article; J. J. C. Smart, *Outlines of a Utilitarian System of Ethics* (Melbourne, 1961); and J. J. C. Smart and Bernard Williams, *Utilitarianism: For and Against* (Cambridge University Press, 1973).

8. The example is Judith Jarvis Thomson's.

9. Cf. Anthony Quinton, *Utilitarian Ethics* (Macmillan, 1973), p. 49f for a good discussion of this and other similar points. My discussion is indebted to Quinton.

10. This example is derived from Anthony Quinton.

11. Bernard Williams, "A Critique of Utilitarianism," in Smart and Williams, *Utilitarianism: For and Against*, p. 98f.

12. In his *The Method of Ethics* (Oxford, 1874) the famous utilitarian Henry Sidgwick argued that utilitarians should keep their views a secret for the good of society.

13. See Peter Railton, "Alienation, Consequentialism, and the Demands of Morality," *Philosophy and Public Affairs* (1984), pp. 134–171, reprinted in Pojman, *Ethical Theory*, pp. 197–213, for an excellent defense of sophisticated utilitarianism on this point.

For Further Reflection

1. Consider three of the purposes of morality mentioned in Chapter 1: (1) to promote human flourishing, (2) to ameliorate human suffering, and (3) to resolve conflicts of interest justly. Which of these does utilitarianism fulfill and which does it fail to fulfill?

2. W. D. Ross argued that utilitarianism should be rejected because it is counterintuitive. Consider two acts, A and B, that will both result in 100 hedons (units of pleasure or utility). The only difference is that A involves telling a lie and B involves telling the truth. The utilitarian must maintain that the two acts are of equal value. Do you agree?

3. One criticism of utilitarianism is that it fails to protect people's rights. Consider the case of five sadists who get a total of 100 hedons while torturing an innocent victim who is suffering 10 dolors (units of pain). On a utilitarian calculus this would result in a total of 90 hedons. If no other act would result in as many or more hedons, the utilitarian would have to endorse this act, arguing that the victim has a duty to submit to the torture and that the sadists have a duty to torture the victim. What do you think of this sort of reasoning? How much does it count against utilitarianism?

4. With respect to the trolley car example in this chapter, many people agree that we ought to kill one in order to save five. But how do you feel about a similar case (given by Gilbert Harman): Suppose you are a doctor and have five needy patients, all of whom are in danger of dying unless you obtain suitable organs within the day. One needs a heart transplant, two need one kidney each, one a lung, and another a liver. A tramp who has no family walks into the hospital for a routine checkup. By killing him and using his organs for your patients, you could save five people, restoring them to health. If you don't kill the tramp, are you negatively responsible for the deaths of the five patients? What is the difference, if any, between these two examples?

5. In his False Analogy Argument, John Rawls argues that utilitarianism errs in applying to society the principle of personal choice. That is, we all would agree that an individual has a right to forgo a present pleasure for a future good: I have a right to go without a new suit so that I can save the money for my college education or so that I can give it to my favorite charity. But utilitarianism prescribes that we demand that you forgo a new suit for someone else's college education or for the overall good of the community—whether you like it or not or whether you agree to it or not. That is, utilitarianism takes the futuristic notion of agent-utility maximization and extends it to cover society in a way that violates the individual's rights. Is this a fair criticism?

6. At the beginning of this chapter we quoted Francis Hutcheson: "The Greatest Happiness for the Greatest Number." Do you find anything puzzling about this motto? Notice that it has two superlatives. Recall the situation mentioned in this chapter: I tell you that I am going to give a $1,000 prize to the person who runs the greatest distance in the least time. Three people sign up and run. Here are the results.

Person	Distance	Time
John	7 miles	50 minutes
Joe	5 miles	31 minutes
Jack	1 mile	6 minutes

Who should get the prize? How could this become a problem for utilitarian calculus? How does the utilitarian go about deciding how to distribute goods to different groups of people?

Suppose we have a situation involving three social policies that will divide up welfare payments between three equal groups of people (see Figure 2). In Policy I, Group A will receive 75 units, Group B 45 units, and Group C 25 units, for a total of 145 units. In Policy II, A will receive 50 units, and B and C will receive 45 units each, for a total of 140 units. In Policy III, A will receive 100 units and B and C 25 units each, for a total of 150 units (see the diagram on next page). Suppose that it is agreed that 30 units is necessary for a minimally acceptable social existence. Which policy should the utilitarian choose?

Figure 2   Units of Welfare

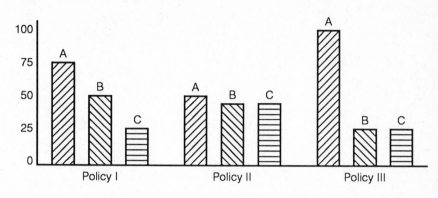

For Further Reading

Bentham, Jeremy. *Introduction to the Principles of Morals and Legislation*, ed. W. Harrison. Oxford University Press, 1948.

Brandt, Richard. "In Search of a Credible Form of Rule-Utilitarianism," in H. N. Castaneda and George Nakhnikian, eds. *Morality and the Language of Conduct*. Wayne State University Press, 1953. This oft-anthologized article is one of the most sophisticated defenses of utilitarianism.

Brandt, Richard. *A Theory of the Good and the Right*. Clarendon Press, 1979.

Brink, David. *Moral Realism and the Foundation of Ethics*. Cambridge University Press, 1989. Chapter 8 is an excellent discussion of utilitarianism.

Brock, Dan. "Recent Work in Utilitarianism," *American Philosophical Quarterly* 10, 1973.

Hardin, Russell. *Morality Within the Limits of Reason*. University of Chicago Press, 1988. A cogent contemporary defense of utilitarianism.

Hare, R. M. *Moral Thinking*. Oxford University Press, 1981.

Lyons, David. *Forms and Limits of Utilitarianism*. Oxford University Press, 1965.

Mill, John Stuart. *Utilitarianism*. Bobbs-Merrill, 1957.

Miller, Harlan B., and William Williams, eds. *The Limits of Utilitarian-*

ism. University of Minnesota Press, 1982. Contains important but advanced articles.

Parfit, Derik. *Reasons and Persons.* Oxford University Press, 1984.

Railton, Peter. "Alienation, Consequentialism and the Demands of Morality," in *Philosophy and Public Affairs* 13, 1984.

Quinton, Anthony. *Utilitarian Ethics.* Macmillan, 1973. A clear exposition of classical utilitarianism.

Sen, Amartya, and Bernard Williams, eds. *Utilitarianism and Beyond.* Cambridge University Press, 1982. Contains important readings.

Smart, J. J. C., and Williams, Bernard. *Utilitarianism: For and Against.* Cambridge University Press, 1973. A classic debate on the subject.

Taylor, Paul. *Principles of Ethics.* Dickenson, 1975.

CHAPTER 6

Kantian and Deontological Systems

Kant's Groundwork of the Metaphysic of Morals is one of the small books which are truly great: it has exercised on human thought an influence almost ludicrously disproportionate to its size. In moral philosophy it ranks with the Republic of Plato and the Ethics of Aristotle; and perhaps it shows in some respects a deeper insight even than these. Its main topic—the supreme principle of morality—is of the utmost importance to all who are not indifferent to the struggle of good against evil. Its message was never more needed than it is at present, when a somewhat arid empiricism is the prevailing fashion in philosophy.

H. J. PATON, PREFACE TO KANT'S GROUNDWORK OF THE
METAPHYSIC OF MORALS

TWO TYPES OF DEONTOLOGICAL SYSTEMS

WHAT MAKES A right act right? The teleological answer to this question is that it is its good consequences that make it right. Moral rightness and wrongness are determined by nonmoral values (for example, happiness or utility). To this extent the end justifies the means. The deontological answer to this question is quite the opposite. It is not its consequences that determine the rightness or wrongness of an act, but certain features in the act itself or in the rule of which the act is a token or example. The end never justifies the means. For example, there is something right about truth-

91

telling and promise-keeping even when acting thusly may bring about some harm, and there is something wrong about lying and promise-breaking even when acting thusly may bring about good consequences. Acting unjustly is wrong even if it will maximize expected utility. Referring to our examples at the beginning of the previous chapter, as a deontologist you would very likely keep your promise and give the $2 million to the New York Yankees and share or flip a coin for the food on the raft.

Act-Deontological Theories

Deontological theories are of two kinds: act- and rule-deontological systems, or particularists and generalists. Act-deontologists consider each act to be a unique ethical occasion and believe that we must decide on what is right or wrong in each situation by consulting our conscience or intuitions or by making a choice apart from any rules. As suggested by this description, there are two types of act-deontological ethics: intuitionists and decisionists. Intuitionists believe that one must consult one's conscience in every situation in order to *discover* the morally right (or wrong) thing to do. Decisionists, sometimes called existentialists, believe that there is no morally right answer until the agent chooses for himself or herself what is right or wrong; nothing is in itself right or wrong, but choosing makes it so. The existentialist Jean-Paul Sartre (1905–1980) held such a position. We have already examined and rejected this sort of radical relativism in Chapter 2, so we may concentrate on act-intuitionism (to be distinguished from rule-intuitionism).

An expression of intuitional act-deontological ethics is found in the famous moral sermons of the Bishop of Durham, Joseph Butler (1692-1752):

> [If] any plain honest man, before he engages in any course of action, ask himself, Is this I am going about right, or is it wrong? . . . I do not in the least doubt but that this question would be answered agreeably to truth and virtue, by almost any fair man in almost any circumstance.[1]

Butler believed that we each have a conscience that is able to discover what is right and wrong in virtually every instance. This belief is consistent with those who give such advice as "Let your conscience be your guide." We do not need general rules to learn what is right and wrong; our intuition will inform us of those things. The judgment lies in the moral perception and not in some abstract, general rule.

Act-deontological systems have some serious disadvantages. First, it is difficult to see how any argument could take place with an intuitionist:

Either you both have the same intuition about lying or you don't, and that's all there is to it. If I believe that a specific act of abortion is morally permissible and you believe that it is morally wrong, we may ask each other to look more deeply into our consciences, but we cannot argue about the subject.

Second, it seems that rules are necessary to all reasoning, let alone moral reasoning. As R. M. Hare says:

> To learn to do anything is never to learn to do an individual act; it is always to learn to do acts of a certain kind in a certain kind of situation; and this is to learn a principle. . . . Without principles we could not learn anything whatever from our elders. . . . Every generation would have to start from scratch and teach itself. But . . . self-teaching, like all other teaching, is the teaching of principles.[2]

You may test this by thinking about learning to drive a car, do long division, or type. Even though the initial principles may eventually be internalized as habits so that we are unconscious of them, nevertheless a rule could be cited that covers our action. For example, a driver may no longer remember the rules for accelerating an automobile, but there was an original experience of learning the rule, which he continues unwittingly to follow. Moral rules, such as 'Keep your promises' and 'Don't kill innocent people' seem to function in a similar way.

Third, there seem to be common features that different situations share, so that it would be inconsistent for us to prescribe different moral actions. Suppose you believe that it is morally wrong for John to cheat on his math exam. If you also believe that it is morally permissible for you to cheat on the same exam, don't you need to explain what it is that makes your situation different from John's? If I say that it is wrong for John to cheat on exams, am I not implying that it is wrong for anyone relevantly similar to John (for example, any student at all) to cheat on exams? That is, morality seems to involve a universal aspect or what is called the principle of **universalizability**: If one judges that X is right (or wrong) or good (or bad), one is rationally committed to judging that anything relevantly similar to X is right (wrong) or good (bad). If this principle is sound, then act-deontological ethics are misguided.

Rule-Deontological Theories

Most deontologists have been of the rule variety. Rule-deontological systems accept the principle of universalizability as well as the notion that in making moral judgments we are appealing to principles or rules. Such rules as 'We ought never lie,' 'We ought always to keep our promises,'and 'We ought never to execute an innocent person' constitute a set of valid prescriptions regardless of the outcomes.

There are different types of rule-deontological systems. We may distinguish between rule-intuitionists and rule-rationalists and between objectivists and absolutists. W. D. Ross (1877–1971) is a good example of an objectivist rule-intuitionist. He believed that intuition both discovered the correct moral principles and applied them correctly. The moral principles are self-evident upon reflection to any normal person, but they are not absolute; every rule has exceptions.

In order to make this point clear, Ross speaks of two kinds of rules or duties: **prima facie** (Latin for "at first glance") or conditional duties and *actual duties*. Prima facie duties are not actually duties but may become such, depending on the circumstances. Ross listed seven prima facie duties: promise-keeping, fidelity, gratitude for favors, beneficence, justice, self-improvement, and nonmaleficence. If we make a promise, for example, we put ourselves into a situation in which the duty to keep promises is a moral consideration. It has presumptive force, and if there is no conflicting prima facie duty that is relevant, then the duty to keep our promises automatically becomes an actual duty.

What about situations of conflict? For an absolutist an adequate moral system can never produce moral conflict, nor can a basic moral principle be overridden by another moral principle. But Ross was no absolutist. He allowed for overridability of principles. Suppose that you have promised your friend that you will help her with her Ethics homework at 3 P.M. As you are going to meet her, you encounter a lost, crying child. There is no one else around to help the little boy, so you help him find his way home, but in so doing you miss your appointment. Have you done the morally right thing? Have you broken your promise? It is possible to construe this situation as constituting a conflict between two moral principles:

1. We ought always to keep our promises.
2. We ought always to help people in need when it is not unreasonably inconvenient to do so.

In helping the child find his way home you have decided that the second principle overrides the first. This does not mean that the first principle is not a valid principle, only that the "ought" in it is not an absolute ought. The principle has objective validity, but it is not always decisive, depending on which other principles may be applicable to the situation.

Although the idea of prima facie duties has merit, it can be detached from **intuitionism** and appropriated by rationalists and naturalists. The first objection against intuitionism still has force. If we are thorough intuitionists, we cannot use reason in arguing for or against various courses of action. It is this desire to be able to build rational arguments that has led many deontologists to opt for a rational form of deontological ethics. The most famous of these forms is the one put forth by Immanuel Kant, to which we now turn.

KANT'S RULE-DEONTOLOGICAL SYSTEM:
THE CATEGORICAL IMPERATIVE

Immanuel Kant (1724–1804), the greatest philosopher of the German Enlightenment and one of the most important philosophers of all time, was both an absolutist and a rationalist. He believed that we could use reason to work out a consistent, nonoverridable set of moral principles.

The first thing to note is that Kant wanted to remove moral truth from the realm of contingency and empirical observation and place it securely in the realm of necessary, absolute, universal truth. Morality's value is not based on the fact that it has instrumental value—that it often secures nonmoral goods such as happiness—but rather it is valuable in its own right:

> Even if it should happen that, owing to special disfavour of fortune, or the niggardly provision of a step-motherly nature, this [good] will should wholly lack power to accomplish its purpose, if with its greatest efforts it should yet achieve nothing, and there should remain only the good will . . . then, like a jewel, it would still shine by its own light, as a thing which has its whole value in itself. Its usefulness or fruitfulness can neither add to nor take away anything from this value.[3]

All mention of duties (or obligations) can be translated into the language of imperatives or commands. As such moral duties can be said to have imperative force. Kant distinguishes between two kinds of imperatives: hypothetical and categorical. The formula for a **hypothetical imperative** is *if you want to A, then do B* (for example, 'If you want to get a good job, get a good education' or 'If you want to be happy, stay sober and live a balanced life'). The formula for a categorical imperative is simply *Do B!* (that is, Do what reason discloses to be the intrinsically right thing to do, for example, 'Tell the truth!'). Hypothetical or means/ends imperatives are not the kinds of imperatives that characterize moral actions. Categorical or unqualified imperatives are the right kind of imperatives, for they show proper recognition of the imperial status of moral obligations. This imperative is an intuitive, immediate, and absolute injunction that all rational agents understand by virtue of their rationality.

Moral duty must be done solely for its own sake ('Duty for duty's sake'). Some people conform to the moral law because they deem it to be in their own enlightened self-interest to be moral, but they are not moral because they do not act for the sake of the moral law. For example, a businessman may believe that 'honesty is the best policy'; that is, he may judge that it is conducive to good business to give his customers correct change and high-quality products. But unless he does these acts *because* they are his duty, he is not acting morally, even though his acts are the same acts that he would do if he were acting morally.[4]

The kind of imperative that fits Kant's scheme as a product of reason is one that universalizes principles of conduct. He names it the **categorical imperative** (CI): "Act only on that maxim whereby thou canst at the same time will that it would become a universal law." This is given as the criterion (or second-order principle) by which to judge all other principles.

By 'maxim' Kant means the general rule in accordance with which the agent intends to act, and by 'law' he means an objective principle, a maxim that passes the test of universalizability. The categorical imperative is the way to apply the universalizability test. It enables us to stand outside our personal maxims and estimate impartially and impersonally whether or not they are suitable as principles for all of us to live by. If you could consistently will that everyone would do some type of action, then there is an application of the categorical imperative enjoining that type of action. If you cannot consistently will that everyone would do some type of action, then that type of action is morally wrong. The maxim must be rejected as self-defeated.[5]

The process looks like this:

Maxim (M)

↓

Second Order Principle (CI) ⟶ rejected maxims

↓

First Order Principle (P) (surviving maxims)

Kant gave four examples of applying this test: (1) making a lying promise, (2) suicide, (3) neglecting one's talent, and (4) refraining from helping others. Let's illustrate how the CI works by applying it to each of these maxims.

The Test for Making a Lying Promise

Suppose I need some money and consider whether it would be moral to borrow the money from you. Suppose also that I promise to repay it without ever intending to do so. Could I say to myself that everyone makes a false promise when he is in difficulty from which he cannot otherwise escape? The maxim of my act is M:

> M. Whenever I need money, I should make a lying promise while borrowing the money.

Can I universalize the maxim of my act? By applying the universalizability test to M, we get P:

> P. Whenever anyone needs money, that person should make a lying promise while borrowing the money.

But something has gone wrong, for if I universalize this principle of making promises without intending to keep them, I would be involved in a contradiction: "I immediately see that I could will the lie but not a universal law to lie. For with such a law [that is, with such a maxim universally acted on] there would be no promises at all.... Thus my maxim would necessarily destroy itself as soon as it was made a universal law."[6] The resulting state of affairs would be self-defeating, for no one in his right mind would consider promises to be promises unless there was the expectation of fulfillment. So the maxim of the lying promise fails the universalizability criterion; hence, it is immoral. Now I take the opposite maxim, one based on keeping my promise:

> M1. Whenever I need money, I should make a sincere promise while borrowing it.

Can I successfully universalize this maxim?

> P1. Whenever anyone needs money, he or she should make a sincere promise while borrowing it.

Yes, I can universalize M1, for there is nothing self-defeating or contradictory in this. So, it follows that making sincere promises is moral; we can make the maxim of promise-keeping into a universal law.

The Test for Suicide

Some of Kant's illustrations do not fare as well as the duty to keep promises. For instance, he argues that the categorical imperative would prohibit suicide, for we could not successfully universalize the maxim of such an act. If we try to universalize it, we obtain the principle 'Whenever it looks like one will experience more pain than pleasure, one ought to kill oneself', which is, according to Kant, a self-contradiction because it would go against the very principle of survival upon which it is based. But whatever the merit of the form of this argument, we could modify the principle to read 'Whenever the pain or suffering of existence erodes the quality of life in such a way as to make nonexistence a preference to suffering existence, one is permitted to commit suicide'. Why couldn't this (or something close to it) be universalized? It would cover rare instances in which no hope is in sight for terminally ill patients or for victims of torture or deep depression, but not cover the normal kinds of suffering and depression that most of us experience in the normal course of life. Kant seems unduly absolutist in his prohibition of suicide.

The Test for Neglecting One's Talent

Kant's other two examples of the application of the CI are also questionable. In his third example he claims that we cannot universalize a maxim to refrain from developing our talents. But again, could we not qualify this and stipulate that under certain circumstances it is permissible not to develop our talents? Perhaps Kant is correct, in that if everyone refrained from developing any talent, society would soon degenerate into anarchy; but couldn't one universalize the following maxim M3?

> M3. **Whenever I am not inclined to develop a talent and this refraining will not seriously undermine the social order, I may so refrain.**

The Test for Refraining from Helping Others

Kant's final example of the way the CI functions regards the situation of not coming to the aid of others whenever I am secure and independent. He claims that I cannot universalize this maxim because I never know whether I will need the help of others at some future time. Is Kant correct about this? Why could I not universalize a maxim never to set myself a goal the achievement of which appears to require the cooperation of others? I would have to give up any goal as soon as I realized that cooperation with others was required. In what way is this contradictory or self-defeating? Perhaps it would be selfish and cruel to make this into a universal law, but there does not seem to be anything contradictory or self-defeating in the principle itself. The problems with universalizing selfishness are the same ones we encountered in analyzing egoism, but it's dubious whether Kant's categorical imperative captures what is wrong with egoism. Perhaps he has other ways to capture what is wrong with egoism. We will return to this later.

Kant thought that he could generate an entire moral law from his categorical imperative. It seems to work with such principles as promise-keeping and truth-telling and a few other maxims, but it doesn't seem to give us all that Kant wanted it to. Some critics have objected that Kant's CI is both too wide and too unqualified.

The charge that it is too wide is based on the perception that it seems to justify some actions that we would consider trivial and even immoral. Consider, for example, principle P:

P. Everyone should always tie one's right shoe before one's left shoe.

Can we universalize P without contradiction? Why not? Just as we universalize that people should drive cars on the right side of the street rather than on the left, we could make it a law that everyone should tie the right shoe before the left shoe. But it seems obvious that there would be no point to such a law; it would be trivial. But it is justified by the categorical imperative.

One could object that all this counterexample shows is that it may be permissible to live by the principle of tying the right shoe before the left, for we could also universalize the opposite maxim (tying the left shoe before the right) without contradiction. That seems correct.

Another counter example is offered by Fred Feldman.[7] Maxim M:

M. Whenever I need a term paper for a course and don't feel like writing one, I shall buy a term paper from Research-Anonymous and submit it as my own work.

Now we universalize this maxim into a universal principle P:

P. Whenever anyone needs a term paper for a course and doesn't feel like writing one, one should buy one from a suitable source and submit it as one's own work.

But this procedure seems to be self-defeating. It would undermine the whole process of academic work, for teachers wouldn't believe that any-one's research papers really represented the work of those who turned them in. Grades would be meaningless and so would transcripts, and the whole institution of education would break down, so that whole purpose of cheating would be defeated.

But suppose we made a slight adjustment to M and P, inventing M^1 and P^1:

M^1. Whenever I need a term paper for a course and don't feel like writing one, and no change in the system will occur if I submit a store-bought one, then I shall buy a term paper and submit it as my own work.

and

P^1. Whenever anyone needs a term paper for a course and doesn't feel like writing one, and no change in the system will occur if he submits a store-bought one, then he shall buy a term paper and submit it as his own work.

Does P^1 pass as a legitimate expression of the categorical imperative? It might seem to satisfy the conditions, but Kantian students have pointed out that in order for a principle to be universalizable or law-like, one must ensure that it is public.[8]

But if it were public and everyone were encouraged to live by P^1, it would be exceedingly difficult to prevent an erosion of the system. Teachers would take precautions against it. Would cheaters have to announce themselves publicly? In sum, the attempt to universalize even this qualified form of cheating would undermine the very institution that makes cheating possible. So P^1 may be a thinly veiled oxymoron: Do what will undermine the educational process in such a way that it doesn't undermine the educational process.

Another type of counterexample might be used to show that the CI refuses to allow us to do things that common sense permits. Suppose I need to flush the toilet. So I formulate my maxim M:

M. At time t_1 I would flush the toilet.

I universalize this maxim:

P. At time t_1 everyone should flush their toilets.

But I cannot will this if I realize that the pressure of millions of toilets flushing at the same time will cause the destruction of the nation's plumbing systems, so I cannot flush the toilet.

The way out of this problem is to qualify the original maxim M to read:

M*. Whenever I need to flush the toilet and have no reason to believe that it will cause the impairment or destruction of the community's plumbing system, I may do so.

From this we can universalize to P*:

P*. Whenever anyone needs to flush the toilet and has no reason to believe that it will cause the destruction of the community's plumbing system, he or she may do so.

So Kant seems to be able to respond to some of the objections to his theory.

More serious is the fact that the categorical imperative seems to justify acts that we judge to be horrendously immoral. Suppose I hate people of a certain race or ethnic group. Suppose it is Americans that I hate and that I am not an American. My maxim is 'Let me kill anyone who is American'. By the universalizability test we get P^2:

P^2. Always kill Americans.

Is there anything contradictory in this injunction? Could we make it into a universal law? Why not? Americans might not like it, but there is no logical contradiction involved in such a principle. Had I been an American when this command was in effect, I would not be around to write this book, but the world would have survived my loss without too much inconvenience. If I suddenly discover that I am an American, I would have to commit suicide, but so long as I am willing to be consistent, there doesn't seem to be anything wrong with my principle so far as its being based on the categorical imperative is concerned.

Of course, it would be possible to universalize the opposite—that no one should kill innocent people—but that only shows that either type of action is permissible.

Some may object that Kant presupposed that only rational acts could be universalized, but this won't work, for the CI is intended to be the criterion for rational action.

It may be that when we come to Kant's second formulation of the categorical imperative he will have more ammunition with which to defeat P^2.

Finally, Kant thought that the categorical imperative yielded unqualified absolutes. The rules that the categorical imperative generates are universal and without exception. In his *Lectures on Ethics* [9] Kant illustrates this point with regard to truth-telling. Suppose that an innocent man comes to your door, begging for asylum, because a group of gangsters is hunting him down in order to kill him. You take the man in and hide him in your third-floor attic. Moments later the gangsters arrive and inquire after the innocent man. "Is he in your house?" they inquire. What should you do? Kant's advice is to tell them the truth: "Yes, he's in my house."

What is Kant's reasoning here? It is simply that the moral law is sacrosanct and has no exceptions. It is your duty to obey its commands, not to reason about the likely consequences. You have done your duty: You have hidden an innocent man and you told the truth when asked a straightforward question. Thus you are absolved of any responsibility for the harm that comes to the innocent man; it's not your fault that there are gangsters in the world.

To many of us this kind of absolutism seems counterintuitive. There are two ways in which we might alter Kant's theory here. The first way is simply to include qualifications to the universal principles, changing the sweeping generalization 'Never lie' to the more modest 'Never lie except in order to save an innocent person's life'. The trouble with this way of solving the problem of the sweeping generalization is that there seem to be no limits on the qualifications that would need to be attached to the original generalization, for example: 'Never lie *except* to save an innocent person's life (except when trying to save the innocent person's life will undermine the entire social fabric)' or 'Never lie *except* to save an innocent person's life (except when this will undermine the social fabric) or when lying will spare people of great anguish (for example, telling a cancer patient the truth about her condition)'. And so on. The process seems infinite and time-consuming and thus impractical.

A second way of qualifying the counterintuitive results of the Kantian program is to follow W. D. Ross (mentioned earlier in this chapter) and distinguish between actual and prima facie duties. The prima facie duty that wins out in the comparison is called the *actual duty* or the *all-things-considered duty*. We may apply this distinction to Kant's innocent man example. First we have the principle L: 'Never lie'. Next we ask whether any other principle is relevant in this situation and we discover that principle P 'Always protect innocent life', also applies. But we cannot obey both L and P (we assume for the moment that silence will be a giveaway). We have two general principles but neither is to be seen as absolute or nonoverridable, but rather as prima facie. We have to decide which of the two overrides the other, which has greater moral force. This is left up to our considered judgment (or to the considered judgment of the reflective moral community). Presumably, we will opt for P over L, so that lying to the gangsters becomes our actual duty.

Will this maneuver save the Kantian system? Well, it changes it in a way that Kant might not have liked, but it seems to make sense: It transforms Kant's absolutism into an objectivist system. But now we need to have a separate criterion to adjudicate the conflict between two objective principles.

We conclude, then, that whereas the categorical imperative is an important criterion for evaluating moral principles, it needs supplementation. In itself it is purely formal and leaves out any understanding about the content or material aspect of morality. The categorical imperative along with its universalizability test, constitutes a necessary condition for being a valid moral principle, but it does not provide us with a sufficiency criterion. That is, if any principle is to count as rational or moral, it must be universalizable—it must apply to everyone and to every case that is relevantly similar. If I believe that it's wrong for others to cheat on exams, then unless I can find a reason to believe that I am relevantly different from others, it is also wrong for me to cheat on exams. If premarital heterosexual coitus is prohibited for women, then it must also be prohibited for men (otherwise, with whom would the men have sex?). But this formal consistency does not tell us whether cheating itself is right or wrong or whether premarital sex is right or wrong. That decision has to do with the material content of morality, and we must use other considerations to help us decide about that.

KANT'S OTHER FORMULATIONS
OF THE CATEGORICAL IMPERATIVE

Kant offered three formulations of the categorical imperative. We've already discussed the first formulation; now we'll consider the other two.

The Principle of Ends

The second formulation of the categorical imperative, referred to as the principle of ends, is 'So act as to treat humanity, whether in your own person or in that of any other, in every case as an end and never as merely a means only'. Each person qua rational has dignity and profound worth, which entails that he or she must never be exploited or manipulated or used merely as a means to our idea of what is for the general good (or to any other end).

What is Kant's argument for considering rational beings to have ultimate value? It goes like this: In valuing anything, I endow it with value; it has no value apart from someone's valuing it. As a valued object, it has *conditional* worth—worth derived from my valuation. On the other hand, the person who values the object is the ultimate source of the object, and as such the person belongs to a different sphere of beings. We, as valuers, must conceive ourselves as having *unconditional* worth. We cannot think of our personhood as a mere thing, for then we would have to judge it to be without any value except that given to it by the estimation of other people. But then that person would be the source of value, and there is no reason to suppose that one person should have unconditional worth and not another who is relevantly similar. Therefore, we are not mere objects. We have unconditional worth, and so we must treat all such value-givers as valuable in themselves—as ends, not merely means. I leave it to you to evaluate the validity of this argument, but most of us do hold that there is something exceedingly valuable about human life.

Kant thought that this formulation—the principle of ends—was substantively identical with his first formulation of the categorical imperative, but most scholars disagree with him. It seems better to treat this principle as a supplement to the first—as an addition of content to the purely formal categorical imperative. In this way, Kant would limit the kinds of maxims that could be universalized. Egoism and the principle enjoining the killing of Americans (P^2 above) would be ruled out at the very outset, for they involve a violation of the dignity of rational persons. The process would be as follows:

1. Maxim formulated
2. Ends-Test (Does the maxim involve violating the dignity of rational beings?)
3. Categorical imperative (Can the maxim be universalized?)
4. Successful moral principles survive both tests.

Does the principle of treating persons as ends in themselves fare better than the original version of the categorical imperative? Three problems soon emerge. The first problem has to do with Kant's setting such a high value on rationality. Why does reason and only reason have intrinsic worth? Who gives this value to rational beings and how do we know that they have this value? What if we believe that reason has only instrumental value?

Kant's notion of the high inherent value of reason is more plausible to those who believe that humans are made in the image of God and who interpret that belief, as the mainstream of the Judeo-Christian tradition has, to imply that our rational capabilities are the essence of being created in God's image: We have value because God created us with worth (that is, with reason). But even nontheists may be persuaded that Kant is correct in veiwing rationality as inherently good. It is one of the things rational beings value more than virtually anything else, and it is a necessary condition to what we judge to be a good life or an ideal life (a truly happy life).

Kant seems to be correct in valuing rationality. It does enable us to engage in deliberate and moral reasoning, and it lifts us above lower animals. Where he may have gone wrong is in neglecting other values or states of being that may have moral significance. For example, he believed that we have no obligations to animals because they are not rational. But surely the utilitarians are correct when they insist that the fact that animals can suffer should constrain us in our behavior towards them: We ought not cause them unnecessary harm. Perhaps Kantians can supplement their system to accommodate this objection.

This brings us to our second problem with Kant's second formulation. If we agree that reason is an intrinsic value, then does it not follow that those who have more of this quality should be respected and honored more than those who have less?

1. Reason is an intrinsic good.
2. The more we have of an intrinsically good thing, the better.[10]
3. Therefore, those who have more reason than others, are intrinsically better.

Thus on Kantian logic people should be treated in exact proportion to their ability to reason, and so geniuses and intellectuals should be given privileged status in society (as Plato and Aristotle might argue). Kant could deny the second premise and argue that rationality is a threshold quality, but the objector could come back and argue that there really are degrees in ability to use reason, ranging from gorillas, chimpanzees, and dolphins all the way through to the upper limits of human genius. Should we treat gorillas, chimps, and dolphins as ends in themselves, but exploit small babies and severely senile people because the former do not yet act rationally and the latter have lost what rational ability they had? If we accept Kantian principles, what should be our view on abortion?

There is a third problem with Kant's view of the dignity of rational beings. Even if we should respect them and treat them as ends, this does not tell us very much. It may tell us not to enslave them or act cruelly toward them without a good reason, but it doesn't tell us what to do in instances of conflict. For example, what does it tell us to do about a terminally ill patient who wants us to help her die? What does it tell us to do in a war when we are about to aim our gun at an enemy soldier? What does it mean to treat a rational being as an end? What does it tell us to do with regard to the innocent victim and the gangsters who have just asked us about the whereabouts of the victim? What does it tell us about whether we should steal from the pharmacy in order to procure medicine we can't afford to pay for in order to bring healing to a loved one? It's difficult to see how the notion of the kingdom of ends helps us much in these situations. However, in fairness to Kant, we must say that virtually every moral system has trouble with dilemmas and that it might be possible to supplement Kantianism to solve some of them.

The Principle of Autonomy

The final formulation of the CI invokes the principle of **autonomy**. Every rational being is able to regard himself or herself as a maker of universal law. That is, one does not need an external authority—be it God, the state, one's culture, or anyone else—to determine the nature of the moral law. One can discover this for oneself, and the Kantian faith proclaims, everyone who is ideally rational will legislate exactly the same universal moral principles.

The opposite of autonomy is **heteronomy**. The heteronomous person is one whose actions are motivated by the authority of others, whether it be religion, the state, one's parents, or one's peer group. The following illustration may serve as an example of the difference between these two states of being.

In the early 1960s Stanley Milgram of Yale University conducted a series of experiments in social psychology in order to determine the degree to which the ordinary citizen was obedient to authority. Volunteers from all walks of life were recruited to participate in "a study of memory and learning." Two people were taken into the laboratory. One was to play the role of the teacher and the other was to play the role of the learner; the experimenter explained the process to both. The "teacher" was put in a separate room where he or she could still hear the "learner." He was instructed to ask the "learner" to choose the correct correlate to a given word, and the learner was to choose from a set of options. If the "learner" got the word correct, fine, they moved on to the next word. But if the learner chose the incorrect word, he or she was punished with an electric shock. The "teacher" was given a sample shock of 45 volts just to get the feeling of the game. Each time the "learner" made a mistake the shocks were increased by 15 volts (starting with 15 volts and continuing to 450 volts). The meter was marked with verbal designations: slight shock, moderate shock, strong shock, very strong shock, intense shock, extreme intensity shock, danger: severe shock, and XXX.

As the experiment proceeded, the "learner" could be heard grunting at the 75 volt shock, crying out at 120 volts, begging for release at 150 volts, and screaming in agony at 270 volts. Around 300 volts there was dead silence.

Now unbeknownst to the "teacher" the "learner" was not actually experiencing the voltage shocks. The "learners" were really trained actors who were simulating agony.

The results of the experiment were astounding. Whereas Milgram and associates expected that only a small proportion of citizens would comply with their instructions, actually 60 percent were completely obedient to their authority and carried out the experiment to the very end. Only a handful refused to participate in the experiment at all once they discovered what it involved. Some 35 percent left at various stages of the experiment. Milgram's experiments were later replicated in Munich, West Germany, where 85 percent of the subjects were found to be completely "obedient to authority."

There are two ways in which the problems of autonomy and heteronomy are illustrated by this example. In the first place, the experiment seems to show that the average citizen acts less autonomously than we might have suspected. People are basically heteronomous, herd-followers. But in the second place, there is the question about whether Milgram should have subjected people to these experiments. Was he violating their autonomy and treating them as means (rather than as ends) in deceiving them in the way he did? Perhaps a utilitarian would have an easier time justifying these experiments than would a Kantian.

In any case, for Kant it is our ability to use reason in universalizing the maxims of our actions that sets rational beings apart from nonrational beings. As such, rational beings belong to a Kingdom of Ends. Kant thought that as fully rational, autonomous legislators, each of us would be able to reason to exactly the same set of moral principles—the ideal Moral Law.

KANT'S ETHICS AND RELIGION

Although Kant thought of ethics as fully autonomous, there is a deep religious dimension to his system. Indeed, it is difficult to separate Kant's system from Judeo-Christian faith, which was his childhood heritage. His view of the unconditional worth and equal dignity of humanity, of natural purposes in nature and in human nature, and of the ultimate justification of morality all seem deeply rooted in religious faith. We have already mentioned these first two points. Now let's consider breifly how religion provides an ultimate justification for the moral point of view.

First we must distinguish between the nature of ethics and its ultimate justification. With regard to the nature of ethics, Kant held to the doctrine of the autonomy of ethics. There could be no difference between valid religious ethics and valid philosophical ethics: Both God and humanity have to obey the same rational principles, and reason is sufficient to guide us to these principles.

Kant's system exalts ethics to an intrinsic good; indeed, we ought to do our duty for no other reason but that it is our duty. Ethics constitutes the *summum bonum*, the supreme good. As such it is related to religion; it is our duty to God because God desires that we attain the highest good. God's commands are exactly those of morality, so there cannot be a conflict between morality and religion.

God loves the virtuous and will finally reward the virtuous with happiness in proportion to their virtue. In fact, God and immortality are necessary postulates of ethics, without which ethics would not be fully justified.

Immortality is necessary in this way: We are commanded by the moral law to be morally perfect. Because 'ought' implies 'can', we must be *able* to reach moral perfection. But we cannot attain perfection in this life, for the task is an infinite one. So there must be an afterlife in which we continue to make progress toward this ideal.

God is a necessary postulate in that there must be someone to enforce the moral law. That is, to be completely justified the moral law must end in a just recompense of happiness in accordance to virtue, what Kant refers to as the "complete good." From the standpoint of eternity, the complete good requires that happiness should be proportioned to virtue in such a way that those who deserve happiness should obtain it in proportion to their moral merit. Likewise, evil people must be punished with unhappiness in proportion to their vice. This harmonious correlation of virtue and happiness does not happen in this life, so it must happen in the next life. So there must be a God, acting as judge and enforcer of the moral law, without which the moral law would be unjustified.

Kant is not saying that we can *prove* that God exists or that we ought to be moral *in order* to be happy. Rather, the idea of God serves as a completion of our ordinary ideas of ethics.

Kant's moral theology has been criticized as being inconsistent with his overall system. Arthur Schopenhauer (1788–1860) thought it was antithetical to Kant's idea of moral autonomy and to the notion that morality is not prudence. If these religious notions are accepted, morality becomes the supreme act of prudence. Kant's defenders respond that criticisms like Schopenhauer's miss the mark by confusing reasons for actions for a total justification of the enterprise of morality. One should not take prudence into account in deciding what to do, but rather one must have faith in the divine harmony in order for the enterprise of morality to be fully justified.

Other critics point out that we can use Kant's argument against him. If his thesis is true and the justification of morality depends on the existence of God, then if we do not find convincing evidence for the existence of God, we are justified in rejecting morality! Yet many people are more confident of their moral beliefs than they are of their religious views, so that it would seem wiser to separate religion from morality and free the justification of ethics from the necessity of religion. We shall examine this issue more fully in Chapter 10.

A RECONCILIATION PROJECT

In Chapters 5 and 6 we have examined two radically different types of moral theories. Some people seem to gravitate to a deontological position and some to a utilitarian position, but many people find themselves dissatisfied with both positions. They find something valid in each type of theory, but at the same time something is deeply troubling about each of them. Utilitarianism seems to catch the spirit of the purpose of morality (human flourishing and the amelioration of suffering) but undercuts justice in a way that is counterintuitive. Deontological systems seem right in their emphasis on the importance of rules and the principle of justice but tend to become rigid or lose focus on the central purposes of morality.

One philosopher, William Frankena of the University of Michigan, has responded to this sense of bifurcation by attempting to reconcile the two types of theories in an interesting way. He calls his position "mixed deontological ethics," for it is basically rule-centered but in such a way as to take account of the teleological aspect of utilitarianism.[11] Utilitarians are right about the purpose of morality; all moral action involves doing good or alleviating evil. However, utilitarians are wrong to think that they can measure the amounts of good and evil or that they are always obligated to bring about the "greatest balance of good over evil," as articulated by the principle of utility.

In place of the principle of utility Frankena puts forth a near relative, the principle of beneficence, which calls on us to strive to do good without demanding that we be able to measure or weigh good and evil. Under the principle of beneficence he lists four hierarchically arranged subprinciples that are contained by the main principle. They are:

1. One ought not to inflict evil or harm.
2. One ought to prevent evil or harm.
3. One ought to remove evil.
4. One ought to do or promote good.

In some sense 1 takes precedence over 2, 2 over 3, and 3 over 4, all other things being equal. These are prima facie principles that may be overridden by the principle of justice.

The principle of justice is the second principle in Frankena's system. It involves treating every person with equal respect because that is what each is due. To quote John Rawls, "Each person possesses an inviolability founded on justice that even the welfare of society as a whole cannot override. . . . The rights secured by justice are not subject to political bargaining or to the calculus of social interests."[12] There is always a presumption of equal treatment unless a strong case can be made for overriding this principle. So, even though both the principle of beneficence and the principle of justice are prima facie principles, the principle of justice enjoys a certain hegemony, a priority. All other duties can be derived from these two fundamental principles.

Of course, the problem with this kind of two-principle system is that we have no clear principle for adjudicating between them in cases of moral conflict. In such cases, Frankena opts for an intuitional approach: We need to use our intuition whenever the two rules conflict in such a way as to leave us undecided on whether beneficence should override justice. Perhaps we cannot decisively solve every moral problem, but we can solve most of our problems successfully and make progress toward refining our subprinciples in a way that will allow us progressively to reduce the undecidable areas. At least we have improved on strict deontological ethics by outlining what the moral perception is supposed to envision.

Notes

1. Joseph Butler, *Five Sermons* (Liberal Arts Press, 1949), p. 45.

2. R. M. Hare, *The Language of Morals* (Oxford University Press, 1952), p. 60f.

3. Immanuel Kant, *Foundations of the Metaphysics of Morals*, tr. L. W. Beck (Bobbs-Merrill, 1959), section 1.

4. An excellent example of a Kantian sense of duty is conveyed by the Danish existentialist Soren Kierkegaard (1813–1855):

"When I was five years old I was sent to school. I made my appearance at school, was introduced to the teacher, and then was given as my lesson for the following day the first ten lines of Balle's *Lesson Book* which I was to learn by heart. Every other impression was then obliterated from my soul, only my task stood out vividly before it. As a child I had a good memory, so I had soon learned my lesson. My sister had heard me recite it several times and affirmed that I knew it. I went to bed, and before I fell asleep I catechized myself once more; I fell asleep with the firm purpose of reading the lesson over the following morning. I awoke at five o'clock, got dressed, got hold of my lesson-book, and read it again. At this moment everything stands as vividly before my eyes as if it had occurred yesterday. To me it was as if heaven and earth might collapse if I did not learn my lesson, and on the other hand as if, even if heaven and earth were to collapse, this would not exempt me from doing what was assigned to me, from learning my lesson .... I had only one duty, that of learning my lesson, and yet I can trace my whole ethical view of life to this impression." [Soren Kierkegaard, *Either/Or* vol.II, tr. Walter Lowrie, (Anchor Books, 1959) p. 271f]

5. A note on consequences in Kant: Universal principles may be known a priori independently of their consequences. This does not means that Kant entirely ignores consequences—he doesn't. We may take them into account in order to apply a maxim (to see whether it qualifies as a moral law), but not in order to establish the validity of the principle or to make an exception to it. We should not ask what the consequences of this particular principle would be, but rather what the consequences of everyone's acting on this principle would be. This would show whether or not the law somehow yielded either a self-defeating state or an impossible situation. If it did, the principle was proscribed; if it didn't, it was permitted.

6. Kant, *Foundations*, p. 19.

7. Fred Feldman, *Introductory Ethics* (Prentice-Hall, 1978), p. 114f.

8. Three of the students in my ethical theory course at the University of Mississippi— Scott Morris, Clayton Overton, and John Ates— pointed this out to me almost simultaneously.

9. Immanual Kant, *Lectures on Ethics*, tr. Louis Infield (Harper Torchbooks, 1963).

10. One of my students, Scott Morris, has pointed out that the proposition 'the more of a good thing, the better' is not a necessary truth: Food and sex are good, but you can have too much of these good things. This is true, but the proposition seems to work better with intrinsic goods like love, happiness, knowledge, health, and reason. Still even here we might argue that if one intrinsically good thing were to crowd out another intrinsically good thing, it would serve a bad purpose (for example, if in our quest for knowledge or aesthetic excellence we were to neglect our duties to our family or friends).

11. William Frankena, *Ethics*, 2nd. ed. (Prentice-Hall, 1973), pp. 43–53.

12. John Rawls, *A Theory of Justice* (Harvard University Press, 1971), p. 3.

For Further Reflection

1. Do you think that the Kantian argument that combines the categorical imperative with the notion of the kingdom of ends is successful? Is the notion of the kingdom of ends clear enough to be significantly action-guiding? Does it cover some intelligent animals but not severely retarded people? Are fetuses and infants included in it? Why or why not?

2. Note the comments of the anti-Kantian, Richard Taylor:

If I were ever to find, as I luckily never have, a man who assured me that he really *believed* Kant's metaphysical morals, and that he modeled his own conduct and his relations with others after those principles, then my incredulity and distrust of him as a human being could not be greater than if he told me he regularly drowned children just to see them squirm [Richard Taylor, *Good and Evil* (Macmillan, 1970), p. xii].

He and others have criticized Kant for being too rigid. Many people use the idea of moral duty to keep themselves and others from enjoying life and showing mercy. Do you think that there is a basis for this criticism?

3. Kant has been criticized for stifling spontaneous moral feelings in favor of the deliberate will, so that the person who successfully exercises his or her will in overcoming a temptation is superior to the person who isn't tempted at all but acts rightly spontaneously. For example, the person who through a strenuous act of the will just barely resists the temptation to shoplift would be, on this criterion, morally superior to the person who isn't tempted to shoplift at all. Based on your analysis of Kant, do you think that this is a fair interpretation of Kant, and if so, does it undermine his ethics?

4. Many people besides Richard Taylor have a negative reaction to Kant's moral theory. Evaluate the following quotation from Oliver Wendell Holmes, Jr.:

From this it is easy to proceed to the Kantian injunction to regard every human being as an end in himself and not as a means. I confess that I rebel at once. If we want conscripts, we march them up to the front with bayonets in their rear to die for a cause in which perhaps they do not believe. The enemy we treat not even as a means but as an obstacle to be abolished, if so it may be. I feel no pangs of conscience over either step, and naturally am slow to accept a theory that seems to be contradicted by practices that I approve" [Oliver Wendell Holmes, Jr., *Collected Legal Papers* (Harcourt Brace Jovanovich, 1920), p. 340].

For Further Reading

Acton, Harry. *Kant's Moral Philosophy*. Macmillan, 1970.

Baier, Kurt. *The Moral Point of View*. Cornell University Press, 1958.

Broad, C. D. *Five Types of Ethical Theory*. Routledge & Kegan Paul, 1930.

Donagan, Alan. *The Theory of Morality*. University of Chicago Press, 1977.

Feldman, Fred. *Introductory Ethics*. Prentice-Hall, 1978, Chapters 7 and 8. A clear and critical exposition.

Gewirth, Alan. *Reason and Morality*. University of Chicago Press, 1978. Important but advanced.

Harris, C. E. *Applying Moral Theories*. Wadsworth, 1986, Chapter VII. An excellent exposition of contemporary deontological theories, especially of Gewirth's work.

Kant, Immanuel. *Foundations of the Metaphysic of Morals*, tr. Lewis White Beck. Bobbs-Merrill, 1959.

Kant, Immanuel. *Critique of Practical Reason*, tr. Lewis White Beck, Bobbs-Merrill, 1956.

Kant, Immanuel. *Lectures on Ethics*, tr. Louis Infield, Harper Torchbooks, 1963.

Larmore, Charles. *Patterns of Moral Complexity*. Cambridge University Press, 1987. A very good discussion of particular duties and the complexity of the moral life.

Nell, Onora. *Acting on Principle: An Essay on Kantian Ethics*. Columbia University Press, 1975.

Raphael, D. D. *Moral Philosophy*. Oxford University Press, 1981. Chapter 6.

Ross, W. D. *Kant's Ethical Theory*. Clarendon Press, 1954.

Ward, Keith. *The Development of Kant's Views on Ethics*. Basil Blackwell, 1972.

Wolff, Robert P. *The Autonomy of Reason: A Commentary on Kant's "Groundwork of the Metaphysics of Morals"*. Harper & Row, 1973.

CHAPTER 7

Virtue-Based Ethical Systems

*The virtues are sentiments, that is, related families
of dispositions, and properties regulated by a
higher-order desire, in this case a desire to act from
the corresponding moral principles.*

JOHN RAWLS, A THEORY OF JUSTICE

*Suppose however that in articulating the problems of
morality the ordering of evaluative concepts has been miscon-
ceived by the spokesman of modernity and more particularly
of liberalism; suppose that we need to attend to
virtues in the first place in order to understand
the function and authority of rules.*

ALASDAIR MACINTYRE, AFTER VIRTUE

*Morality is internal. The moral law . . . has to be expressed in
the form, "be this," not in the form "do this." . . . [T]he true
moral law says "hate not," instead of "kill not." . . .
[T]he only mode of stating the moral law must
be as a rule of character.*

LESLIE STEPHEN, THE SCIENCE OF ETHICS

JOHN HEARS THAT 100,000 people are starving in Ethiopia. He feels
deep sorrow about this and sends $100 of his hard- earned money to a
famine relief project in Ethiopia. Joan hears the same news but doesn't feel
anything. However, out of a sense of duty she sends $100 of her hard-
earned money to a famine relief project in Ethiopia.

Jack and Jill each have the opportunity to embezzle $1 million from the
bank at which they work. Jill never even considers embezzling; the possibility is not an option for her. Jack wrestles valiantly with the temptation

and almost succumbs to it, but through a grand effort of will barely succeeds in resisting the temptation.

Who, if anyone, in each of these cases is the more moral person?

Whereas most ethical theories have been either duty- or action-oriented (**deontic** from the Greek word for "obligation")—either deontological or teleological—there is a third tradition that goes back to Plato and, especially, Aristotle, and that receives support in the writings of the Epicureans, Stoics, and members of the early Christian church, as well as in some sections of the New Testament. I refer to the virtue-based systems, sometimes called **aretaic ethics** (from the Greek word *arete*, which we translate 'excellence' or 'virtue'). Rather than seeing the heart of ethics as based in actions or duties, virtue ethics centers in the heart of the agent—in the character and dispositions of people. Whereas action or deontic ethics emphasizes *doing*, virtue or agent ethics emphasizes *being*, being a certain type of person who will no doubt manifest his or her being in actions or nonactions.

For traditional duty-based ethics, the question is, What should I do? For aretaic ethics the question is, What sort of person should I become? Aretaic ethics seeks to produce excellent people, who both act well out of spontaneous goodness and serve as examples who inspire others. It seeks to create people like Moses, Socrates, Jesus, St. Francis, Gandhi, Martin Luther King, Jr., and Mother Teresa, who stand out as "jewels who shine in their own light." There is a teleological aspect in aretaic ethics, but it is different from the kind usually found in utilitarianism, which asks what sort of action will maximize happiness or utility. The aretaic concept of teleology focuses, rather, on the *goal* of life: living well and achieving excellence.

In this chapter we will examine the nature of the virtues and the possibility of a virtue-based ethic within the context of the ongoing battle between deontic and virtue ethics. First we will look at four charges brought against rule-governed ethics by the aretaic camp. Then, we will examine the nature of virtue ethics, and finally we will address the question of the relationship between deontic systems and aretaic systems. Do virtue ethics supplement action-based ethical systems, or can they be entirely accounted for by action-based systems?

THE ARETAIC CRITIQUE OF ACTION-BASED (DEONTIC) ETHICAL SYSTEMS

Virtue ethics has reemerged as a major ethical theory largely due to a dissatisfaction with rule-governed or action-centered ethical systems.

Since 1958 such philosophers as Elizabeth Anscombe, Philippa Foot, Alasdair MacIntyre, Bernard Mayo, Edmund Pincoffs, and Richard Taylor have become disenchanted with the promises of the mainstream of the modern ethical tradition and have argued for a return to a virtue-based theory.[1] Specifically, four criticisms have been lodged against rule-governed ethics: (1) they lack a motivational component, (2) they are founded on a theological-legal model that is no longer appropriate, (3) they ignore the spiritual dimension of morality, and (4) they overemphasize the principle of autonomy and neglect the communal context of morality. Let's look more closely at these charges.

Action-Based Ethics Lack a Motivational Component

Critics claim that action-based ethics are uninspiring, even boring—and largely negative. They fail to motivate or inspire to action. Ethics becomes a sort of mental plumbing, or a moral casuistry, or a set of hair-splitting distinctions, that somehow loses track of the purpose of morality altogether. But what good are such rules without the dynamo of character that propels the rules to action?

This uninspiring feature is illustrated by the largely negative character of deontological systems. Most of the commandments and rules in such systems are inherently negative: 'Thou shalt not ___!' As John Stuart Mill complained about the so-called "Christian morality" of the Victorian Age:

> Christian morality (so-called) has all the characters of a reaction; it is, in great part, a protest against Paganism. Its ideal is negative rather than positive, passive rather than active; Innocence rather than Nobleness; Abstinence from Evil, rather than energetic Pursuit of the Good; in its precepts "Thou shalt not" predominates unduly over "Thou shalt." Whatever exists of magnanimity, highmindedness, personal dignity, even the sense of honor, is derived from the purely human, not the religious part of our education, and never could have grown out of a standard of ethics in which the only worth, professedly recognized, is that of obedience.[2]

There is something unsatisfactory about a morality that is so disproportionately defined in terms of "Thou shalt not's," stressing innocence rather than an "energetic Pursuit of the Good." Deontological and contractual systems (such as Hobbes's) focus on an egoistic, minimal morality, the basic principles of which seem to be more preventive than positive. The only sure principle is a reciprocal duty to do no harm. This sort of theory places a very low value on morality, judging it primarily as a necessary evil. The aretaist rejects this judgment, seeing morality as an intrinsically worthwhile activity.

Action-Based Ethics Are Founded on a Theological-Legal Model That Is No Longer Appropriate

Moral language in traditional schemes usually has a structure that resembles law. Typically, the notions of right and wrong occur within the structure of a legal context in which there is a clear authority. Traditional, natural-law ethics used this model with integrity, for it considered moral principles to be analogous to law and God to be the analogue to the sovereign. Now, however, ethics has been detached from its theological moorings—it has become an autonomous activity—leaving the legal model without an analogue, so that it has become an incoherent metaphor. The virtue ethicist rejects this model. Rather than spend time on moral hair-splitting and puzzle-solving, ethics should help us develop admirable characters that will generate the kinds of insights needed for the exigencies of life.

In this regard, the legalistic bent of modern moral theory has the effect of undermining the spirit of morality: "Morality was made for man, not man for morality." Rules often get in the way of kindness and spontaneous generosity. An illustration of this is the passage from Mark Twain's *Huckleberry Finn*, in which Huck sees that his duty is to obey the law and turn in his black friend, the runaway slave Jim. Huck's principles tell him to report Jim to the authorities:

> Conscience says to me: "What had poor Miss Watson done to you, that you could see her nigger go off right under your eyes and never say one single word? What did that poor old woman do to you, that you could treat her so mean?" I got to feeling so mean and miserable I most wished I was dead. . . . My conscience got to stirring me up hotter than ever, until at last I says to it: "Let up on me—it ain't too late, yet—I'll paddle ashore at first light and tell."

Huck intends to report Jim, and soon he has the opportunity when two men hunting for runaway slaves ask him whether the man on his raft is black. But something in his character prevents Huck from turning Jim in. Virtue ethicists point out that Huck does the right thing because of his character, not his principles, and that sometimes, at least, our moral principles actually militate against deeper moral action that arises out of character.[3]

Action-Based Ethics Often Ignore the Spiritual Dimension of Ethics

Action-based ethics reduce all moral judgments to judgments about actions ("deontic judgments") and neglect the spiritual qualities of gratitude, self-respect, sympathy, having one's emotions in proper order, and aspiring to become a certain kind of person.

Consider Jack and Jill's situations mentioned at the beginning of this chapter. Both have the opportunity to embezzle. For Jack it is a strenuous effort of will that enables him to resist the temptation to embezzle, whereas for Jill the temptation does not even arise. She automatically rejects the fleeting thought as out of range of her character. Now it might be said that Jack has the important virtue of considerable strength of will, but he lacks the virtue of deep integrity that Jill possesses. Whereas stringent action-based ethics (such as Kant's, which puts the emphasis on conscientiousness, or doing one's duty for duty's sake) would say that Jack is the only one of the two who is moral, virtue ethics would say that Jill is the superior moral being; she has something good about her character that Jack lacks. Or consider John and Joan: Both send money to charity, but John does it with deep feeling of sympathy for the famine victims, whereas Joan does it simply out of a sense of duty. The virtue ethicist would argue that John has the right moral feelings, whereas Joan is merely a cold, calculating moral machine who lacks the appropriate warmth of judgment toward the starving.

Virtue ethicists often cite Kant's theory as a paradigm of an antivirtue ethics. They point out that an examination of Kant's extreme action-centered approach reveals the need for a virtue alternative. For Kant, natural goodness is morally irrelevant; the fact that you actually want to help someone (because you like them or just like doing good deeds) is of no moral importance. In fact, because of the emphasis put on the good will (doing duty for duty's sake), it would seem that Kant's logic would force him to conclude that you are actually moral in proportion to the amount of temptation that you have to resist in performing your duty: For little temptation you receive little moral credit; if you experience great temptation, you receive great moral credit for overcoming it.

To virtue ethicists this is preposterous. Taken to its logical conclusion, the homicidal maniac who always just barely succeeds in resisting his perpetual temptation to kill is actually the most glorious saint, surpassing the "natural saint" who just does good because of a good character. True goodness is spontaneously, cheerfully, and enjoyably to do what is good. As Aristotle said,

> We may even go so far as to state that the man who does not enjoy performing noble actions is not a good man at all. Nobody would

call a man just who does not enjoy acting justly, nor generous who does not enjoy generous actions, and so on.[4]

It is not the hounded neurotic who barely manages to control himself before each passing temptation, but the natural saint— the one who does good out of habit and from the inner resources of good character—who is the morally superior person.

Action-Based Ethics Overemphasize Autonomy and Neglect the Communal Context of Ethics

This criticism, set forth by Alasdair MacIntyre in *After Virtue* (1981), claims that rule-governed ethics is a symptom of the Enlightenment, which exaggerated the principle of autonomy—the ability of each person to arrive at a moral code by reason alone. In fact, all moral codes are rooted in practices that are themselves rooted in traditions or forms of life. We do not make moral decisions as rational atoms in a vacuum, and it is sheer ideological blindness that allows this distorted perception. MacIntyre does not want to embrace relativism. His point is that we can discover *better* ways of living, but they will probably be founded on an account of what the good life is and what a good community is.

It is in communities that such virtues as loyalty, natural affection, spontaneous sympathy, and shared concerns arise and sustain the group. It is out of this primary loyalty (to family and friends and community) that the proper dispositions arise and flow out to the rest of humanity. Hence, moral psychology is more important than traditional ethics has usually recognized. Seeing how people actually learn to be moral and how they are inspired to act morally is vital to moral theory itself, and this, it seems, has everything to do with the virtues.

In sum, rule-governed systems are uninspiring and unmotivating, negative, improperly legalistic, neglectful of the spiritual dimension, overly rationalistic, and atomistic. Against this background of dissatisfaction with traditional moral theory, virtue ethics has reasserted itself by offering something that captures the essence of the moral point of view.

THE NATURE OF VIRTUE ETHICS

Virtue ethics says that it is important not only to do the right thing, but also to have the requisite dispositions, motivations, and emotions in being good and doing right. It is important that normally we are not even tempted to steal, lie, or cheat and that normally we enjoy doing good because we are good. Virtue ethics is not only about action but about emotions, character, and moral habit. As Richard Taylor puts it, it is an ethics of aspiration rather than an ethics of duty.[5] It calls us to aspire to be an ideal person. The virtues are excellences of character—trained behavioral dispositions that result in habitual acts. Traditionally, they may be divided into two types: moral and nonmoral virtues, the criterion of difference being either intuitive or tied to moral principles.[6]

1. Moral virtues: honesty, benevolence, nonmalevolence, fairness, kindness, conscientiousness, gratitude, and so forth
2. Nonmoral virtues: courage, optimism, rationality, self-control, patience, endurance, industry, musical talent, cleanliness, wit, and so forth

The exact classification of various virtues is debatable. Courage is sometimes in the "moral" camp, and virtues like kindliness (as opposed to impartial benevolence) might fit into either camp. The moral virtues are more closely associated with what has been deemed essential for the moral life and incompatible with the immoral life, but the distinction seems rough and inexact, for many of the "moral" virtues could be used for bad purposes (for example, in the case of the benevolent person who always makes things worse). The nonmoral virtues are generally considered to be those that contribute to the moral life but are more easily expropriated for immoral purposes (for example, those possessed by the courageous criminal who is more dangerous than the cowardly one).

Although most virtue systems do not deny that there are principles of action that serve as action-guides (at least as rules of thumb), these entities are not the essence of morality. Likewise, it is sometimes appropriate to reason about what to do, but such reasoning or deliberating should give significant attention to such feelings as sympathy and loyalty, and the like. The primary focus is not on abstract reason but on ideal types of people or on actual ideal people. Discovering the proper moral example and imitating the person or ideal type thus replace casuistic reason as the most significant aspects of the moral life. Eventually, the apprentice-like training in virtue gained by imitating the ideal model results in a virtuous person who spontaneously does what is good.

Let's look more closely at this exemplary model aspect of virtue ethics. As mentioned above, there are two different ways that this comes into focus: either through an examination of ideal types of people or through following someone who is an ideal type. We'll examine each of these in turn.

The Ideal Type: Aristotle's *Nicomachean Ethics*

In Aristotle's classic work on the virtues, written more than three centuries before Christ, the virtues are simply those characteristics that enable individuals to live well in communities. In order to achieve a state of well-being (*eudaimonia*, often translated as 'happiness'), proper social institutions are necessary. Thus the moral person cannot really exist apart from a flourishing political setting that enables him or her to develop the requisite virtues for the good life. For this reason ethics is considered a branch of politics.

For Aristotle, humanity has an essence or function. Just as the function of a doctor is to cure the sick and restore health, the function of a ruler is to govern society well, and the function of a knife is to cut well, so it is the function of humans to use reason in pursuit of the good life (*eudaimonia*, happiness or flourishing). The virtues indicate the kind of moral-political characteristics necessary for people to attain happiness.

After positioning ethics as a part of politics, Aristotle explains that the moral virtues are different from the intellectual ones. Whereas the intellectual virtues may be taught directly, the moral ones must be lived in order to be learned. By living well we acquire the right habits; these habits are in fact the virtues. The virtues are to be sought as the best guarantee to the happy life. But again, happiness requires that one be lucky enough to live in a flourishing state. The morally virtuous life consists in living in moderation, according to "the Golden Mean." By "the Golden Mean" Aristotle means that the virtues are a kind of midpoint between excess and deficiency (for example, courage is the mean between cowardice and foolhardiness; liberality is the mean between stinginess and unrestrained giving).

Aristotle was an elitist who didn't believe that everyone was capable of the virtues; some people were worthless, natural slaves. Even for those who were capable of developing moral dispositions, external circumstances could prevent them from reaching the goal of happiness. The moral virtues were a necessary but not a sufficient condition for happiness. One must, in addition to being virtuous, be healthy, wealthy, wise, and have good fortune.[7]

Aristotle hardly mentions principles; one may, however, read them into his thought. For example, his condemnation of adultery may be read as a principle ('Thou shalt not commit adultery'). But Aristotle seems to think that such activities as adultery or murder are inherently and obviously bad, so that it is laboring the point to speak of a rule against adultery or killing innocent persons.

The Ideal Individual

Most of us learn by watching others and imitating them; this is a hallmark of virtue ethics. Rules cut up moral reality in fragmented and unnatural ways, but lives exhibit appropriate attitudes and dispositions in wholistic fashion. The life of a Socrates, a Jesus, a Gandhi, or a Mother Teresa shows us what ideals there are and inspires us to become ideal types. We have in the exemplar living proof and a picture of the moral life to which we may aspire by imitation. The lesson of the exemplar is, "If this person can overcome temptation and live a deeply moral life, so can I."

Perhaps no figure has served as an exemplar for more people in Western culture than Jesus of Nazareth.[8] An example of how his image has helped form the moral conscience of individuals is related in the biography of the agnostic ethicist G. E. Moore. As his biographer, Paul Levy, puts it:

> The habit of examining one's conscience by asking oneself "What would Jesus do?" is conducive to the frame of mind required to enable one to ask oneself "What is the right (or the good) thing to do?" And it is only a short step from asking oneself what Jesus would do, to the realization that one is not asking an historical question such as "What in fact did Jesus do?", but a question that means "What would Jesus have done in these circumstances?" In the end . . . he is appealing to the idea of Jesus as a perfectly moral human being to give him ethical standards.[9]

TYPES OF RELATIONSHIPS BETWEEN VIRTUE AND ACTION ETHICS

There are three basic relationships between principles and virtues in the history of ethical theory. All of them are positions held today. In the following sections we will examine these positions. After listing the relationship, I have listed the names of some contemporary philosophers who might be considered to espouse the position in question.

1. *Pure aretaic ethics.* The virtues are dominant and have intrinsic value; moral principles or duties are derived from the virtues. For example, if we claim that we have a duty to be just or beneficent, then we must discover the virtues of fairness and benevolence in the good person. This view is attributed by some to Aristotle and is held by Philippa Foot, Alasdair MacIntyre, and Richard Taylor.[10]

2. *The standard deontic view: subordinate nonaretaic ethics.* Action-guiding principles are the essence of morality. The virtues are derived from the principles and are instrumental in performing right action. For each virtue there is a corresponding principle that is the important aspect of the relationship. This view can be found in the works of William Frankena, Bernard Gert, Alan Gewirth, John Rawls, and Geoffrey Warnock.

3. *Complementarity ethics*. Also referred to as pluralistic ethics, which holds that both deontic and aretaic models are necessary for an adquate or complete system. Neither the virtues nor principles are primary; rather, but they both complement each other, and both may have intrinsic value. Robert Louden, Walter Schaller, and Gregory Trianosky are among those holding this view.

Pure Aretaic Ethics

Even though the formula for pure aretaic ethics sometimes accurately describes how a moral act is generated (that is, we sometimes act spontaneously out of a good heart), it hardly seems to cover all ethical actions; sometimes we do use rules and moral reasons in order to decide on what to do. The question is, Are these rules really irrelevant to the essence of morality? To date no one has worked out a complete pure aretaic account, and so it is difficult to know whether it can be done. Pure aretaic ethics seems to suffer from two major types of problems; one is epistemological and the other is practical. We turn to these problems.

Epistemological Problems What habits and emotions are genuine or proper virtues? How do you know which ones? Who is the virtuous person? Suppose you ask me, "What is the right thing to do?" I answer, "Do what the virtuous person would do!" But you counter, "Who is the virtuous person?" To which I reply, "The man who does the right thing." The reasoning is circular. As Frankena has stated, "Virtues without principles are blind." We need something to serve as a criterion for the virtues.

Related to this epistemological problem is the problem of virtue relativism. What counts as a virtue changes over time and place. Whereas Aristotle valued pride as a special virtue, Christians see it as a master vice. A caveman armed only with a spear and confronted by a herd of mastodons would be thought by his community to have "excessive" fear if he abandoned his fellow tribesmen and fled; contemporary society would make no such judgment. Capitalists view acquisitiveness as a virtue, whereas Marxists see it as a vice.[11]

The Problem of Moral Direction One of the perennial criticisms of virtue-based ethical systems is that such theories provide no guidance for resolving an ethical dilemma.[12] In Aristotle's *Nicomachean Ethics,* precious little is said about what we are supposed to *do*. One would think that ethics should be, at least to some extent, action-guiding. Aristotle's answer seems to be, Do what a good person would do. But the question arises, Who is the good person, and how shall I recognize him or her? Furthermore, even if we could answer that question without reference to kinds of actions or principles addressed by the nonvirtue-oriented ethicists, it is not always clear what ideal people would do in our situations. Sometimes Aristotle writes as though the right action is that intermediate or "Golden Mean" between two extremes, but it is often difficult, if not impossible, to determine how to apply this. As J. L. Mackie says:

> As guidance about what is the good life, what precisely one ought to do, or even by what standard one should try to decide what one ought to do, this is too circular to be very helpful. And though Aristotle's account is filled out with detailed descriptions of many of the virtues, moral as well as intellectual, the air of indeterminacy persists. We learn the names of the pairs of contrary vices that contrast with each of the virtues, but very little about where or how to draw the dividing lines, where or how to fix the mean. As Sidgwick says, he "only indicates the whereabouts of virtue."[13]

In sum, virtue ethics has a problem of application: It doesn't tell us what to do in those particular instances in which we most need direction. We turn next to two rule-governed systems that incorporate the virtues: the standard deontic view and the complementarity view.

The Standard Deontic View: The Correspondence Thesis

The standard deontic view asserts three theses:[14]

1. Moral rules require people to perform or omit certain actions, and these actions can be performed by people who either lack or possess the various virtues. For example, both the benevolent and those who lack that virtue can perform beneficent acts like giving to charity.

2. The moral virtues are dispositions to obey the moral rules— that is, to perform or omit certain actions. For example, the virtue of benevolence is a disposition to carry out my duty to perform beneficent acts. According to the correspondence theory of virtues, each virtue corresponds to an appropriate moral principle.

3. The moral virtues do not have intrinsic value, but rather instrumental and derivative value. Agents who have the virtues are more likely to do the right acts—that is, to obey the rules. The virtues are important only because they motivate right action.

On the standard view it is important to make two different but related assessments within the scope of morality: We need to make separate evaluations of the agent and the act. Both are necessary to a full ethical assessment, but it is the act that is logically prior in the relationship. Why is this?

It has to do with the nature of morality. If we agree that the general point of morality is to promote human flourishing and to ameliorate suffering, then we may judge that it is good or right kinds of acts that are, in the end, of utmost importance. But if we agree that there is a general tendency in human affairs for social relations to run down due to natural inclinations toward self-interest, then we can see that special forces must be put in motion in order to countervail natural selfishness. One of these forces is the external sanctions produced by the law and social pressure. But a deeper and more enduring force is the creation of dispositions in people to do what is morally commendable. As Geoffrey Warnock says, "It is necessary that people should acquire, and should seek to ensure that others acquire, what may be called *good dispositions,* that is, some readiness on occasion voluntarily to do desirable things which not all human beings are just naturally disposed to do anyway, and similarly not to do damaging things."[15]

Warnock identifies four such countervailing virtues that are necessary for social well-being. Because we naturally have a tendency to inflict damage on others (especially those outside the circle of our sympathies) in the competitive struggle for goods, there is a need for the virtue of nonmaleficence. But we will all do better if we are not simply disposed to leave each other alone, but instead are positively disposed to help each other whenever social cooperation is desirable; so we should cultivate the virtue of beneficence. Because there is also a natural tendency to discriminate in favor of one's loved ones or one's own interests, we must train ourselves to be just, impartial judges who give each person his or her due: We must acquire the virtue of fairness. Finally, there is a natural temptation to deceive others in one's own interest; we lie, cheat, and give false impressions when it is to our advantage. But this deception tends to harm society at large by generating suspicion, which in turn undermines trust and leads to the breakdown of social cooperation; so we must cultivate the disposition to honesty or truthfulness. And we must value and praise those who have the right dispositions and safeguard ourselves against those who lack these virtues.

Duty-based ethical theorists who hold to the standard account do not deny the importance of character. But they claim that the nature of the virtues can only be derived from right actions or good consequences. To quote Frankena once more, ". . . traits without principles are blind."[16] Whenever there is a virtue, there must be some possible action to which the virtue corresponds and from which it derives its virtuosity. For example, the character trait of truthfulness is a virtue because telling the truth, in general, is a moral duty. Likewise, conscientiousness is a virtue because we have a general duty to be morally sensitive. There is a correspondence between principles and virtues, the latter being derived from the former, as the following suggests:

The Correspondence Theory of Virtues

The Virtue which derives from	*The Principle* (prima facie)
Nonmaleficence	Duty not to harm
Truthfulness	Duty to tell the truth
Conscientiousness	Duty to be sensitive to one's duty
Benevolence	Duty to be beneficent
Faithfulness	Duty to be loyal or faithful
Fairness	Duty to be just
Love	Duty to do what promotes another's good

Although they are derived from the right kind of actions, the virtues are nonetheless very important for the moral life: They provide the dispositions that generate right action. In a sense, they are motivationally indispensable. To complete the passage quoted above, ". . . principles without traits are impotent and traits without principles are blind." Frankena modifies the above position, distinguishing two types of virtues: the standard moral virtues that correspond to specific kinds of moral principles, and nonmoral virtues, such as natural kindliness or gratefulness, industry, courage, and intelligence or rationality, which are "morality-supporting." They are sometimes called "enabling virtues" because they make it possible for us to carry out our moral duties.

The relationship looks something like this:

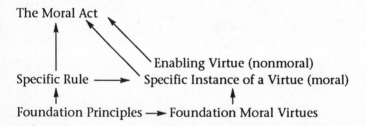

For example, consider a situation in which you have an obligation to save a drowning child in spite of some risk to your own life. The specific rule 'Always come to the aid of drowning people' is grounded in a foundational principle of general beneficence, which in turn generates the foundation virtue of benevolence. In this case, it gives rise to a tendency to try to save the drowning child, but whether or not you actually dive into the water may depend on the enabling (nonmoral) virtue of courage.

Courage itself is not a moral virtue, as benevolence or justice are, for it is the kind of virtue that enhances and augments both virtues and vices (for example, think of the courageous murderer).

The Standard Deontic View's Responses to the Aretaic Critique

Can the correspondence theory answer the objections leveled against it earlier in this chapter? Let's consider the kinds of initial responses available to it.

To the charge that it lacks an adequate motivational component (p. 116), philosophers like Warnock would insist that we can bring up children to prize the correct principles and embody them in their lives. Moral psychology will help us develop the necessary virtues in such a way as to promote human flourishing.

A deontic ethicist can honor the virtues and use them wisely without distorting their role in life. The sophisticated deontic ethicist can even insist that we have a duty to obtain the virtues as the best means to achieve success in carrying out our duties, and that we have a special duty to inculcate in ourself and others the virtue of conscientiousness (the disposition to do one's duty) which will help us achieve all our other duties. This kind of thinking shows that the story of Huck Finn's conscience is not really a good counterexample to deontic ethics. Sometimes our character is ahead of our principles, but that has nothing to do with the essential relationship between virtue and rule.

To the charge that action ethics is based on an improper theological-legal model (p.117), the action-based ethicist responds that we can separate the rational decision-making procedures from the theological ones without violating those procedures. To the charge that this still leaves us with a skewed process of casuistry or hair-splitting, they answer that it is important to come as close as possible to working out a consistent system, for we want to have all the guidance for our actions that is possible. Appropriate modesty will inform us of our limits in this respect, but at least we have rules as guides—unlike the extreme aretaist, who only has dispositions.

To the charge that deontic ethics neglects the spiritual dimension of morality (p.118), the action ethicist responds that we can honor the virtues without making them into a religion. It is better to have a virtue (for example, benevolence) than not to have it because having the virtue gives us the best chance of acting rightly. However, there is no intrinsic value in the virtue; what really is important is *doing* the right act. This is not to deny that there may be aesthetic value in having correct attitudes or virtues besides their morally instrumental value, but we ought not confuse ethical value with aesthetic value. In our opening example in this chapter, there is something satisfying about John's feeling sorrow over the starving Ethiopians, but it is an aesthetic satisfaction. Note the language of describing deeply altruistic people: They are "jewels who shine in their own light." The very metaphor should signal the fact that beyond their moral worth (in the actions they perform) we find something aesthetically attractive in the virtuous life.

Finally, to MacIntyre's criticism that morality emerges in communities and cultures (p. 119), the action ethicist responds that if this is taken as the whole story, then it implies ethical relativism, in which case the virtues have no objective status either. On the other hand, if he allows that we can discover the good for humanity in the context of an Aristotelian naturalism, then we can derive a core set of principles as well as the right virtues.

Complementarity or Pluralistic Ethics

The aretaic ethicist will not be satisfied with the correspondence theory because it is still reductionistic—it treats the virtues like second-class citizens, like servants of the master rules.[17] Even though he may agree that aretaic ethics cannot stand alone, the aretaist will not accept reductionism. There must be true complementarity, a recognition of the importance of both rules and virtues in ways that do not exhaust either. Some instances of carrying out the rule may be done without a virtue and some virtues will be prized for their own sake even without any correspondence to a moral duty.

Let's examine the virtue ethicist's response to the three theses of the standard deontic view. Recall the three theses:

1. Moral rules require people to perform or omit certain actions, and these actions can be performed by people who either lack or possess the various virtues.

2. The moral virtues are dispositions to obey the moral rules—that is, to perform or omit certain actions. According to the correspondence theory of virtues, each virtue corresponds to an appropriate moral principle.

3. The moral virtues do not have intrinsic value, but rather instrumental and derivative value. The virtues are important only because they motivate right action.

The virtue ethicist rejects all three theses of the standard deontic view: the action-nature of the rules thesis, the reductionist thesis, and the instrumental value thesis. The complementarity ethicist still holds to the essential Aristotelian idea that the virtues are excellences that have value in their own right, not merely *instrumental* to, but *constitutive* of the good life. The virtues are not wholly derivative, but rather partly intrinsic; their value is at least partially independent of the rightness of the actions to which they are related. And finally, sometimes the rules require not action but the right kind of sentiments or attitudes. Let's look at these points in greater detail, taking each of the standard deontic view's theses in order.

    1. **The moral rules require people to perform (or omit) certain actions, and these can be performed by people who either lack or possess the virtues.**

There are two problems with the first thesis of the standard deontic view from the virtue ethicist's perspective. First of all, it neglects the close causal link between virtue and action. Doing right without the requisite disposition is like a person who has never played baseball before hitting a home run against a leading major league pitcher: He may have had luck this time, but he shouldn't count on it again. Likewise, without the virtues we shouldn't expect right conduct, even though we may occasionally be surprised both by the right act of the nonvirtuous and the wrong act of the virtuous. Because of the close causal connection, it is statistically improbable that the good will do wrong and the bad or indifferent will do right.

But second, the thesis fails to point out that we have moral obligations to be certain kinds of people—that is, to have the requisite dispositions and attitudes for their own sake. It specifies only rules that require action, but there are other types of moral rules as well—those that require virtue.

The second thesis of the standard deontic view is the reductionist thesis—that virtues are dispositions that correspond to principles of action. What is at issue here is whether the virtues are more than just dispositions to act— whether they include attitudes that may not involve action.

Kant pointed out that love (in the passional or emotional sense) could not be a moral duty because it could not be commanded, for we have no direct control over our emotions. Even though the moral law may require me to give a part of my income to feed the poor, I don't have to like them; I give my money because it is right to do so.

The virtue ethicist rejects this kind of thinking. Although we don't have direct control over our emotions, we do have indirect control over them. We cannot turn our dispositions on and off like water faucets, but we can take steps to inculcate the right dispositions and attitudes. If we recognize the appropriateness of certain emotions in certain situations, we can use meditation, sympathetic imagination, and therapy (and, if one is religious, prayer) in order to obtain those attitudes in the right way. We are responsible for our character; we must not only be good, but we must love the Good. As Aristotle said, "There must first be a disposition to excellence, to love what is fine and loathe what is base."[18]

Consider two people, John and Joan, whose actions are equally correct. However, there is a difference in their attitudes. John tends to rejoice in the success of others and feel sorrow at their mishaps. Joan, on the other hand, tends to feel glee at their mishaps and envy at their success. So long as their outward actions (and will to do right) are similar, the action ethicist regards them as equally moral. But not the virtue ethicist. John has, but Joan lacks, the requisite moral attitude—and Joan has a moral duty to change that attitude.

Thomas Hill tells the story of a deferential wife who always does what is morally right or permissible but does it out of a motive borne of low self-esteem.[19] She doesn't respect herself but defers to her husband and children with an attitude of self-depreciation. Self-respect doesn't appear to be easily parsed out into types of action, yet it seems plausible to believe that it is a virtue, one that we have a duty to inculcate (assuming that we are intrinsically worthy qua rational beings). If this is correct, the duty to respect oneself is yet another counterexample to the second thesis.

There are reactive attitudes or emotions, such as grief, gratitude, respect, and sensitivity that seem appropriate in many situations for their own sake, regardless of whether or not they can be acted upon. The action view neglects this feature of morality; it reduces morality to actions.

The third thesis of the standard deontic view is that the virtues have only derivative and instrumental value. The aretaist rejects this thesis: The virtues have intrinsic value and are not merely derivative but part of what constitutes the good life.

The Good is not simply good for others, but it's good for you as well. The virtues are an inextricable part of what makes life worth living— having the right dispositions and attitudes to the right degree expressed in the right way. John is a better person for grieving with the suffering and rejoicing with the successful. He has an appropriate attitude, whereas Joan doesn't, and this reflects on the quality of their happiness. It is not enough to do the right thing—even to do the right thing for the right reason; it is also important to do it with the right attitude and to have the right attitude and dispositions even when no action is possible.

The difference between the standard deontic view and the pluralist aretaic view is this: Both recognize that the promotion of human flourishing is an essential goal of morality, but the action ethicist thinks that morality only has to do with the kinds of actions that produce this state of affairs, whereas the virtue ethicist believes that the virtues are constitutive of the state of affairs itself—that the unvirtuous (virtue-indifferent or vicious) life is not worth living.

CONCLUSION

It is doubtful whether the action ethicist will be satisfied with the complementary thesis of virtues as just set forth, but we must leave the matter here—exactly where it is in the contemporary debate. If nothing else, virtue ethicists have been successful in drawing attention to the importance of the virtues. There is a consensus in moral philosophy that the virtues have been neglected and that it is important to work them into one's moral perspective. There is also some consensus that a pure virtue-ethic cannot stand alone without a strong deontic component; principles of action are important largely in the way deontological and utilitarian accounts have said they were. The question is not whether these accounts were wrong in what they said, but whether they said enough. The current debate centers on whether the virtues can be successfully incorporated into an actional account, or whether they are worth pursuing for their own sake as well as for the external benefits they bring. The debate is likely to go on, and you are challenged to come to your own judgment in this matter.

Notes

1. See "For Further Reading" for books and articles by authors mentioned.

2. John Stuart Mill, *Essay on Liberty* (Penguin Books, 1974), p. 112.

3. See J. Bennett, "Conscience of Huckleberry Finn," *Philosophy* (1974), pp. 123–134.

4. Aristotle, *Nicomachean Ethics*, 1099a.

5. Richard Taylor, *Ethics, Faith and Reason* (Prentice-Hall, 1985).

6. Contemporary virtue ethicists want to reorganize this classification, but as far as I know no complete theory has been forthcoming. This may be partly due to the fact that virtue ethicists often applaud a piecemeal, antitheoretical approach to ethics. [See Edmund Pincoffs, *Virtues and Quandaries* (University of Kansas Press, 1986).] I am indebted to Robert Loudan's article, "Virtue Ethics and Anti-Theory," (*Philosophia*, 1989) on this subject.

7. On Aristotle's elitist and functional view of human nature: His view flourishing quality of life; (b) the centrality of the moral-political domain wherein most people are judged as worthless, natural slaves who should

not play a dominant role in the political process; (c) the idea that the highest form of life is the life of pure reason, of contemplation; and (d) the idea that the ideal life is that of the great-souled man (megalopsychia) who is proud, patronizing, and indifferent to ordinary hardship to himself or others.

8. An example of the exemplary model may be found in Sidney Lanier's encomium to Jesus:

But Thee, O sovereign Seer of Time,
But Thee, O poet's Poet, Wisdom's Tongue,
But Thee, O man's best Man, O love's best Love,
O perfect life in perfect labor writ,
O all men's Comrade, Servant, King or Priest—
What if and yet, what mole, what flaw, what lapse,
What least defect or shadow of defect,
What rumor, tattled by an enemy,
Of inference loose, what lack of grace
Even in torture's grasp, or sleep's or death's—
Oh, what amiss may I forgive in Thee,
Jesus, good Paragon, thou Crystal Christ?

9. Paul Levy, *Moore* (Oxford, 1979), p. 41f.

10. See the works listed under the various authors in "For Further Reading". This schema is an oversimplification, meant only to indicate the general direction of the position held by each author.

11. See Gregory Pence, "Recent Work on Virtues" (*American Philosophical Quarterly*, p.282f) for a discussion of this point.

12. For an excellent discussion of the problems connected with virtue ethics, see Robert Louden, "Some Vices of Virtue Ethics," *American Philosophical Quarterly* (1984), pp. 227–236, reprinted in Louis Pojman, ed., *Ethical Theory* (Wadsworth, 1989), pp. 311–320.

13. J. L. Mackie, *Ethics: Inventing Right and Wrong* (Penguin Books, 1977), p.186.

14. I am indebted to Walter Schaller's "Are Virtues No More than Dispositions to Obey Moral Rules?" (unpublished paper) for these theses; I have altered them slightly. Schaller illustrates them from the works of Gert, Gewirth, and Rawls.

15. Geoffrey Warnock, *The Object of Morality* (Methuen, 1971), p. 76.

16. William Frankena, *Ethics* , 2nd ed. (Prentice Hall, 1973), reprinted in Pojman, *Ethical Theory*, pp. 305–310.

17. I have been greatly influenced by the works of Walter Schaller (cf. note 14) and Gregory Trianosky (cf. "For Further Reading") in formulating the pluralist position.

18. Aristotle, *Nicomachean Ethics*.

19. Thomas Hill, "Servility and Self-Respect," *The Monist* (1973), pp. 87–104

For Further Reflection

1. Examine the four criticisms of traditional ethics discussed in this chapter (pp.116–119). How valid are they? How would such moral philosophers as Frankena and Warnock, who hold to a correspondence theory of virtues, reply to them?

2. Consider again Aristotle's statement: "There must first be a disposition to excellence, to love what is fine and loathe what is base." Virtue ethicists maintain that it is not enough habitually to do the right act in order to be counted a virtuous person; one must also have the proper emotions. Are there moral emotions? Is it important not only to act kindly to people in distress but to feel sympathy for them? Is it morally significant not simply to do good, but to take pleasure in doing good—to enjoy it—and, conversely, is a lack of the appropriate degree of proper emotions at the right time a sign of weak character?

3. Is moral character, as described by virtue ethicists, really an aesthetic, rather than a moral, category? Note the language of the aretaic philosopher: The good person "is a jewel who shines in his own light." Is it at best only accidental that certain habits and emotions are connected with doing the morally right act? Or is there something necessary about the connection between the right act and good habits and appropriate emotions?

4. Robert Fulgram has written that the rules of life are fairly basic and simple, and that most of us learned them in kindergarten:

> Wisdom was not at the top of the graduate school mountain, but there, in the sandbox at nursery school. These are the things I learned: Share everything. . . . Play fair. . . . Don't hit people. . . . Put things back where you found them. . . . Clean up your own mess . . . . Don't take things that aren't yours. . . . Say you're sorry when you hurt somebody. . . . Wash your hands before you eat. . . . Flush . . . . Warm cookies and cold milk are good for you. . . . Live a balanced life. . . . Learn some and think some and draw and paint and sing and dance and play and work some every day. . . . Take a nap every afternoon. . . . When you go out into the world watch for traffic, hold hands and stick together. . . . Be aware of wonder. . . .

[*All I Really Need to Know I Learned in Kindergarten* (Villard Books, 1988), p. 6]

Do you agree with Fulgram? What implications does this have for the action/virtues debate?

For Further Reading

Anscombe, Elizabeth. "Modern Moral Philosophy," *Philosophy* 33, 1958.

Blum, Lawrence A. *Friendship, Altruism and Morality.* Routledge & Kegan Paul, 1980. A pioneering work in contemporary virtue theory, including a sustained critique of both utilitarian and Kantian ethics.

Foot, Philippa. *Virtues and Vices.* Blackwell, 1978. A collection of articles by one of the virtuosos of virtue ethics.

Frankena, William. *Ethics.* Prentice-Hall, 1973.

French, P. A., T. E. Uehling, and H. K. Wettstein, eds. *Midwest Studies in Philosopy.* Vol XIII (Ethical Theory: Character and Virtue). University of Notre Dame, 1988.

Gert, Bernard. *The Moral Rules,* 2nd ed. Harper & Row, 1966, Chapter 9.

Gewirth, Alan. "Rights and Virtues," *Review of Metaphysics* 38, 1985.

Hardie, W. F. R. *Aristotle's Ethical Theory.* Clarendon Press, 1968.

Hill, Thomas. "Servility and Self-Respect," *The Monist* 57 1973.

Kruschwitz, Robert, and Robert Roberts, eds. *The Virtues.* Wadsworth, 1987. Contains excellent readings and bibliography.

Louden, Robert. "Some Vices of Virtue Ethics," *American Philosophical Quarterly* 21, 1984.

MacIntyre, Alasdair. *After Virtue.* University of Notre Dame Press, 1981.

Mayo, Bernard. *Ethics and the Moral Life.* Macmillan, 1958.

Murdoch, Iris. *The Sovereignty of Good.* Schocken Books, 1971.

Pence, Gregory. "Recent Work on Virtues," *American Philosophical Quarterly* 24 1984. A comprehensive survey.

Pincoffs, Edmund. *Quandaries and Virtues.* University of Kansas Press, 1986.

Roberts, Robert, "Will Power and the Virtues," *Philosophical Review* 93, 1984.

Taylor, Richard. *Ethics, Faith and Reason.* Prentice-Hall, 1985.

Trianosky, Gregory. "Supererogation, Wrongdoing and Vice: On the Autonomy of the Ethics of Virtue," *Journal of Philosophy* 83, 1986.

———— . "Virtue, Action and the Good Life: A Theory of the Virtues," *Pacific Journal of Philosophy*, 1988.

Wallace, James. *Virtues and Vices*. Cornell University Press, 1978.

Warnock, Geoffrey. *The Object of Morality*. Methuen, 1971.

CHAPTER 8

The Fact-Value Problem: Metaethics in the 20th Century

I cannot forbear adding to these reasonings an observation, which may, perhaps, be found of some importance. In every system of morality which I have hitherto met with, I have always remarked, that the author proceeds for some time in the ordinary way of reasoning, and establishes the being of a God, or makes observations concerning human affairs; when of a sudden I am surprised to find that, instead of the usual copulations of propositions, is, and is not, I meet with no proposition that is not connected with an ought, or an ought not. This change is imperceptible; but is, however, of the last consequence. For as this ought, or ought not, expresses some new relation or affirmation, it is necessary that it should be observed and explained; and at the same time that a reason should be given, for what seems altogether inconceivable, how this new relation can be a deduction from others, which are entirely different from it. But as authors do not commonly use this precaution, I shall presume to recommend it to the readers; and am persuaded, that this small attention would subvert all the vulgar systems of morality, and let us see that the distinction of vice and virtue is not founded merely on the relations of objects, nor is perceived by reason.

DAVID HUME, A TREATISE ON HUMAN NATURE

IN THIS CLASSIC QUOTATION from David Hume's work on philosophical anthropology, the question of the relationship of 'is' to 'ought'—of facts to values—is raised. Hume suggests that there is something illicit in arguing from facts to values. This illicitness is sometimes referred to as "Hume's Fork" or the "naturalistic fallacy."

In this chapter we will consider various 20th-century responses to Hume's question. We want to know whether values are essentially different from facts or whether they are derived from facts, and whether value statements can be true and false like factual statements are. Ultimately, we want to understand the nature of moral language and of moral justification. So we are trying to understand how to think about ethics itself. Sometimes this second-order reflection is called **metaethics,** as opposed to normative ethics. Whereas ethics is a philosophical examination of morality, metaethics is philosophizing about ethics—that is, about the very terms and structure of ethical theory.

To get us started in our inquiry, consider the following situation. Jill is currently getting a "D" in her philosophy course and sees an opportunity to raise her grade by cheating on an exam. She would like to get a higher grade, for if she doesn't do better, her father will very likely take away her automobile, and her chances of getting into professional school will be severely diminished. So Jill considers cheating. Yet she is troubled by the thought of cheating. Ought she cheat? The statement "Jill wants to cheat" is a factual one, but is it a fact that she *ought* to cheat? Where does the value term 'ought' come in? What if her boyfriend, Jack, asserts that "Jill ought not cheat"? How could we decide who was right? Does an action-guiding directive—an obligation either to cheat or not to cheat—follow from some descriptions of Jill, for example, that she desperately needs to get a higher grade in her philosophy course? From the premises

1. Jill is in need of a "B" in her philosophy course
2. Jill can get a "B" in her philosophy course by cheating

can we infer the conclusion that

3. Jill ought to cheat in her philosophy course?

Or can we infer from the premise

1a. Jack wants Jill to refrain from cheating in her philosophy course because it will undermine the integrity of the academic process

to the conclusion that

2a. Jill ought not to cheat in her philosophy course?

What is the relationship between facts and values and between descriptive statements and prescriptive judgments?

In this part of our inquiry we will consider several 20th-century responses to Hume's question concerning the relationship of facts to values: naturalism, intuitionism, noncognitivism (emotivism and prescriptivism) and neonaturalism (descriptivism). Essentially, naturalism is the theory that value statements can be defined in terms of factual statements. By 'fact' we refer to what is signified by empirically verifiable statements—for example, that Jill cheated on her exam. By 'value' we refer to what is signified by an evaluative sentence—for example, 'cheating is wrong'. When we claim that something is a fact, we imply that some object or state of affairs exists. When we make a value judgment, we are evaluating or appraising something.

According to naturalism, from the factual statement about Jill's situation (1 or 1a) and a major premise stating a naturalist principle, we can derive a conclusion (either 3 or 2a). The other theories (intuitionism, emotivism, and prescriptivism) deny this, whereas neonaturalism seeks an innovative compromise, asserting that values can sometimes be derived from facts; that is, certain facts entail values. The history of ethical theory in the 20th century is largely the history of the development of these theories as responses to the fact/value problem.

NONNATURALISM

In 1903 one of the most influential books in the history of ethics was published: G. E. Moore's *Principia Ethica*.[1] It inaugurated a sustained inquiry about the meaning of ethical terms and the relation of fact to values that was to dominate moral philosophy in the 20th century. This mode of inquiry was later to be known as "metaethics"—the philosophizing *about* the very terms of ethics and considering the structure of ethics as an object of inquiry. Whereas philosophers before Moore mainly set forth systematic attempts to describe the correct moral theory, philosophers since Moore have been concerned with the functions of ethical terms, the status of moral judgments, and the relation of ethical judgments to nonethical factual statements (the 'is/ought' problem). Normative concerns (for example, Is it possible to fight a just war?) were replaced by logical and epistemological concerns. The central questions became: What, if anything, is the meaning of the terms 'good' or 'right'? How, if at all, can we justify our moral beliefs? Although these questions were raised prior to Moore, they became as a result of his work the sum and substance of moral philosophy for two generations. It is worth our while to outline Moore's argument here.

Moore begins *Principia Ethica* by announcing that philosophers have been muddled about ethical problems largely because they have not first clearly defined the province of ethics and limited the kinds of questions that philosophers were able to ask and answer. Philosophers must first determine the exact domain of ethics before they can deal with the further implications of ethics: "That province may indeed be defined as the whole truth about that which is at the same time common to all such judgments and peculiar to them."

Ultimately, Moore was interested in making ethics a science with clear decision-making procedures, and getting clear on the domain of ethics is but the first step in this direction. Moore thought that the way to understand the 'right', as in 'right action'—which has often been the subject matter of ethics—is first to discover the meaning of the term 'good'. At first glance this seems odd, for we generally think of the domain designated by the term 'good' to be the general domain of axiology (including aesthetics and prudence as well as ethics). Moore may have been broadening the notion of 'ethics' to be coterminous with axiology, or else he thought that axiology is the door to ethics; he did not make this clear.

The philosopher, qua philosopher, is not concerned with morality—with right or wrong behavior—but with the meaning of fundamental terms:

> There are far too many persons, things, and events in the world, past, present, or to come for a discussion of their individual merits to be embraced in any science. Ethics, therefore, does not deal at all with facts of this nature, facts that are unique, individual, absolutely particular . . . and, for this reason, it is not the business of the ethical philosopher to give personal advice or exhortation.

On the contrary, Moore explains, the sole task of ethics proper is to define the term 'good':

> That which is meant by 'good' is, in fact, except its converse 'bad', the only simple object of thought which is peculiar to Ethics. . . . Unless this first question be fully understood, and its true answer clearly recognized, the rest of Ethics is as good as useless from the point of view of systematic knowledge.

'Good', Moore concludes, must be a simple notion like yellow, and, just as you cannot explain to anyone who does not already know it what yellow is, so you cannot explain what 'good' is. No further analysis is possible, for analysis always is the making of the complex simpler; but the Good is already a simple fact and the sort of atomic fact that we use to build up more complex ideas. Here Moore contrasts the notion 'good' with 'horse', which is complex and in need of further analysis.

We come to the heart of Moore's argument against naturalism. Moore's argument may be compared to David Hume's version of the naturalist fallacy in the passage quoted at the beginning of this chapter. Hume believed that naturalists confuse facts with values. His point is that we cannot go from fact statements ('is' statements) to value statements ('ought' statements) without including a value statement as one of our premises. He is criticizing those who argue in the following manner:

A. 1.   Jill wants to cheat in order to realize an important goal.

   2.   Therefore, Jill ought to cheat.

or

B. 1a. Cheating will undermine the integrity of the academic enterprise.

   2a. Therefore, Jill ought not to cheat.

or

C. 1b. God has commanded us to love our neighbor.

   2b. Therefore, we ought to love our neighbor.

According to Hume, all of these arguments are invalid because they commit the naturalist fallacy of moving from a factual statement to a value statement without including a value statement in the premises. They have the form:

1. Fact
2. Therefore, value

or

1. 'Is'
2. Therefore, 'Ought'

This is an invalid form, because in order to get a value in the conclusion, we need to have one in at least one of the premises.

But Moore means more even than simply this,[2] for Hume could still allow that ethical terms could be reduced to nonethical ones. He could fill out the above arguments by adding a second premise that includes a value statement in the following way:

A. 1.   Jill wants to cheat in order to realize an important goal.

   2.   Anyone who wants to cheat in order to get an important goal ought to cheat.

    3. Therefore, Jill ought to cheat.

and

   C. 1b. God has commanded us to love our neighbor.

       2b. We ought to do what God commands.

       3b. Therefore, we ought to love our neighbor.

A Humean could define 'good' in terms of a natural property, such as meeting human need (or desire) or obedience to God; that is, a Humean could be a self-reflective naturalist—one who answers in the affirmative his own question about whether one can derive an 'ought' from an 'is'.

But Moore would not accept this reasoning. His views are more radical than Hume, for according to Moore's interpretation of the naturalistic fallacy, we cannot reduce ethical (normative) terms to nonethical (natural) terms. Ethical characteristics are different in kind from nonethical ones, and hence we cannot deduce ethical propositions from nonethical ones in the way that many Humeans would allow (for many followers of Hume would allow, but Moore would not, that ethical terms are definable by nonethical terms.

In order to expose the naturalist's error and show that all forms of naturalism are false, Moore set forth what he called "the open question argument." He asks us to imagine some naturalistic definition for 'good', such as Bertrand Russell's suggestion that "'good' means that which we desire to desire." But when we analyze this statement carefully, we find a problem: We can still ask, 'Is it good to desire to desire X?', which reduces to 'Is the desire to desire X one of the things that we desire to desire?' or to 'Do we desire to desire to desire to desire X?', which seems ridiculous and not at all equivalent to the question 'Is X good?', which seems to be a simple question, not at all complex.

Stated formally, the argument goes as follows: First we define the term 'good' by a natural property, F: (1) Good = df* F. We can still always ask (2) 'Are F's good?' But by substitution for 'good' in (2), we get a tautology (3) 'Are F's F?', which is not a meaningful question. So presumably 'good' cannot be identified with F. Equivalently,

    1. Good = df* F.

    2. X is F.

    3. X is F, but is X good?

    4. By substitution 1, statement 3 becomes 'X is good, but is X good'?, which is a tautology.

* =df means "equals the definition of."

5. But statement 3 is not a tautology, so statements 3 and 4 are not equivalent.

6. Therefore, statement 1 is false and we cannot define 'good' in terms of a natural property.

Let's illustrate this. Suppose you say that "Pleasure is good" and I respond, "Torturing children gives me pleasure, but is it good?" I seem to have a counterexample to your claim. If we say "Jogging is pleasant, but is it pleasant?", we see that the sentence makes no sense, for we are asking a tautological question (of the form: X is F, but is it F?); but if we say "Jogging is pleasurable, but is it good?", we have asked a meaningful question— something nontautological—which it would be if 'good' meant 'that which gives pleasure'. We could apply this test to any candidate for a definition of 'good', and Moore would contend that the result will be the same: We will find that we cannot define 'good'.

Moore's conclusion is that because the good cannot be defined, there are only two alternatives: Either it is a simple, indefinable property, or it doesn't refer to anything at all (and hence there is no subject of ethics). Because he was convinced that ethics is not an illusion, he inferred that the subject matter of ethics—good—"is a simple, indefinable, unanalyzable object of thought."

One may ask whether Moore was right about all this. Does the open question test show that 'good' is entirely an indefinable, nonnatural property? A tradition going back at least as far as Aristotle had viewed the good as a natural property in terms either of the object of desire or some psychological state (such as pleasure or, more complexly, happiness).

To Moore's open question:—'X has F, but is it good?'—could not the naturalist respond, "Yes"? When Moore points out that this substitution leads to a tautology ('X is good but is it good?'), the naturalist might point out that this difference in meaning doesn't affect the essential referent. Consider the following:

D. 1. This is Venus, but is it the Morning Star?

by Moorean substitution:

D. 2. This is Venus, but is it Venus?

or

E. 1. This is the 41st President of the United States, but is it George Bush?

by Moorean substitution:

E. 2. This is Bush, but is it Bush?

In both cases adequate information convinces us that the answer to both questions is "Yes," even though statements 1 and 2 in each case may not mean the same thing. Likewise, might not the naturalist respond in a similar way to the open question argument? For example, naturalists might say that 'good' means or includes as part of its meaning 'being an object of positive interest' or 'the flourishing of rational (or sentient) beings'.

Whether this sort of move is adequate to save naturalism will be considered toward the end of this chapter. During the first half of the 20th century, the prospects of naturalism looked bleak.

EMOTIVISM

According to Moore, intuitionism was the only satisfactory ethical theory. If 'good' could not be identified with a natural property, it must be definable ostensibly as a nonnatural one, resembling a Platonic form (for example, the Good) that we all know by intuition.[3] It is by adhering to our intuitions, then, that morality "gets off the ground"—that we know its nature and become moral people. The influence of Moore on subsequent ethics cannot be overemphasized. On the one hand, it inspired intuitionism to new endeavors; on the other hand, those who were sceptical of nonnatural properties—forms of the good and other ideals—were nevertheless convinced by his open question argument that ethical terms could not be defined by natural properties.

Recall that Moore said that there were three possibilities with regard to the meaning of 'good': Either it was (1) a complex natural property; (2) a simple, unanalyzable, nonnatural property; or (3) not a property at all, in which case ethics was not a reality at all. Those who accepted the open question argument against naturalism but rejected Moore's Platonism were forced to accept the third possibility—the death of ethical truth. Because there was no subject matter for ethics, they concluded that ethics is only about emotions (hence the school's name, **emotivism**.

It may be helpful at this point to put the matter into a schema. Moore's intuitionism includes four theses:

1. The Humean Thesis: 'Ought' statements cannot be derived from 'is' statements
2. The Platonic Thesis: Basic value terms, including moral statements, refer to nonnatural properties
3. The Cognitive Thesis: Moral statements are either true or false; that is, they are objective, putative claims about reality, which can be known

4. The Intuition Thesis: Moral truths are discovered by the intuition;
they are self-evident upon reflection

Moore held only thesis 3, the cognitive thesis, in common with the
naturalist.

We can best understand emotivism, which was a reaction to intuitionism, as a rigorously empirical analysis of these four theses. Emotivists
accept thesis 1 but deny theses 3 and 4; thesis 2 is the crucial thesis.
Emotivists agree that evaluative statements *claim* to refer to a nonnatural
world, but because there is no way to find out whether there is a nonnatural
world, there is no way to know whether they refer to anything at all.
Because meaningful discourse, according to the emotivists, is made up of
either analytic statements or empirical statements that can be verified, we
must reject evaluative language as meaningless or, as C. L. Stevenson
(1908–1979) did, give it a separate, noncognitive meaning (that is, use the
term 'meaning' in a way that does not depend on whether a sentence is true
or false).[4] For the classical emotivist, value sentences are neither true nor
false; they are without a clear sense, and there is no reason to think that
intuition will save us here. Intuitive speculation is unverifiable and thus a
form of nonsense.

Perhaps the purest example of an ethical emotivist is the Oxford
University philosopher A. J. Ayer (1910–89). In the 1930s Ayer went to
Vienna to study with a group of philosophers called the "Logical Positiv-
ists," who believed that the meaning of a sentence is found in its method
of verification. All meaningful sentences must be either tautologies (of the
form 'A is A', or reducible to such statements) or empirically verifiable (for
example, observations about the world, such as 'The book is red'). Value
statements are neither tautologies nor verifiable statements; hence they are
meaningless. Theological statements were also meaningless—neither true
nor false but simply a form of nonsense—because we cannot state the
manner in which they could be verified.

Compare an empirical statement, (1) "There are cobwebs in the north-
west corner of your dorm room" with (2) "Cheating is wrong" and (3) "A
benevolent, omnipotent being is guiding your life." We have a pretty good
idea what can verify statement 1, but what kinds of observations could
verify statements 2 and 3? It seems difficult to say. So only statement 1 is
meaningful, and statements 2 and 3 are nonsense. To the emotivist all
value and religious and metaphysical utterances are seen as meaningless.

Here is how two of the earliest emotivists put the matter:

"Good" is alleged to stand for a unique, unanalyzable concept . . .
[which] is the subject matter of ethics. This peculiar ethical use of
'good' is . . . a purely emotive use. When so used the word stands for

nothing whatever. . . . Thus, when we so use it in the sentence, "This is good," we merely refer to *this*, and the addition of "is good" makes no difference whatever to our reference. . . . It serves only as an emotive sign expressing our attitude to *this*, and perhaps evoking similar attitudes in other persons, or inciting them to action of one kind or another.[5]

In 1935 Ayer wrote that

the fundamental ethical concepts are unanalyzable, inasmuch as there is no criterion by which one can test the validity of the judgments in which they occur. . . . The reason why they are unanalyzable is that they are mere pseudo-concepts. The presence of an ethical symbol in a proposition adds nothing to its factual content. Thus if I say to someone "You acted wrongly in stealing that money," I am not stating anything more than if I had simply said "You stole that money." In adding that the action is wrong, I am not making any further statement about it.[6]

The argument of both quotations is essentially this:

1. A sentence is cognitively meaningful if and only if it can be verified.
2. Moral sentences cannot be verified.
3. Therefore, moral sentences are not meaningful.

Moral statements are a type of nonsense, albeit a useful type. Even though they cannot be said to be true or false, they express our emotions. "Murder is evil" is really only a shorthand way of expressing our dislike for acts of murder. Saying "Murder is morally wrong" is equivalent to saying "Murder—Boo!", and saying "Helping people is morally good" is like saying "Helping people—hoorah!" The only other function ethical statements have is to persuade others to take the same attitude toward the activity in question: "Murder—Boo! Don't you agree?" The functions of ethical statements thus take two forms:

(1) 'Good' =df expressive of positive emotion (Ayer's version)

or

(2) 'X is good' =df I approve of X, do so as well (Stevenson's version)

So the emotivist notes three things about moral language:
First, moral language is expressive of emotions or feelings; it is subjective. Such sentences are useful like barking is useful to dogs—it provides a

release of feelings. But such sentences are not to be confused with the view of subjective relativism, which says that the truth or falsity of a moral judgment depends on the agent holding that judgment. For the emotivist there is no truth or falsity. The difference is the difference between saying "I have a headache" and holding your head and while grimacing and groaning: In the first case (analogous to subjectivism) my statement is either true or false, but in the second case (analogous to emotivism) my actions are sincere or insincere.

Second, moral language is imperative: It commands ('Cheating is wrong' means 'Don't cheat, please!'). It is not at all descriptive.

Third, moral language aims at persuading: It has a magnetic force aimed at influencing another person's actions. According to Stevenson, 'This is right' means 'I approve of this; do so as well'.

Because moral statements are said to be without truth-value (are neither true nor false), they could be said to be without cognitive content. The term **noncognitivism** was used to designate them, separating them from ethical theories that held that moral statements did have truth-value, designated 'cognitivism' (held by naturalists, nonnaturalists, and intuitionists).

In "The Emotive Meaning of Ethical Terms," (1937) and *Ethics and Language* (1944), Stevenson gives us a more sophisticated version of emotivism. He does not deny that moral language has meaning, as Ayer does. It is just that it has a different sort of meaning: emotive meaning rather than descriptive meaning. Stevenson provides a careful analysis of the term 'good', arguing that any adequate analysis must meet three criteria: We must be able to disagree about whether something is good; 'goodness' must possess a magnetism, a tendency to act in its favor; and it must not be discoverable solely through scientific investigation. He then argues that naturalist theories fail for one reason or another to satisfy these criteria, but that emotivism, which emphasizes the difference between descriptive and emotive meaning, does satisfy all the criteria in the following ways.

Disagreement over whether something is good, Stevenson argues, is simply disagreement in attitude. If you say stealing is bad and I say that it is good, we simply are manifesting different attitudes toward stealing. This "attitude theory" emphasizes that it is precisely the magnetic aspect of the term 'good' that is important, that the term has laudatory meaning. And finally, emotivism recognizes that fundamental disagreements (those not rooted in mere disagreement in beliefs about some nonmoral facts) will not be resolved by empirical methods; if I have a pro-stealing attitude and have considered all the facts relevant to that activity, reason and science are impotent to effect a change in me.

A Critique of Emotivism

Several objections against emotivism were soon forthcoming. First of all, the verification theory of meaning, upon which Ayer's emotivism was founded, was discovered to be problematic. Specifically, it didn't pass its own test; that is, the principle either couldn't be verified or couldn't describe its method of verification, and so, on its own terms, it was meaningless. There is no reason to confine meaningfulness to empirical statements.

Second, if the emotivist theory of meaning is correct, one cannot easily distinguish between the effects and the meaning of a value term. The term 'good' may cause others to approve, but it is doubtful whether this causal power is part of the meaning of 'good'. The term 'evil' attached to a noun, as in "that evil man" may repel us and cause us to avoid the person in question, but the effect is not part of the meaning of the term 'evil'. There is a difference between *giving reasons* why someone should do something and *getting* him to do something.

Third, if ethical disagreement is fundamentally a disagreement in attitude (as the emotivist alleges) then a good reason is one that causally resolves a disagreement in attitude. But we think that our reasons for action are separable from the causes that change our attitudes. For example, manipulating some neurons in my temporal lobe may cause a change in attitude toward cheating, but that would not be the same as giving me reasons to believe that the good accomplished by certain instances of cheating would far outweigh the bad effects. It is difficult to separate reasons from persuasive manipulation on the emotivist account, for on that account, the two come to the same thing. According to Alasdair MacIntyre, emotivism obliterates the distinction between manipulation and nonmanipulative behavior in social relations.[7]

Fourth, morality seems deeper than mere emotions or acting on feelings or attitudes. Morality is based on reasons (as we alleged in the third objection above), but moral judgments are also universalizable: If it is wrong for Jill to steal, then it is wrong for anyone relevantly similar to Jill to steal. That is, morals are not simply isolated emotive ejaculations or attitudes, but principles that guide actions.

Finally, not only does emotivism fail to note the universality of moral principles by treating moral statements as isolated, atomic, verbal ejaculations; it also fails to note that this feature enables us to argue about moral judgments. As universal action-guides, moral principles form the bases of reasoning about morality. So we indeed can argue (and not merely emote) about right and wrong. These last two points are emphasized in the next metaethical theory we'll discuss: prescriptivism.

PRESCRIPTIVISM

Emotivism is not the only kind of noncognitivism. Another version, first set forth by R. M. Hare (1919-) in *The Language of Morals* (henceforth LM) and called prescriptivism,[8] accepts Moore's open question argument against naturalism along with the emotivists' radical separation of facts from values. Although he agrees with the emotivists that we cannot ascribe truth or falsity to moral statements and that moral judgments are attitudinal, Hare changes the emphasis regarding moral terms from feelings of approval (or disapproval) to certain types of judgment that include a universalizability feature and a prescriptive element.[9]

According to Hare there are "three most important truths about moral judgments." Moral judgments are (1) prescriptive judgments, that are (2) distinguished from other prescriptions in that they are universalizable, and they (3) exhibit logical relations; that is, they involve a rational procedure based on the fact that there are logical relations between prescriptive judgments.[10] All of this presupposes a fourth, even more fundamental notion—that moral judgments involve principles which in turn call for the weighting of principles in cases of conflict in order to arrive at an overriding principle. Let us examine each of these four metaethical theses.

Prescriptivity

We have already noted that moral judgments seem to do more than simply describe states of affairs. The statement 'Jill should not cheat' is not primarily a description of behavior but rather a prescription for behavior. Moral judgments are given in order to guide actions—to answer questions of the form 'What shall I do?'

Moral judgments are a species of value judgments (which include aesthetic evaluations and are centered in the idea of the Good). Following Hume, Hare believes that there is a logical distinction between a statement's descriptive element and its evaluative element. In a sense, value judgments are something extra or superfluous ("supervenient" is the word in fashion) beyond the plain description. For example, when I say of a particular automobile that it is a good car, I mean that it has certain characteristics: It doesn't often break down, it isn't rusted, it will go over 50 mph, it goes at least 20 miles per gallon of gasoline, it serves its owner well for several years, and so forth. But I need not call all of this 'good'; I could just as well describe my car item by item. Putting the adjective 'good' next to the noun 'car' simply means that I, like most people, would commend such an automobile. But Hot-Rod Harry, who has a passion for fast cars and is a skilled mechanic (so that he doesn't mind frequent breakdowns), might not agree with my evaluation; he might agree with my description of a given car and yet not agree that it was a good car. To me my 1979 Chevy is a good car, but to Harry it is a bad car and he wouldn't be seen dead in it:

> Description: Car C has features a, b, c, . . . n.
>
> Evaluation: 'Good' is always an attribution relative to some standard.

Hot-Rod Harry and I differ in calling car C good because we have different standards of reference. We can choose whatever standard of reference we like; any such standard is not intrinsic to the nature of cars.

The point is that the descriptive meaning of 'good' does not exhaust its meaning. There is something added—something "supervenient"—that is the value factor. And this value aspect, the commending-nature of 'good', is a matter of choice. "When we commend or condemn anything, it is always in order, at least indirectly, to guide choices, our own or other people's, now or in the future" (LM, p. 127).

Now if I know that someone needs a car and has similar needs and values as mine, I can commend a used Chevy sedan like mine to him. "It's a good car," I might say. Or "If you want a good used car, get a Chevy sedan" or "You ought to buy an inexpensive second-hand Chevy like mine." All of these speech acts have the same logical force. The first sentence is an indicative value statement; the second is a hypothetical imperative (of the form 'If you want X, do A'); the third is an indicative sentence containing the prescriptive verb 'ought'.

Value judgments cannot be equated with imperatives, but they do have something in common with them: They are both prescriptive. A moral judgment entails an imperative. 'You ought not cheat' is just another way of saying 'Don't cheat, please!' When I accept the judgment that cheating is wrong—that people ought not to cheat—I am committing myself to live by that prescription myself. My moral judgment that you ought not to do X is meant to "guide" your action, not in the sense that it necessarily moves you to do X, but in the sense that your accepting my judgment commits you to doing X and your not doing X implies that you have rejected my judgment.

The Logic of Moral Reasoning

A particular feature of Hare's theory that advances the program of noncognitivism is the idea that there is a logic to prescriptive judgments. Although moral judgments do not have truth-value, they do have a logical form. We can argue about particular judgments and use arguments to reach particular prescriptions.

Hare holds two theses about the distinction between 'is' and 'ought'—between descriptive and prescriptive statements as they pertain to logical form:

I. **No indicative conclusion can be validly drawn from a set of premises that cannot be validly drawn from the indicatives among them alone**

and

II. **No imperative conclusion can be validly drawn from a set of premises that does not contain at least one imperative.**

Because the first thesis is controversial, we would do well to focus on the second one. A case of arguing from an indicative premise to an imperative would be:

A. 1. This is a box.

2. Therefore, take this box to the railroad station.

Something is clearly missing. We must add a major premise in the form of an imperative:

1. Take all the boxes to the railroad station.

As a result, the argument becomes:

B. 1. Take all boxes to the railroad station.

2. This is a box.

3. Therefore, take this to the railroad station.

When we recall that 'ought' judgments are a type of imperative and when we apply thesis II to moral judgments, we see that a valid moral argument must contain at least one 'ought' or imperatival premise in order to reach a moral conclusion:

C. 1. Students ought not cheat on tests (imperative form: Never cheat, please!).

2. Jill is taking a philosophy test (indicative statement).

3. Therefore, Jill ought not cheat on her test (imperative form: Therefore, Don't cheat, Jill!).

The form of a moral argument is an example of an Aristotelian practical syllogism, which has the form:

D. 1. Always do X! (universal imperative).

2. This A is a case of X (singular indicative).

3. Conclusion: Do A! (singular imperative).

or

E. 1. Never do X!

2. This A is a case of X.

3. Conclusion: Don't do A!

Universalizability

This is the most important feature of Hare's moral theory, for it gives the theory a formal structure. There is no special content to Hare's system, but there is a method, and the method is essentially Kantian, similar to the categorical imperative: Act in such a way as to be able to will that the principle of your action could be a universal law. What distinguishes Kant's theory from Hare's is Kant's belief that the categorical imperative will generate substantive universal principles.

According to Hare's principle of universalizability, it is a necessary and sufficient condition of any moral judgment that one would impartially enjoin the same principle in any case of the same kind as the one in question. In making a moral judgment one has to say that one would make the same judgment in all similar cases. A judgment is not moral unless the agent is prepared to universalize his or her principle: "To ask whether I ought to do A in these circumstances is to ask whether or not I will that doing A in such circumstances should become a universal law" (LM, p. 70).

For example, to say that "You ought not steal from your boss" entails via the principle of universalizability that the speaker believes that no one should steal in relevantly similar circumstances. Furthermore, for you to say that I should not steal is for you to commit yourself to a principle of forbidding stealing, and it is from that commitment that you are *prescribing* that others live that way also. Universalizability is the recognition that what is "sauce for the goose is sauce for the gander." It constrains our choices to the extent that it warns us that by what judgment we judge we too shall be judged.

Is Hare correct? Is universalizability both a necessary and sufficient condition for moral principles? A strong intuitive case can be made for viewing universalizability as a necessary condition, for if you say that something X has a certain property F and point out that another object Y is exactly similar to X, then we would expect that Y would also have property F. If this cube of sugar is sweet and the one next to it is exactly similar in every relevant way, we should have to conclude that it is also sweet.

Some moral philosophers, however, argue that there are counterexamples to the principle of universalizability. Abraham may have felt that he had an obligation to sacrifice his son Isaac but that no other father had a similar obligation, or I may believe that I have a special duty to give all my money to the poor without believing that everyone has a similar duty.

But I don't think that this analysis is correct. What these examples indicate is that the principle of universalizability must be carefully applied to relevant characteristics and that it is sometimes difficult to specify just what the relevant characteristic is. If Abraham had a special duty to sacrifice Isaac, it was because God demanded this and God had a right to demand this. If this is so, then God has a right to demand of anyone relevantly similar to Abraham (and in a similar situation as Abraham's) that he sacrifice his child. Likewise, there must be some reason why I in particular ought to give all my money to the poor. For example, perhaps I simply feel an overwhelming pity for them, which causes me to believe that I have a duty to give my money to the poor. But if I reflect on this, don't I have to believe that anyone relevantly similar to me who feels a similar overwhelming pity for the poor must also have an obligation?

It seems at least plausible to assert that universalizability is a necessary condition for moral judgment, but it is not as obvious that universalizability is a sufficient condition for moral judgments. Universalizability merely grants moral judgments formal consistency.

Principles

One of the most insightful aspects of Hare's work is his recognition of the centrality of principles in moral reasoning. As we noted above, they serve as major premises in arguments that guide our actions. In order to get a better look at this feature, let's contrast principle-centered systems with a nonprincipled system. One such type of ethics is situational ethics, especially as advocated by Joseph Fletcher in his book *Situation Ethics* (Westminster Press, 1966). Fletcher relates the following story to illustrate his thesis that principles are unnecessary for moral living. During the 1964 election campaign a friend of Fletcher's was riding in a taxi and happened to ask the taxi driver about his political views. The driver said, "I and my father and grandfather . . . and their fathers, have always been straight-ticket Republicans." "Ah," said the friend who was himself a Republican, "I take it that means you will vote for Senator Goldwater," "No" said the driver, "there are times when a man has to push his principles aside and do the right thing." The taxi driver is the hero of Fletcher's book, and his attitude is that we can jolly well do without principles.

But Hare would point out that in Fletcher's mind there is a confusion between viewing principles as rigid absolutes and as reasons that are necessary to inform our deliberations. If Fletcher's friend had pursued the taxidriver a bit further, he no doubt would have gotten him to give some reasons for switching his vote (for example, he might argue that Senator Goldwater wants to escalate the war in Vietnam and such an escalation is both unjust and will lead to terrible consequences).

Indeed, Hare argues that all moral reasoning involves principles and that without principles most teaching would be impossible, for we usually teach not particular items but a set of action-guiding principles; that is, we don't learn isolated individual acts, but classes of acts in classes of situations:

> In learning to drive, I learn, not to change gear *now*, but to change gear when the engine makes a certain kind of noise. If this were not so, instruction would be of no use at all; for if all an instructor could do were to tell us to change gear now, he would have to sit beside us most of the rest of our lives in order to tell us just when, on each occasion, to change gear (LM, p. 60f).

After we have basic principles, we next learn when to use them and when to subordinate them to suit a complex situation. In driving we first learn to draw to the side of the road before stopping. Later we learn that this does not apply when stopping before making a left-hand turn onto a side road, for then we must stop near the middle of the road until it is possible to turn. Still later we learn that in this maneuver it is not necessary to stop at all if it is an uncontrolled junction and we can see that there is no traffic that we will obstruct by turning. And so the process of modifying our driving principles goes on.

> The good driver is one whose actions are so exactly governed by principles which have become a habit with him, that he normally does not have to think just what to do. But road conditions are exceedingly various, and therefore it is unwise to let all one's driving become a matter of habit. . . . The good driver constantly attends to his habits, to see whether they might not be improved; he never stops learning (LM, p. 63).

Now often a dilemma occurs when two accepted principles conflict. Suppose that you are hurrying to make an appointment with your teacher, whom you have promised to meet at 3 P.M. in his office. On the way to his office you come upon an accident and see a woman in need of your attention. If you stop to help her, you will miss your appointment and so be guilty of breaking your promise. But you sense that you also have an obligation to help the woman, which you will be violating if you do not stop. You cannot meet both obligations, so you need to find out which obligation overrides the other. Whenever two of our principles conflict, we must decide on which principle overrides the other in this sort of situation.

But how do we decide which obligation is the greater? Here Hare becomes an existentialist in a way reminiscent of Jean-Paul Sartre's description of the student who must choose between staying with his mother and going abroad to fight with the Free French Army against the German occupiers of his country. Just as Sartre argues that there is no "true" answer to this question, Hare argues that there are no objectively right or wrong things—absolutes given for all time and place, independently of our choosings. One is free to choose one's own principles, but having chosen, one must commit oneself to the principle, thus universalizing it; your being willing to commit yourself to that prescription is a necessary and sufficient condition for the justification of that principle. Hare wrote that

> a complete justification of a decision would consist of a complete account of its effects, together with a complete account of the principles which it observed, and the effects of observing those principles. . . . If pressed to justify a decision completely, we have to give a complete specification of the way of life of which it is a part. This complete specification it is impossible in practice to give; the nearest attempts are those given by the great religions. . . . If the inquirer still goes on asking "But why *should* I live like that?" then there is no further answer to give him, because we have already, *ex hypothesi*, said everything that could be included in this further answer. We can only ask him to make up his own mind which way he ought to live; for in the end everything rests upon such a decision of principle (LM, p. 69).

Hare believes that by using the imagination and putting oneself "in the shoes" of other people, we will be able to arrive at a group of common principles. For although Hare's system, like Ayer's and Stevenson's, seems relativistic, he believes (unlike these emotivists) that if all normal people use his approach, they will in fact end up with a common normative moral theory—some form of utilitarianism. This conclusion has been hotly contested.

At this point it may be useful to provide a diagram[11] of the positions we have surveyed.

	Problems of Meaning	Problems of Justification

Cognitivism [Ethical claims have truth-value and it is possible to know what it is.]

A. Naturalism	Ethical terms are defined in factual terms; they refer to natural properties.	Ethical judgments are disguised assertions of some kind of fact and thus can be justified empirically.
1. Subjective	Their truth originates in individual or social decision.	
2. Objective	Their truth is independent of individual or social decision.	
B. Nonnaturalism	Ethical terms cannot be defined in factual terms; they refer to non-natural properties.	Ethical conclusions cannot be derived from empirically confirmed propositions.
1. Intuitionism		Intuition alone provides confirmation.
2. Religious revelation		Some form of divine revelation provides confirmation.

Noncognitivism [Ethical claims do not have truth-value.]

A. Emotivism	Ethical terms do not ascribe properties, and their meaning is not factual, but rather, emotive.	Ethical judgments are not justifiable factually, rationally, or by intuition.
B. Prescriptivism	Ethical terms do not ascribe properties, and their meaning is not factual, but signifies universal prescriptions.	Ethical judgments are not factually, intuitively, or rationally justifiable, but are existentially justified.

A Critique of Prescriptivism

The first sustained criticism of Hare's strong fact/value dichotomy is Philippa Foot's "Moral Beliefs,"[12] which was delivered at the Aristotelian Society in 1958. It represents the first clear critique of the whole formalist enterprise of the noncognitivists. She argues that the noncognitivists have separated the evaluative meaning from the descriptive meaning of 'good' in an implausible way. There are limits to what we can reasonably prescribe as a moral judgment, and there are some so-called "descriptive" concepts that include moral or valuational overtones: 'dangerous', 'courage', 'injury', and 'justice'. Foot is not a naturalist, or at least not a straightforward naturalist, for she doesn't believe that value terms can be defined by factual statements, but she does try to show that there is not a complete logical gap between facts and values (as all of the other ethicists in this section have maintained in their adherence to the naturalistic fallacy). Certain facts logically entail values. Foot's compromise position was labeled "descriptivism" or "neonaturalism."[13]

Let's look more closely at the kinds of criticisms levelled at Hare's prescriptivism by Foot and others. Essentially, three kinds of criticisms are aimed at the radical, formal dimension of the theory. Prescriptivism is charged with (1) being too broad, (2) permitting the trivial, and (3) allowing the moral substance in life to slip away from ethical theory. We'll now examine each of these charges and then I'll add a fourth criticism of my own.

First, prescriptivism is too broad: It allows terribly immoral agents and acts to count as moral. Hare himself was the first to point this out in Chapter 6 of *Freedom and Reason*. He admitted that the fanatic who prescribed that all people of a certain race should be exterminated could, on his account, be considered as moral judged by his theory. A convinced Nazi could validly use argument A:

A. 1. All Jews ought to be exterminated.
    2. David is a Jew.
    3. Therefore, David ought to be exterminated.

And a McCarthyite or right-wing fanatic could reason:

B. 1. No socialist should be allowed to teach in an American university.
    2. Herbert Aptheker is a socialist.
    3. Therefore, Herbert Aptheker should not be allowed to teach in an American university.

The only constraint on choosing moral principles is that one should use one's sympathetic imagination and put oneself "into the other person's shoes" before making the judgment. But this doesn't hinder the fanatic, who reasons "If I were ever to become a socialist (or be found to be a Jew), I would deserve the same treatment as I am prescribing." Many of us would argue that there is no way to justify these principles. Perhaps the fanatic has been misinformed on the dangers of Jews or socialists, but there is no reason to accept his or her principles as legitimate. There must be something wrong with a theory that is so broad as to allow heinous acts to count as moral. Such a theory seems subject to the same criticisms as subjective relativism (cf. Chapter 2).

Second, prescriptivism allows the most trivial considerations to count as moral judgments. Consider the following arguments:

C. 1. Everyone ought to rub his or her tummy on Tuesday mornings.

2. Today is Tuesday and it is morning.

3. You and I ought to rub our tummies.

D. 1. Everyone ought to tie one's right shoe before one's left shoe.

2. You are about to tie your shoes.

3. Therefore, you have a moral duty to tie your right shoe before your left shoe.

It would seem that any noncontradictory principle or judgment whatsoever could become a moral principle or judgment simply by being chosen (that is, by being prescriptively universalized by some agent). Morality has no special subject matter, no core content.

Third, prescriptivism misses the point of morality: Not only does it allow too much to be counted as moral, it allows too much to slip through the moral net. We generally think that we have some moral obligations, whether we are fully aware of them or not and whether we like it or not. We think it wrong in general to lie or cheat or kill innocent people or harm others without good reason, and any moral theory worth its salt would have to recognize these minimal principles as part of its theory. But there is no necessity to recognize these principles in Hare's theory; the principles 'Killing innocent people is wrong' or 'One ought not to kill innocent people' are not necessary principles in prescriptivism. One may choose the very opposite of that principle if one so wishes: 'One ought to kill innocent people'. So when mass-murderer Mike comes before the judge after being accused of killing 47 children, he may rightly say, "Your Honor, I protest your sentencing me to life-imprisonment. Yes, I broke the law, but morality is higher than the law, and I was only doing what was morally right— killing innocent people. Mine were acts of civil disobedience." A judge who was a prescriptivist would have to agree and reply, "Yes, I can see that you have a different set of moral principles than most of us and that there is no objectively valid way of deciding the issue. But one of my moral principles (indeed, I make my living by it) is to carry out the mandate of the law. So I am sentencing you to life-imprisonment."

Perhaps we could imagine that a conversation like this might actually occur, but there is something counterintuitive about it. We think that morality is (or should be) about important aspects of human existence. Its principles are not something we *invent*, but something we *discover* by reflection.

A fourth criticism—one that I have not seen mentioned in the literature—is that not only are there no limits on what may count as a moral principle, but equally troublesome, there are no logical constraints on altering one's principles or the hierarchy of one's principles as one feels inclined. Hare admits that our moral principles are revisable, but he doesn't seem to notice how damaging this is for a stable moral system. Suppose that you are rich and I am poor, and I universalize the principle that 'The rich ought to help the poor in every way possible,' and suppose also that I convince you to act on this principle. But suppose now that our situations have reversed—I am rich and you are poor—and you notice that I am no longer acting on this principle and accuse me of hypocrisy. I can reply that I am not at all a hypocrite (which implies that one is not living by one's own principles); on the contrary, I am living by my principles— only they are altered principles! I have decided to live by the principle that 'No one has a duty to help the poor'. Of course, if I should become poor again, I might very well change my principles again. You may object that this is insincere, but why should I universalize the principle of universal consistency over time? I am sincere about living by my current principles, and that is all that Hare's moral theory requires. Perhaps this shows a lack of character, but then Hare's theory doesn't give us any objective standards for character. Perhaps I choose to universalize the principle that one may change one's character to suit one's principles. The point here is that there are no nonarbitrary constraints on when and why I may change my moral principles.

THE RENAISSANCE OF NATURALISM

It is the third criticism—that of missing the point of morality—that has been most often hurled against Hare's prescriptivism, and this criticism was first given a sustained form by Geoffrey Warnock. Warnock claims that the formalist nature of noncognitivist moral philosophy is barren and misses the point of morality; that is, morality has a *content*, which, he claims, is to ameliorate the human predicament, which has a tendency to get worse. We can call this claim the entropy principle of social relations. Because of limitations in resources, intelligence, knowledge, rationality, and sympathy, the social fabric tends to come apart, which as a result threatens to produce a Hobbesian state of nature in which chaos reigns. Morality is anti-entropic: It counters the set of such limitations, especially by concentrating on expanding our sympathies, and thus it contributes to "the betterment—or non-deterioration of the human predicament."[14]

Warnock's work paved the way for a new, more sophisticated naturalism. Many philosophers, going back to Aristotle, Hobbes, Kant, and Mill, sought to reinstate a version of naturalistic cognitivism. They endeavored to answer Moore's open question argument by showing that on reflection a natural property is what we mean by moral goodness.

Moore might ask the naturalist, who identifies goodness with some property F, 'X has F, but is it good?' and the naturalist would answer, "Yes." When Moore points out that this substitution leads to a tautology ('X is good but is it good?'), the naturalist might point out that this difference in meaning doesn't affect the essential referent. Consider again the illustrations given earlier in this chapter:

D. 1. This is Venus, but is it the Morning Star?

by Moorean substitution:

D. 2. This is Venus, but is it Venus?

or

E. 1. This is the 41st President of the United States, but is it George Bush?

by Moorean substitution:

E. 2. This is Bush, but is it Bush?

In both cases adequate information convinces us that the answer to both questions is "yes," even though statements 1 and 2 in each case may not mean the same thing. Likewise, we might remain or become naturalists and have an answer to the open question argument. For example, we might say that 'good' means or includes as part of meaning 'the flourishing of rational (or sentient) beings'. The analogous form would look like this:

F. 1. This act promotes the flourishing of rational beings, but is it good?

by substitution:

F. 2. This act promotes the flourishing of rational beings, but does it promote the flourishing of rational beings?

The naturalist answers that, on reflection, we would answer the question in the affirmative. Promoting human flourishing is what we deeply mean by moral goodness. Whether the noncognitivist or the nonnaturalist can show that this sort of answer is illegitimate is a matter that is currently a subject of keen debate.

In fact, it seems to me that Moore's question is itself a problem, for it seems to presuppose a Platonic answer; that is, Moore seems to have reified a concept, treating an idea as though it were a thing. This error is sometimes called the fallacy of hypostatization. Consider this conversation in Lewis Carroll's *Through a Looking Glass*:

> "Just look along the road and tell me if you can see either of the messengers," said the King.
> "I can see nobody on the road," said Alice.
> "I only wish I had such eyes," the King remarked in a fretful tone. "To be able to see Nobody! And at that distance too! Why, it's as much as I can do to see real people, by this light."
> [The messenger arrives.] "Who did you pass on the road?" the King went on, holding out his hand to the Messenger for some more hay.
> "Nobody," said the Messenger.
> "Quite right," said the King, "this young lady saw him too. So of course Nobody walks slower than you."
> "I do my best," the Messenger said in a sullen tone. "I'm sure nobody walks much faster than I do!"
> "He can't do that," said the King, "or else he'd have been here first."[15]

The King makes the ludicrous mistake of treating an indefinite, functional pronoun as a proper noun. In like manner Platonists and Mooreans treat functional common nouns as proper nouns; they seem to treat functional terms such as 'good' as though they were things, just as gold or water are things. This seems wrong.

Consider the way we use 'good' in sentences:

1. "The weather is good today."
2. "That was a good catch" (said of a tight-end who has leaped high into the air to snag a pass).
3. "It's good to increase the GNP."
4. "Telling the truth is a good thing to do, though sometimes it's the wrong thing to do."

It's difficult to give a satisfactory definition of 'good'. Perhaps the closest ones are 'the most general term of commendation' or 'satisfying some requirement'. When the weather suits our aesthetic or prudential desires, we call it "good"—although it is relative to the speaker, for the sunbather and the farmer have different frames of reference. When the tight-end behaves in a manner fitting of his function, we commend his execution. When a nation's productivity is increased, giving promise of a higher standard of living, we express our approval with the adjective "good." Attributing goodness to an activity or artifact represents our approval of that activity or artifact—our judgment that it meets an appropriate standard.

Likewise in ethical discussion, 'good' serves as a term of commendation, expressing the perception that such and such a behavior meets our standards of fitting behavior or contributes to goals we deem positive. When we say that telling the truth is a good thing to do, we do not mean that there is an independently existing form of the Good that truth-telling somehow represents or is "plugged into." If we are reflective, we generally mean that there is something proper or valuable (either intrinsically or extrinsically) about truth-telling. Furthermore, we generally do not judge that the goodness attached to truth-telling is absolute, for it can be overridden in some cases by other considerations. For example, we judge it to be a bad thing to tell the truth to criminals who will use information to murder an innocent person.

We have a notion of good ends that morality serves. Even if we are deontologists, we still think that there is a point to morality, and that point generally has to do with producing better outcomes—truth-telling generally produces better outcomes than does lying. These ends can be put into nonmoral language in terms of happiness, flourishing, welfare, equality, and the like; that is, at least part of our notion of moral goodness is predicated on a notion of nonmoral goodness. A certain logic pertains in what can be called morally good, depending on these nonmoral values.

If this analysis is correct, then it doesn't make much sense to treat the notion of 'good' like a thing (for example, gold or water) and define it in the realist language, any more than it makes sense to treat 'tallness' or 'spectacularity' or 'equality' as things. As my teacher, Gilbert Ryle, has said, It's a category mistake to treat a functional term as though it were a thing.

CONCLUSION

In Warnock's work we have come full circle from the naturalism of Hume, Bentham, and Mill to which the nonnaturalists reacted in the first place some 70 years earlier. If a new naturalism seems more plausible than noncognitivist theories, it has profited importantly from their efforts. Naturalism is different now—almost beyond recognition as a variation of the earlier naturalisms.

One way to see what divides the new cognitivists like Warnock, Kurt Baier, William Frankena, and Kai Nielsen from their noncognitivist predecessors is to note the point at which reason and value come into the various theories. For Ayer, Stevenson, and Hare, we begin with value—we feel an emotion or have an attitude or choose a principle; that is, the 'oughtness' or evaluative element comes in at the outset and solves the is/ought problem. On the other hand, for the cognitivist, the Good or the Right—the proper set of moral principles—is discovered existing, as it were, independently of any particular agent's choice. But a question that never rightly arises for the noncognitivist soon arises for the cognitivist: namely, "Why should I be moral?"

Put another way, reason enters the naturalist's domain right at the start in order to allow choice of the right principles, but then there is an additional problem of choosing the moral point of view. For the noncognitivist (for example, Hare's prescriptivist), the moral point of view is whatever the agent chooses to live by. Reason, then, plays a secondary and formal role in assuring consistency of judgment—that is, in universalizing the principles.

The debate between cognitivism and noncognitivism and between the various renditions of naturalism and nonnaturalism is still going on. I hope that this chapter helps you understand the major aspects of the debate and helps you judge where you stand on these issues.

Notes

1. G. F. Moore, *Principia Ethica* (Cambridge University Press, 1903). All quotes from Moore in this chapter refer to this work.

2. The naturalist fallacy (according to Moore) involves breaking Hume's (is/ought) law by making an invalid inference from a descriptive (is) statement to a prescriptive (ought) statement. The open question argument is used to show that all forms of naturalism are false. For a good discussion of the possibility of annulling the is/ought problem, see the articles in W. D. Hudson, ed., *The Is/Ought Problem* (St. Martin's Press, 1969).

3. Moore's Platonism is nicely brought out in a quote from John Maynard Keynes's memoir: *My Early Beliefs*:

The New Testament is a handbook for politicians compared with the unworldliness of Moore's chapter on the Ideal. I know no equal to it in literature since Plato. And it is better than Plato because it is quite free from *fancy*. It conveys the beauty of the literalness of Moore's mind, the pure and passionate intensity of his vision, unfanciful and undressed up. Moore had a nightmare once in which he could not distinguish propositions from tables. But even when awake, he could not distinguish love and beauty and truth from the furniture. They took on the same definition of outline, the same stable, solid objective qualities and common sense reality. I see no reason to shift from the fundamental intuitions of *Principia Ethica*; though they are much too few and too narrow to fit actual experience. That they furnish a justification of experience wholly independent of outside events has become an added comfort, even though one cannot live today secure in the undisturbed individualism which was the extraordinary achievement of the early Edwardian days. [Quoted in Mary Warnock, *Ethics Since 1900* (Oxford University Press, 1960), p. 54f.]

4. See C. L. Stevenson, *Ethics and Language* (Yale, 1944) and "The Emotive Meaning of Ethical Terms," *Mind* (1937), pp. 14–31.

5. I. A. Richards and C. K. Ogden, *The Meaning of Meaning* (Harcourt Brace Jovanovich, 1923), p. 125.

6. A. J. Ayer, *Language, Truth and Logic*, 2nd ed. (Dover, 1946), p. 107.

7. Alasdair MacIntyre, *After Virtue* (University of Notre Dame Press, 1981), Chapter 1.

8. An interesting fact about Hare's theory is that his ideas were influenced by his experiences in Japanese prison camps in Singapore and Thailand during the Second World War. It was in these "grim and barren prison compounds" that the first draft of his book, *The Language of Morals* (Oxford University Press, 1952) was written (Ved Mehta, "The Bewitchment of the Intellect," *The New Yorker*, Dec. 9, 1961).

9. Here is how Hare states the difference between himself and the emotivists:

The process of *telling* someone to do something, and *getting* him to do it, are quite distinct, logically, from each other. The distinction may be elucidated by considering a parallel one in the case of statements. To tell someone that something is the case is logically distinct from getting (or trying to get) him to believe it. Having told someone that something is the case we may, if he is not disposed to believe what we say, start on a quite different process of trying to get him to believe it (trying to persuade or convince him that what we have said is true). No one, in seeking to explain the function of indicative sentences, would say that they were attempts to persuade someone that something is the case. And there is no more reason for saying that commands are attempts to persuade or get someone to do something; here, too, we first tell someone what he is to do, and then, if he is not disposed to do what we say, we may start on the wholly different process of trying to get him to do it" (*Language of Morals*, pp. 13–14).

Here we see Hare's fundamental disagreement with emotivists like Stevenson on the nature of moral judgments: They are meant not merely to persuade, for if they were, there would be no difference between reasoning and propaganda.

10. R. M. Hare, *Freedom and Reason* (Oxford University Press, 1963), p. 4f.

11. This diagram is modelled on one by Tom L. Beauchamp, *Philosophical Ethics* (McGraw-Hill, 1982), p. 359.

12. Phillipa Foot, "Moral Beliefs," in *Vices and Virtues* (Blackwell, 1978).

13. If one defines a 'naturalist' as one who holds that factual claims entail (or are entailed by) fundamental ethical claims, then one would call Foot a naturalist. In that case we would need to amend our chart to include a form of naturalism that was not definitional (that is, does not define ethical terms by natural ones), but rather broadly logical.

14. Geoffrey Warnock, *The Object of Morality* (Methuen, 1971), p. 26.

15. Lewis Carroll, *Through the Looking Glass* (Pan Books, 1947), p. 232f. Compare this passage to the hypostatization of 'time' in Carroll's *Alice in Wonderland* (Pan Books, 1947), p. 54.

For Further Reflection

1. Review this chapter in order to make sure that you understand the major positions of naturalism, nonnaturalism, noncognitivism, and prescriptivism. Which, if any, seems to capture the truth about moral judgments?

2. P. H. Nowell-Smith, as a noncognitivist, suggests that value words are *multifunctional*: They "are used to express tastes and preferences, to express decisions and choices, to criticize, grade and evaluate, to advise, admonish, warn, persuade, and dissuade, to praise, encourage and reprove, to promulgate and draw attention to rules; and doubtless for other purposes also" [*Ethics* (Penguin Books, 1954), p. 98]. He believes that moral language is primarily used for choosing actions and advising others. Does this description of noncognitivism make the theory more plausible?

3. In a classic article on the subject of the is/ought problem, "How to Derive 'Ought' from 'Is'" (*The Philosophical Review*, 1964), John Searle sets forth the following argument, which he claims shows that we can derive a "fact statement" from a "value statement." He argues as follows:

1. John says, "I promise to pay you (Mary) the $10 you have just loaned me."

2. John promised to pay Mary $10 (description of 1 above).

3. John has put himself under an obligation to pay Mary $10.

4. John has an obligation to pay Mary $10.

5. John ought to pay Mary $10.

According to Searle, we have gone from an 'is' to an 'ought' statement without committing any logical mistake. Is he correct? What does this tell us about the is/ought problem?

4. At the outset of this book we said that morality served four purposes:

to keep society from falling apart, the promotion of human flourishing, the amelioration of suffering, and the just resolution of conflicts of interest. How would each of the theories discussed in this chapter respond to those purposes? Would they argue over whether those were, indeed, the correct purposes in the first place? Would they question whether there was any definite set of purposes that morality played? What are the purposes of morality suggested by each of these theories?

For Further Reading

Blum, Lawrence A. *Friendship, Altruism and Morality*. Routledge & Kegan Paul, 1980. Contains a sustained critique on some aspects of rule-goverened ethics, such as the principles of universalizability and imparti-ality.

Foot, Phillipa. *Vices and Virtues*. Blackwell, 1978. See especially her essay, "Moral Beliefs."

Goodpaster, K. E., ed. *Perspectives on Morality: Essays by William K. Frankena*. University of Notre Dame Press, 1976. Contains important essays on the subject matter of this chapter.

Hancock, Roger. *Twentieth Century Ethics*. Columbia University Press, 1974.

Hare, R. M. *The Language of Morals*. Oxford University Press, 1952.

Hare, R. M. *Freedom and Reason*. Oxford University Press, 1963.

Hudson, W. D., ed. *The Is/Ought Question*. St. Martin's Press, 1969.

Hudson, W. D. *Modern Moral Philosophy*, 2nd ed. Macmillan, 1983. A clear, comprehensive survey of the issues discussed in this section.

Moore, G. E. *Principa Ethica*. Cambridge University Press, 1903. The book that started the major discussion of metaethics in the 20th century.

Nowell-Smith, Patrick. *Ethics*. Penguin Books, 1954.

Pritchard, H. A. *Moral Obligation*. Oxford University Press, 1968.

Ross, David W. *The Right and the Good*. Oxford University Press, 1930.

Searle, John. "How to Derive 'Ought' from 'Is'." *The Philosophical Review* 73, 1964.

Sellars, Wilfred, and John Hospers, eds. *Readings in Ethical Theory*, 2nd ed. Prentice-Hall, 1970. The largest collection of essays on the problems discussed in this chapter.

Stevenson, C. L. *Ethics and Language*. Yale University Press, 1944.

Urmson, J. O. *The Emotive Theory of Ethics*. Hutchinson, 1968.

Warnock, G. J. *The Object of Morality*. Methuen, 1971. The book that signaled the revival of ethical naturalism.

Warnock, Mary. *Ethics Since 1900*. Oxford University Press, 1960. A short, clear exposition of the history of ethics in the 20th century.

CHAPTER 9

Morality and Self-Interest: Glaucon's Question

Nice guys finish last.
LEO DUROCHER, FORMER NATIONAL LEAGUE MANAGER

The Good is good for you.
STATEMENT OF SOCRATIC ETHICS

"Why should people in general be moral?"

and

"Why should I be moral?"

THESE TWO QUESTIONS should not be confused; the former question asks for a justification for the institution of morality, whereas the latter asks for reasons why one personally should be moral, even when it does not appear to be in one's interest. I once knew a student, call him Joe, who cheated his way into medical school. Had he not cheated, he probably would never have become a physician. For Joe, morality and self-interest were clearly at odds, and he chose self-interest.

In the *Leviathan* Thomas Hobbes offers a plausible answer to our first question concerning a justification of morality in general. Unless there is a general adherence to a basic moral code that protects basic values, society itself would be impossible. Without that minimal morality that contains rules against killing the innocent, rape, robbery, the violation of agreements, and the like, we would exist in a "state of nature" deprived of common laws, reliable expectations, and security of person and possessions. There would be no incentive to mutual trust or cooperation, but only chaotic anarchy as egoists tried to maximize personal utility. The result would be a "war of all against all" in which individual life is "solitary, poor, nasty, brutish, and short."[1]

Morality serves as an antidote to this state of nature and allows self-interested individuals to fulfill their needs and desires in a context of peace and cooperation. As such, morality is a mechanism for social control. It is in all of our interests to have a moral system that is generally adhered to so that we can maximize our individual life-plans. Unless there is general adherence to the moral point of view, society will break down. Indeed, many sociologists argue that unless there is a moral consensus, society will break down.[2]

This may not be a full picture of morality, nor a very inspiring one, but it is certainly part of the picture—the part that virtually everyone agrees with. Whatever more there is to morality and whether it is, as Kant said, "a jewel that shines by its own light," is another matter, one that has to do with the second question about morality.

The second question is "Why should I be moral?" Actually, this question may also be divided into two different questions: "Why should I accept the moral point of view at all?" and "Why should I be moral all of the time, that is, even on those rare occasions when I can greatly profit from breaking the moral code?" The first question is the more fundamental one and will occupy us for most of this chapter; then we'll consider the second question.

Why shouldn't I *appear* to be moral and to promote morality in society, so that I can profit egotistically from the docility of the stupid public? Paul Taylor calls this the "Ultimate Question":

> There is one problem of moral philosophy that perhaps deserves, more than any other, to be called the Ultimate Question. It is the question of the rationality of the moral life itself. It may be expressed thus: Is the commitment to live by moral principles a decision grounded on reason or is it in the final analysis, an arbitrary choice?[3]

Is the choice of a moral way of life a rational choice or simply an arbitrary one? The question was first raised over two millenia ago in Plato's dialogue, the *Republic*, in which Plato's brother, Glaucon, asks Socrates whether justice or moral goodness is something that is only a necessary evil; that is, he wants to know whether it is the case that it would be better if we could have complete freedom to indulge ourselves as we will, but that because others could do the same it is better to compromise and limit our acquisitive instincts. Glaucon tells the story of a shepherd named Gyges who comes upon a ring that at his behest makes him invisible. Gyges uses it to escape the external sanctions of society—its laws and censure—and to serve his greed to the fullest. He kills the king, seduces his wife, and becomes king himself. Glaucon asks, Wouldn't we all do likewise?

In order to sharpen his case, Glaucon offers us a thought-experiment that in contemporary terms goes like this. Suppose that there were two brothers, Jim and Jack. Jim is a splendid fellow—kind and compassionate, almost saintly, always sacrificing for the poor, and helping others (including Jack with his homework and chores). In fact he is too good to seem true. As a young man, he was framed by Jack for a serious crime, was imprisoned, gang-raped, and constantly harassed and tortured by the guards and prisoners. When he was released, he was unable to secure employment and was forced to beg for his food. Now he lives as a street-person in a large city, is in poor health, and is without a family or shelter. People avoid him whenever they can, for he looks like a dangerous person. Yet, in truth, his heart is as pure as the driven snow.

Jack, Jim's older brother and the man who framed him, is as evil as Jim is good. He also is as "successful" as Jim is "unsuccessful". He is the epitome of respectability and civic virtue. He is a rising and wealthy corporate executive who is praised by all for his astuteness and integrity (the latter of which he has not an ounce). He is married to the most beautiful woman in the community, and his children all go to the best boarding schools. Jack's wife is not too smart, so she is completely taken in by his performance; and his children, who hardly know him, love him. He is an elder on his church's board of directors and a prominent supporter of its work (he can afford to be, for he is a millionaire who pays no taxes, thanks to tax write-offs). Last year he was voted the Ideal Citizen of his city. Teachers cite him as an example of how one can be both morally virtuous and a successful entrepeneur. He is loved and honored by all, yet he is an evil man.

So, Glaucon wants to know, if you were forced to make a choice between living either of these lives, which life would you choose to live: the life of the unjust man who seems just and is incredibly "successful" or the life of the just man who seems unjust and is incredibly "unsuccessful"? Is it better to be bad but seem good, or to be good but to seem bad? Which would *you* choose?[4]

I don't know which you would choose, but let's consider two initial reasons for choosing to live the life of the seemingly unjust good man, Jim. The first is Socrates' answer to Glaucon—that, in spite of appearances, we should choose the life of the "unsuccessful" just person because it's to our advantage to be moral. He draws attention to the idea of the harmony of the soul and argues that immorality corrupts the inner person, whereas virtue purifies the inner person, so that one is happy or unhappy in exact proportion to one's moral integrity. Asking to choose between being morally good and immoral is like asking to choose between being healthy and sick. Even if the immoral person has material benefits, he cannot enjoy them in his awful state, whereas the good person may find joy in the simple pleasures in spite of poverty and ill fortune.

But is Socrates correct? Is the harm that Jim suffers compensated by the innate goodness of his soul? And is the good that Jack experiences outweighed by the evil of his heart? Perhaps we don't know enough about the hearts of people to state with any assurance who is better off, Jim or Jack. But perhaps we know of (or can imagine) people like Jack who seem to flourish in spite of their wickedness. They may not completely fool us, but they seem satisfied with the lives they are living, moderately happy in their business and personal triumphs. And perhaps we know of some people like Jim who are really very sad in spite of their goodness. They wish they had meaningful work, a loving family, friends, and shelter, but they don't, and their virtue is insufficient to produce happiness. Some good people are unhappy and some bad people seem to be happy. So the Socratic answer on the health-sickness analogy may not be correct.

The second answer to Glaucon is the religious response: God will reward and punish people on the basis of their virtue or vice. The promise is of eternal bliss for the virtuous and some very hard times for the vicious; God sees all and rewards with absolute justice according to our moral merit. Accordingly, in spite of what may be their differing fates here on earth, Jim is infinitely better off than Jack. If ethical monotheism of this sort is true, then it is in our self-interest to be moral: The good is really good for you. The religious person has good reason to choose the life of the destitute saint.

We will take up the relationship of religion to morality in the next chapter, but here we can say this much about the problem: Unfortunately, we do not know for certain whether there is a God or life after death. Many sincere people doubt or disbelieve religious doctrines, and it is not easy to prove them wrong. Even the devout have doubts and probably cannot be sure of the truth of the doctrine of life after death or of the existence of God. In any case, millions of people are not religious, and the question of the relationship between self-interest and morality is a pressing one. Can a moral philosopher give a satisfying answer to secularists as to why they should choose the moral point of view?

THE PARADOX OF
MORALITY AND SELF-INTEREST

Initially we seem to run into a paradox in trying to discuss this issue. On many contemporary accounts of moral duty, one only has a duty to do some act A if one has sufficient reason to do A. But this seems to generate a paradox that involves asking for self-interested reasons as to why we should prefer morality when it conflicts with our self-interest. What David Gauthier has called the paradox of morality and advantage goes like this:

1. If it is morally right to do act A, then it must be reasonable to do act A.
2. If it is reasonable to do A, then it must be in my interest to do A.
3. But sometimes the requirements of morality are incompatible with the requirements of self-interest.
4. Hence, we have an apparent contradiction: It both must be reasonable and need not be reasonable to meet our moral duties.

Because morality is not always in our self-interest, we must wonder whether it is not simply a delusion, an artifice to keep us in place. If it is a delusion, then the rational person will be an egoist and will promote morality for everyone else but will violate it whenever he or she can safely do so.

In order to get us started in our attempt to solve this puzzle, consider the case of the prisoner's dilemma. The secret police in another country have arrested two of our spies, Sam and Sue. They both know that if they adhere to their agreement to keep silent, the police will be able to hold them for only four months: if they each violate their agreement and both of them confess that they are spies, they will each get six years in prison; but if one adheres and the other violates, the one who adheres will get nine years and the one who confesses will be freed immediately. We might represent their plight with the following matrix (for any matrix entry, the figure on the left represents the amount of time Sam will spend in prison under the given alternatives and the figure on the right represents the amount of time that Sue will spend in prison under those alternatives):

The Prisoner's Dilemma

		Sue	
		Adheres	*Violates*
	Adheres	4 months, 4 months	9 years, 0 time
Sam			
	Violates	0 time, 9 years	6 years, 6 years

Initially Sam reasons that either Sue will adhere to the agreement or she will violate it; if Sue adheres, Sam thinks, then I should violate; if Sue violates, then I should still violate. Therefore, I should violate. But Sue reasons exactly the same way about Sam: Either he will adhere or he will violate; if he adheres, I should violate, if he violates, then I should violate. Therefore, I should violate. But if both use reason in this way they will obtain the second-worst position, 6 years each, which we know to be pretty awful. They both can see that it is in their best interests to adhere to an agreement (spoken or unspoken) of adhering to the moral code: So long as they have reasonable expectations of the other's adherence, it is in each person's interest to adhere to the code.

Of course, were this a one-time choice, one could argue that it might be in either person's interest to gamble that the other will adhere and thereby try to benefit from that move. But the real prisoner's dilemma is an ongoing relationship of the individual with other individuals in society; each violation weakens the rational, general adherence to the moral code and moves society toward chaos.

We may conclude that rational self-interest over the long run advises Sam and Sue to adhere to their agreement. This is their second choice; it limits their freedom, but it ensures a certain modest happiness.

As David Gauthier puts it, "Morality is a system of principles such that it is advantageous for everyone if everyone accepts and acts on it, yet acting on the system of principles requires that some persons perform disadvantageous acts."[5] The prisoner's dilemma illustrates that morality is the due we each have to pay to keep the minimal good we have in a civilized society; we have to bear some disadvantage (analogous to paying our dues) so that we can have protection from the onslaughts of chaos. The alternatives would look like this:

		B	
		Adheres	*Violates*
	Adheres	orderly society	slavery, royalty
A			
	Violates	royalty, slavery	chaos

The best state for an individual would still occur when that individual violated the code when all others kept it; but if all or most violated it, the society would dissolve. Because an orderly society is no small benefit, the egoist will allow his or her freedom to be limited. So there is no real paradox between morality and self-interest in this sense: We allow some disadvantage in order to reap an overall, long-term advantage.

Still, it may be conceded that this is not quite the same as accepting the moral point of view, for the prudent person will still break the moral code whenever he or she can do so without unduly undermining the whole system. The clever amoralist takes into account the overall consequences on the social system and cheats whenever a careful cost-benefit analysis warrants it. With "the proceeds of his embezzlement" he will perhaps "give a tithe" to moral education so that more people will be more dedicated to the moral code, which in turn will allow him to cheat with greater impunity.

So even though the prisoner's dilemma informs us that even the amoralist must generally adhere to the moral code, it doesn't tell us why he or why *I* should be moral—why I should not act egoistically when it is in my self-interest to do so. The problematic premise seems to be premise 2. Let's examine it again:

> 2. If it is reasonable to do A, then it must be in my interest (or at least not against my interest) to do A.

Might we not doubt premise 2? Could we not have good reasons to do something that went against our interests? Suppose Lisa sees her child about to get run over by a car and hurls herself at the child, knowing all the while the danger to herself of doing this.

You may object that this is not a good example, for Lisa's interest is bound up with that of her child, so that she is not unambiguously going against her own interest in striving to save the child. But suppose that it's a stranger's child that is about to be hit by the car. Lisa's interest is in no way tied up with the life of that child, but she still tries to save its life at great risk to her own. Isn't this a case of having a reason to go against one's self-interest?

I think that it is such a reason. Premise 2 seems unduly based on the doctrine of psychological egoism, which we showed to be false in Chapter 3. Sometimes we have reasons to do things that go against our perceived self-interest: The nonreligious person who gives away needed funds to help the poor or hungry does so, as apparently does the student who refrains from cheating when he knows that he could easily escape detection. Being faithful, honest, generous, and kind often requires us to act against our interests.[6]

But you may object to this reasoning by saying, "It is perhaps *against* our immediate or short-term interests to be faithful, honest, generous, or kind, but really in the long run it is likely to be in our best interests. For the moral and altruistic life promises benefits and satisfactions that are not available to the immoral and the stingy."

There seems to be merit in this response. The basis of it seems to be a plausible view of moral psychology that stipulates that character formation is not like a bathroom faucet that you can turn on and off at will. To have the benefits of the moral life—friendship, mutual love, inner peace, moral pride or satisfaction, and freedom from or forgiveness of moral guilt— one has to have a certain kind of reliable character. All in all, these benefits are eminently worth having; indeed, life without them may not be worth living. So we may assert that for every rational being, qua rational being, the deeply moral life is the best sort of life that he or she can live. Hence it follows that it is prudent to develop such a deeply moral character—or to continue to develop it (because our upbringing partly forms it for most of us).

If one has been raised in a normal social context, then one will feel deep psychic distress at the thought of harming others or doing what is immoral, and deep psychic satisfaction in being moral. For these persons the combination of internal and external sanctions may well bring prudence and morality close together. But this situation may not apply to persons not brought up in a moral context. Should this dismay us? No. As Gregory Kavka says, we should not perceive "an immoralist's gloating that it does not pay him to be moral . . . as a victory over us. It is more like the pathetic boast of a deaf person that he saves money because it does not pay him to buy opera records."[7] He is a Scrooge who takes pride in not having to buy Christmas presents because he has no friends.

We want to say, then, that the choice of the moral point of view is not an arbitrary choice, but a rational one. Some kinds of lives are better than others: A human life without the benefits of morality is not an ideal or fulfilled life; it lacks too much that makes for human flourishing.

The occasional acts through which we sacrifice our self-interests within the general flow of a satisfied life are unavoidable risks that reasonable people take. For although you can lose by betting on morality, you are almost certain to lose if you bet against it.

So premise 2 must be restated:

2'. If it is reasonable to choose a life plan L, which includes the possibility of doing A, then it must be in my interest (or at least not against it) to choose L, even though A itself may not be in my self-interest.

If it is to take into consideration the above discussion, the whole argument needs to be restated:

1'. If it is morally right to do act A, then the life-plan L into which act A fits must be a reasonable one.

2'. If it is reasonable to choose a life-plan L, which includes the possibility of doing A, then it must be in my interest (or at least not against it) to choose L, even though A itself may not be in my self-interest.

3. Sometimes the requirements of morality are incompatible with the requirements of self-interest.

This argument, however, does not result in a paradox, for even though the individual moral act may occasionally conflict with one's self-interest, the entire life-plan in which the act is embedded and from which it flows is not against the individual's self-interest.

Thus the paradox is resolved and Glaucon's question has been successfully answered. Not only is it sometimes reasonable to act for reasons that do not immediately involve our self-interests, but, more importantly, a life without such spontaneous or deliberate altruism may be one not worth living.

WHY SHOULD I BE MORAL ALL THE TIME?

But the question may arise: Haven't we assumed a false dilemma—either deep morality or complete immorality? Isn't there a middle ground—a semimorality wherein we live according to morality most of the time, but break the moral code on rare occasions when the advantages to ourselves are especially great? For many people, semimorality, it may be argued, is the best that they can do—for them, the price of deep morality is simply too costly! How can they have sufficient reason to do what they are not in the least motivated to do? Here we must point out an ambiguity in the notion of 'sufficient reason'. There is a difference between there being a good reason for doing some act X and your being motivated by that reason; that is, there may be a sufficient reason for you to do something, but you may not now be able to be motivated by that reason. There is a good reason for inebriated Eddie not to stick his head in the goldfish bowl, but Eddie cannot be motivated by that reason now—but had he chosen not to get drunk, he could have been motivated by it. You can be held responsible for your current inability to be motivated by a reason only when you are responsible for getting yourself into the current nonmotivating state. We can also say that if a person is rational, there still is a reason for him or her to become moral, even if becoming so is now inoperative or impossible; that is, he or she cannot be motivated by that reason because of previous free actions. My argument comes to something like this:

1. For every rational being B, qua rational being, the deeply moral life (DML) is the best sort of life they can live [better than the semi-moral life and certainly better than the immoral life].

2.   If B has chosen correctly (or had the proper upbringing) at time t, then B is living the DML at t+1.

3.   If B is living the DML at t+1, B has at t+1 sufficient reason to do what morality requires, even if that deed is opposed to B's apparent interests.

4.   Therefore, the best sort of life may require B (and us) to do what is opposed to apparent self-interest.

If this is sound, then we can "have our cake and eat it too." It may be the case that for many people it is not worth the "transition costs"[8] to become deeply moral, but this is a tragedy, not a defect in the DML. Let me illustrate this further.

Recall the analogy we made above to the effect that the immoralist's apparent advantage is like the "advantage" of someone who doesn't need to spend money on musical records because she is deaf or the person who saves money at Christmas because he has no friends to buy presents for.

Suppose that an ordinary music-lover responds that we have set forth a false dilemma and that there is, in fact, an advantage for the ordinary music-lover in remaining just that—an ordinary music-lover—rather than becoming a deep music-lover, for the pain that the former must necessarily suffer is simply unacceptable to the latter. Wouldn't this count against becoming a deep music-lover? I think not—or not necessarily.

Suppose that the deep music-lover (Debra) and the ordinary music-lover (Oliver) have different capacities for music appreciation, so that Debra has the capacity to get 98 total hedons (on a scale ranging from –100 to +100) listening to classical music wherein she necessarily suffers –20 units of pain (dolors) in the process. Oliver only has the potential to get 20 hedons but is satisfied with that because he only suffers 1 dolor, which is about all the pain he has the capacity to suffer.

Granted that now at time t+1 it may be impossible (or not cost-effective) for Oliver to get anywhere near Debra's musical appreciation, but it still would be better if Oliver could attain that level, and if Oliver had been brought up better or had not ruined himself listening to rock music in grammar school, he would now have Debra's capacity, which we all agree is a superior state of being than Oliver's capacity. It simply is better to have a combination of high aesthetic enjoyment and suffering than not to have either ("Better to have loved and lost than never to have loved at all").

This point is even better illustrated by Semi-Scrooge, who loves only his wife and children. It would be better if he could love others too, but perhaps his power to love others has atrophied and he is now unable to do so. But there was a time when, had he chosen differently (or been brought up better), he would now be able to enjoy more love and suffer with others more than he now does. (Note, too, that the more one loves, the more vulnerability and risk of suffering one has.) Scrooge has less capacity for suffering than does Semi-Scrooge, and Semi-Scrooge has less capacity than Anti-Scrooge, who leaves himself open to enormous suffering, but that seems an acceptable risk and price to pay for deep human relations. So we can deeply pity Scrooge and partly pity Semi-Scrooge for their inability both to enjoy the deliverances of love and to accept the suffering as part of love's dues.

"Why shouldn't I as a moral person occasionally be immoral when great gain is possible?" Even though it may be against our immediate self-interest to do what is moral on specific occasions, it may be eminently reasonable, given the long-term view of what the good life consists of. Because of our character and internal sanctions (guilt and moral satisfaction), we will try to do what is moral in spite of these occasional disadvantages. There is something alienating in trying to go against one's deepest principles (which is what morality consists of for the moral person). If we are truly moral, we will have a difficult time acting against character; and if we succeed, the horrors of guilt, which accommodate willing violations of our principles, will accompany us and sour the success. (I am reminded now that I neglected to mention earlier that Joe, the student who cheated his way into medical school, was eventually so haunted by moral guilt that he repented and became a missionary).

This conclusion is close to the Socratic solution. In a sense, the Good is good for you, but in another sense, doing the Good can cause your downfall: The moral person may pay a debt that results in his or her own bankruptcy and subsequent depression. In general, the more just the political order, the more likely it will be that the Good will prosper and morality and self-interest will converge.[9]

Perhaps there are occasions when it may seem that it would be better for us to act immorally in order to save ourselves, but it will be very difficult for the moral person to do this. Concerning his illustration of a father who has good reason to act immorally in saving his criminal son by helping him escape to Brazil, where he will live a good life, Bruce Russell muses that "it would be wrong of you to help him escape, but why isn't it true that what you have most reason to do is to help your son escape justice?"[10]

There are two ways to respond to Russell's example. My first inclination is to question Russell's assumption that it would be wrong for the father to help his son escape. Fathers have special obligations to their children, and these obligations conflict with obligations to the society at large. It may be, in this case, that the duty to his son (who will live a good life in Brazil) outweighs the father's duty to the state; a utilitarian might argue this way.

On the other hand, it might be the case that a utilitarian or a deontologist might conclude quite the reverse—that the son deserves to be turned in. The father, who is deeply moral, simply must supress his sentiment for his child and do that which morality requires. For deeply moral people, it seems, moral reasons always override nonmoral ones, for that is part of what it means to be deeply moral. It may not be the case for the garden-variety moral person, but that may be because he or she is not in the proper state of being.

It may be that a less moral person can succeed and prosper better than a deeply moral person in some situations. In this sense, choosing the moral point of view does have a risk factor built into it, for life is tragic. In some situations, morality may be dangerous to your health and wealth; but on the other hand, a life without deep morality may not be worth living.

Notes

1. Thomas Hobbes, *Leviathan*, 1651; reprinted in Louis Pojman, *Ethical Theory* (Wadsworth, 1989), p. 62.

2. Cf. Steven Lukes, *Emile Durkeim: His Life and Work* (Harper & Row, 1972), Chapter 21, and Brigette and Peter Burger, *The War Over the Family* (Doubleday, 1983).

3. Paul Taylor, *Problems of Moral Philosophy* (Dickenson, 1978), p. 483.

4. In case you think that this story is artificial, let me cite a quote (given to me by an anonymous reviewer) from Joseph Kennedy on the prospects of his son, John F. Kennedy, becoming a congressman. When the elder Kennedy's daughter expressed doubt that John could ever be a successful congressman, he replied, "You must always remember, it isn't what you are, but what people *think* you are, that counts." [In Peter Collier and David Horowitz, *The Kennedy's* (Summit Books, 1984).

5. David Gauthier, "Morality and Advantage," *Philosophical Review* (1967: 460–475; reprinted in Pojman, *Ethical Theory*, pp. 497–504.

6. Perhaps, following a suggestion made by Bruce Russell, we should amend premise 2 to read:

> 2* If it is reasonable to do A, then doing A must maximize the satisfaction of my considered preferences.

Then we should amend premise 3 to read:

> 3* Sometimes acting in accordance with the requirements of morality does not maximize the satisfaction of my considered preferences.

We would obtain statement 4, the paradox of morality again, and so we would not have a reason for always acting according to the moral code. Perhaps 3* is true for some people, but I am inclined to think that their characters are something less than ideal; they are defective beings, who if they reasoned correctly, would want to have a deeper commitment to morality.

7. Gregory Kavka, "Reconciliation Project," *Morality, Reason and Truth*, eds. D. Copp and D. Zimmerman (Rowman and Allanheld, 1984). In this article, Kavka attempts to resolve the paradox and reconcile prudence with morality. Beginning with an analysis of a Hobbesian approach to the problem (one similar to Gauthier's), Kavka argues that this sort of approach, although illuminating and partially correct, "cannot take us far enough" and ultimately is invalid because of its assumption of psychological egoism (cf. Chapter 3 of this book), which assumes that all motivation must be self-interested. What needs to be added to the Hobbesian picture is an account of internal sanctions, the kind of in-built constraints that are an important part of socialization.

8. The phrase is Bruce Russell's, as are the objection and counterexample to which I am responding.

9. In a state of nature no lives seem ideally worthwhile, whereas in a perfectly just society there will be a high correlation between morality and worthwhile lives. As the justice in a society decreases, so does the likelihood of the convergence between morality and the worthwhile life. Morality is a necessary but not a sufficient condition for a worthwhile life.

10. Bruce Russell, "Two Forms of Ethical Skepticism," in Pojman, *Ethical Theory*, pp. 460–471. I owe Russell a debt of gratitude for his incisive criticisms of an earlier draft of this chapter.

For Further Reflection

1. Consider the following situation proposed by John Hospers in *Human Conduct* (Harcourt Brace Jovanovich, 1961), p. 174: "Suppose someone whom you have known for years and who has done many things for you asks a favor of you which will take considerable time and trouble when you had planned on doing something else. You have no doubt that helping out the person is what you ought to do, but you ask yourself all the same *why* you ought to do it. Or suppose you tell a blind news vendor that it's a five-dollar bill you are handing him, and he gives you four dollars and some coins in change, whereas actually you handed him only a one-dollar bill. Almost everyone would agree that such an act is wrong. But some people who agree may still ask, 'Tell me why I shouldn't do it just the same.'" What would you say to such people?

2. Hospers believes that the question "Why should I be moral?" can only be answered by the response "Because it's right." Self-interested answers just won't do, for they come down to asking for self-interested reasons for going against my self-interest, which is a self-contradiction. Is Hospers correct about this, or is there something more we can say about being moral?

3. Whether or not you believe that there are always self-interested reasons for being moral will largely depend on whether and to what degree you believe that some forms of life are objectively better than others (as we discussed in Chapter 4). Explain how this statement goes back to the question of whether values are subjective or objective?

4. Could a person understand that something was his or her duty and yet not be motivated to do it? If there is no necessary connection between duty and motivation, then Kant would seem to be wrong when he wrote that "ought implies can"; but it seems odd to say that I have a duty to do what it is impossible for me to do. On the other hand, if I must be motivated to do X before I can be said to have an obligation to do X, why don't I always do my duty? What is the connection between having a duty and being motivated to do it?

For Further Reading

Baier, Kurt. *The Moral Point of View*. Cornell University Press, 1959.

Frankena, William. *Thinking About Morality*. University of Michigan Press, 1980.

Gauthier, David, ed. *Morality and Rational Self-Interest*. Prentice-Hall, 1970.

Gauthier, David. *Morality by Agreement*. Clarendon Press, 1986.

Hospers, John. *Human Conduct: An Introduction to the Problems of Ethics*. Harcourt Brace Jovanovich, 1961.

Kavka, Gregory. "A Reconciliation Project," *In Morality, Reason and Truth*, eds. D. Copp and D. Zimmerman. Rowman and Allanheld, 1984.

Nielsen, Kai. "Why Should I Be Moral?" *Methodos* XV, 1963. This comprehensive article appears in several anthologies.

Nielsen, Kai. "Is 'Why Should I Be Moral?' an Absurdity?" *Australasian Journal of Philosophy* 36, 1958.

Phillips, D. Z. "Does It Pay to Be Good?" *Proceedings of the Aristotelian Society* 65, 1964–1965.

Richards, David. *A Theory of Reasons for Action* . Oxford University Press, 1971.

Taylor, Richard. *Good and Evil*. Macmillan, 1970. See especially Chapter 5.

CHAPTER 10

Religion and Ethics

*Does God love goodness because it is good,
or is it good because God loves it?*

*The attempts to found a morality apart
from religion are like the attempts of
children who, wishing to transplant
a flower that pleases them, pluck it from the
roots that seem to them unpleasing and
superfluous, and stick it rootless into the ground.
Without religion there can be no real,
sincere morality, just as without roots
there can be no real flower.*

LEO TOLSTOY, "RELIGION AND MORALITY"
IN LEO TOLSTOY: SELECTED ESSAYS

DOES MORALITY DEPEND on religion? Are religious ethics essentially different from secular ethics? These two related but different questions will be considered in this chapter. Unlike many religions found in the ancient world, Judaism, Islam, and Christianity are ethical monotheisms. They not only promise salvation to the faithful but tie ethical responsibility into the matrix of salvation in a very close way, either by making the moral life a necessary condition for God's favor or a consequence of it. In this chapter we will explore the relationship between theistic religion and morality. First we will examine the claim that morality is logically dependent on God's commands. Then we will look at the opposite contention—

that religion is inimical to morality in that it stultifies rational autonomy. Finally, we will consider the possible benefits of religion to the moral life.

DOES MORALITY DEPEND ON RELIGION?

The Divine Command Theory

The first question is whether moral standards themselves depend on God for their validity or whether instead there is an autonomy of ethics, so that even God is subject to the moral order. The question first arises in Plato's dialogue, the *Euthyphro* in which Socrates asks the pious Euthyphro, "Do the gods love holiness because it is holy, or is it holy because the gods love it?"[1] Changing the terms but still preserving the meaning, we want to know whether God commands what is good (or right) because it is good (or right), or whether the good (right) is good (right) because God commands it. According to one theory, called the **Divine Command Theory** (DCT), ethical principles are simply the commands of God. They derive their validity from God's commanding them, and they *mean* 'commanded by God'; without God, there would be no universally valid morality. Here is how the theologian Carl F. H. Henry stated this view:

> Biblical ethics discredits an autonomous morality. It gives theonomous ethics its classic form—the identification of the moral law with the Divine will. In Hebrew-Christian revelation, distinctions in ethics reduce to what is good or what is pleasing, and to what is wicked or displeasing to the Creator-God alone. The biblical view maintains always a dynamic statement of values, refusing to sever the elements of morality from the will of God. . . . The good is what the Creator-Lord does and commands. He is the creator of the moral law, and defines its very nature.[2]

The logic of this reasoning would lead us to agree with Ivan Karamazov in Dostoevsky's *Brothers Karamazov*, when he concludes that "if God doesn't exist, everything is permissible"; nothing is forbidden or required. Without God we have moral nihilism.

Upon analysis we can see that the DCT has three separate theses:

1. Morality (that is, rightness and wrongness) originates with God

2. "Moral rightness" simply means 'willed by God' and "moral wrongness" means 'being against the will of God'

3. Because morality essentially is based on divine will—not on independently existing reasons for action—no further reasons for action are necessary

There are modified versions of the divine command theory (one of which we will soon examine) that drop or qualify one or more of the three theses, but the strongest form includes all three theses. We may characterize the position thus:

1. Necessarily, for any person S and for all acts A, if A is forbidden of S, then God commands that not-A for S. Likewise, if A is permitted for S, then God has neither commanded A nor not-A for S.

Bringing out the implications of this, we may list four propositions:

1. Act A is wrong if and only if it is contrary to the command of God.
2. Act A is right (required) if and only if it is commanded by God.
3. Act A is morally permissible if and only if it is permitted by the command of God.
4. If there is no God, then nothing is ethically wrong, required, or permitted.

The opposing viewpoint—call it the **autonomy thesis** (standing for the independence of ethics)—denies all three theses: (1) morality does not originate with God (though the way God created us may affect the specific nature of morality); (2) rightness and wrongness are not based simply on God's will; and (3) essentially, there are reasons for acting one way or the other, which may be known independently of God's will. In sum, ethics is autonomous and even God must obey the moral law, which exists independently of himself, just as the laws of mathematics and logic do. Just as even God cannot make a three-sided square or make it the case that he never existed, so even God cannot make what is intrinsically evil good or make what is good evil.

Theists who espouse the autonomy thesis may well grant some epistemological advantage to God. God *knows* what is right—better than we do, and because he is good, we can always learn from consulting him. But in principle we act morally for the same reasons that God does: We both follow moral reasons that are independent of God. We are against torturing the innocent because it is cruel and unjust, just as God is against torturing the innocent because it is cruel and unjust. If there is no God on this account, then nothing is changed; morality is left intact, and both theists and nontheists have the very same moral duties.

The motivation for the divine command theory is to preserve or do justice to the omnipotence or sovereignty of God. God somehow is thought to be less sovereign or necessary to our lives if he is not the source of morality. It seems inconceivable to many believers that anything having to do with goodness or duty could be "higher" than or independent of God, for he is the supreme Lord of the believer's life, and what the believer means by "morally right" is that "the Lord commands it—even if I don't fully understand it." When the believer asks what the will of God is, it is a direct appeal to a personal will, not to an independently existing rule.

There are two problems with the divine command theory that need to be faced by those who hold it. One problem is that the DCT would seem to make the attribution of 'goodness' to God redundant. When we say "God is good," we think that we are ascribing a property to God; but if 'good' simply means 'what God commands or wills,' then we are not attributing any property to God. Our statement "God is good" merely means 'God does whatever he wills to do' or 'God practices what he preaches,' and the statement "God commands us to do what is good" merely is the tautology 'God commands us to do what God commands us to do.'

A second problem with the divine command theory is that it seems to make morality into something arbitrary. If God's fiat is the sole arbiter of right and wrong, it would seem to be logically possible for such "heinous" acts as rape, killing the innocent for the fun of it, and gratuitous cruelty to become morally good actions—if God suddenly decided to command us to do these things. The radicality of the DCT is set forth by a classic statement of William Occam:

> The hatred of God, theft, adultery, and actions similar to these actions according to common law, may have an evil quality annexed, in so far as they are done by a divine command to perform the opposite act. But as far as the sheer being in the actions is concerned, they can be performed by God without any evil condition annexed; and they can even be performed meritoriously by an earthly pilgrim if they should come under divine precepts, just as now the opposite of these in fact fall under the divine command.[3]

The implications of this sort of reasoning seem far-reaching. If there are no constraints on what God can command—no independent measure or reason for moral action—then anything can become a moral duty and our moral duties can change from moment to moment. Could there be any moral stability? The proponent of the DCT may object that God has revealed what is his will in his word, the sacred scriptures. But the fitting response is, How do you know that God isn't lying? For if there is no independent criterion of right and wrong except what God happens to will, then how do we know God isn't willing to make lying into a duty (in which case believers have no reason to believe the Bible)?

If God could make what seems morally heinous morally good simply by willing it, wouldn't morality be reduced to the right of the powerful—Friedrich Nietzsche's "Might Makes Right"? Indeed, what would be the difference between the devil and God if morality were an arbitrary command?

Suppose we had two sets of commands, one from the devil and one from God. How would be know which set was which? Could they be identical? What would make them different? If there is no independent criterion by which to judge right and wrong, then it's difficult to see how we could know which was which; the only basis for comparison would be who won. God is simply "the biggest bully on the block" (granted it is a pretty big block —the entire universe).

The Modified Divine Command Theory

Sophisticated divine command theorists seek to answer these two criticisms (the "redundancy" and "arbitrariness" objections) without giving up the essential insights of the DCT. One example of a modified version of the divine command theory (MDCT) is that of Robert Adams.[4] Adams is moved by the objection that the DCT allows for the possibility that God could command acts that are patently vicious. For example, he could command me "to make it my chief end in life to inflict suffering on other human beings, for no other reason than that He commanded it" (p. 526). This will not do. Accordingly, Adams suggests a modification to the DCT:

> According to the modified divine command theory [MDCT], when I say 'it is wrong to do X' [at least part of] what I mean is that it is contrary to God's command to do X. 'It is wrong to do X' *implies* 'It is contrary to God's commands to do X.' But 'it is contrary to God's commands to do X' *implies* 'It is wrong to do X' only if certain conditions are assumed—namely, only if it is assumed that God has the character which I believe Him to have, of loving His human creatures. If God were really to command us to make cruelty our goal, then He would not have that character of loving us, and I would not say it would be wrong to disobey Him (p. 527).

On the MDCT, God's command is a necessary but not sufficient condition for full ethical validity. The command must also be issued from the motive of love or, at least, be consistent with the character of love.

Because we have other values (our secular "ethical" values), it would not be "wrong" for us to disobey a command of God to make gratuitous suffering the goal of life. If God did command this, "my concept of ethical wrongness (and my concept of ethical permittedness) would 'break down'." Although this is logically possible, it is "unthinkable that God should do so" (p. 528).

If I understand Adams, his theses boils down to these:

1. Necessarily, for any person S and for all acts A, if A is forbidden of S, then God commands that not-A for S. Likewise, if A is permitted for S, then God has commanded neither A nor not-A for S. That is, God's command defines our ethical duties as the divine command theory affirms.

2. It is logically possible for God to issue command C: S must engage in gratuitous cruelty.

3. If C, S would be permitted (nonmorally) to disobey God (because S has other values besides ethical ones). In this case, ethics would break down for S.

4. Because God is love, it is unthinkable for God to command C.

A fully ethical act is defined in this way:

5. Necessarily, for any person S and for all acts A, A is forbidden of S, if and only if God commands that not-A (A) for S and the command is issued in a state of love. Likewise, A is permitted for S, if and only if God, in a state of love, has neither commanded A nor not-A for S.

A complete moral command is so if and only if it fulfills two necessary and jointly sufficient conditions: God commanded it, and He did so in a state of love. There seems to be two levels of meaning to the words 'wrong', 'permitted', and 'right'—an ethical one and a nonethical one that actually may override the ethical use. Although Adams refers to the second type of use as 'nonmoral', it has all the features of a moral obligation or permission: It overrides other duties. So let's call this type of duty our 'secular ethical duty' because it refers to those values that we arrive at through reason. On the one hand, God's command makes something an ethical duty; but on the other hand, we may not be required to obey the command if it is not made in love.

Adams states rather mystically that the believer will have a Platonic/ Moorean view of ethical goodness as an unanalyzable, nonnatural property residing in God, and our attribution of the term 'good' to God suggests that "God has some important set of qualities which one regards as virtuous in human beings" (p. 534). Adams argues that it makes no sense to say that God has duties, for that implies that there must be some higher outside authority whence come commands, which is logically impossible.

A Critique of the Modified Divine Command Theory

A critic may challenge Adams's ingenious reformulation of the divine command theory and argue that his version of the MDCT is not a divine command theory at all, but merely a modified version of the autonomy thesis. It is an example of *act-agapism*—the theory that one has a duty to act out of love and never to act against what is the loving thing to do. Agapism is suggested by certain passages in the New Testament, such as: "God is love" (I John 4:8) and "Love is patient and kind. . . . Love does not insist in its own way. . . . It does not rejoice in wrong but rejoices in the right. . . . Make love your aim" (I Corinthians 13:4–6; 14:1).

Love turns out to be the criterion of highest value, and a command is not a fully ethical command unless it is done in love. God can, but must not, act out of character. Here is how we might reconstruct the MDCT as offered by Adams in terms of the Euthyphro Dilemma.

1. God doesn't command (in the sense of require) the right because it is right, but rather the right is right because God commands it (DCT); that is, God's command is what makes an act *formally ethical*.

2. But God must properly command what is (consistent with) loving. Otherwise, the command is not an ethical command that we must obey (one that overrides all other duties); that is, although an unloving command might be formally right, we would be permitted to disobey it. The secular ethic may override the formally ethical obligation.

3. But love is defined as being benevolently concerned for the good of its object; it has to do with human flourishing. So even God cannot make something ethically good that does not conform to what is good for his creatures.

4. So God can properly only command what is good. His love connects the right to the good, so that he commands us to do what is right independent of his commands.

5. Therefore, there is a contradiction between arguments 1 and 4. One of the premises must be rejected.

If we prefer the MDCT to the DCT, then we must say that the DCT is false, and the MDCT becomes equivalent to the autonomy thesis: God commands the Good (or right) because it is good (or right), and the Good (right) is not good (right) simply because God commands it. Furthermore, if this is correct, then we can discover our ethical duties independently of

God's command through reason. For what is good for his creatures is objectively good, (for example, being tortured gratuitously is not good for them, and being happy and wise is good for them). We do not need God to tell us that it is bad to cause unnecessary suffering or that it is good to ameliorate suffering; reason can do that. It begins to look like the true version of ethics is what we called "secular ethics."

Adams might reply that this argument doesn't represent his position, for he distinguishes the good from the right. It is God's command that defines the right, but other values (for example, love) may define the Good, so that the right and the Good may not be in harmony. When the 'right' defies the 'good', the 'good' may override the 'right'. According to Adams, it would not be wrong to disobey God when he commanded something that was heinous from the point of view of our deepest notion of the good. The believer's "positive valuation of doing whatever God may command is not clearly greater than his independent negative valuation of cruelty" — even if God should command it. But normally we think of morality as being that which overrides all other duties, as our highest duty. Indeed, isn't that part of the motivation of the divine command theory in the first place—to link God to our highest moral duty? By bifurcating our value system in this way, Adams leaves us with a dual value system, which seems to create more problems than it solves.

If my revisionist interpretation of Adams's argument is correct, then by making love a necessary condition for God's proper command, Adams' modification of the DCT transforms the DCT into its opposite, the autonomy thesis. He does not seem to recognize that love serves MDCT ethics in exactly the same way that the Good serves autonomous ethics. Even as an act is right (at least in teleological systems) only if it serves the Good, so likewise with the MDCT an act is right only if it issues from love. Proponents of the autonomy thesis typically make Goodness a necessary condition for rightness, whereas the MDCT makes love a necessary condition; and love, it turns out, is simply a functional term for the Good.

Of course, Adams would probably reply that, at most, what this shows is that the autonomy thesis is part of the MDCT but not the whole: It is Goodness plus God's command that determines what is right. But the question arises, what does God add to rightness that is not there simply with Goodness? It is not simply that God *knows* more outcomes than we, for the autonomy thesis would gladly grant that. If love or Goodness prescribes act A, what does A gain by being commanded by God? Materially, nothing at all.

In a later article, "Divine Command Metaethics Modified Again" (see Note 4), Adams seeks to make a distinction that might answer the objection just made. He tries to distinguish between two senses of ethics: the real one and the functionally equivalent one. Both the DCT and autonomous ethics might result in the same principles, but they are nonetheless not the same. He refers to Saul Kripke's thesis of natural kinds. It goes something like this: Suppose that on some other planet (or someplace on our planet) there is a substance W that seems functionally equivalent to what we call water. Would 'W' be water? Kripke says no. Water is necessarily H_2O, and anything that is functionally equivalent to water but not H_2O would not be water, no matter how similar in taste, touch, and physiological effects. Likewise, avers Adams, although ethical principles that do not arise from God may be functionally equivalent to those that do, they are nonetheless not really *ethical* principles; they are simply look-alikes.

How valid is this analogy between water and ethics? It seems to be a distinction without a difference. For if both ethics (MDCT) and secular ethics have human (or 'sentient beings') flourishing as the goal, what difference should it make whether the very same principle issues from a special personal authority (God) or from the authority of reason? After all, don't we need to use reason even to adjudicate revelatory claims to divine authority? Otherwise, how could we distinguish the devil's commands from God's?

If we reject this position and with it the divine command theory itself, then we need to consider the implications of the second horn of Euthyphro's dilemma—that which posits God commanding the Good because it is good.

At this point it must be asked whether there is any need for theists to go to such enormous pains in order to save the divine command theory. Why should they be threatened by the autonomy thesis? If there is an inherent logic to goodness that precludes God's inventing right and wrong, why should that bother religious people? It is widely recognized that God's omnipotence isn't threatened by the fact that the laws of logic exist independently of him. Why should the fact that there is a logic to ethics threaten the notion of God's sovereignty or omnipotence? Couldn't it be the case that God's sovereignty comes in, not at the point of inventing morality once creation is in place, but at the point of deciding what kinds of beings to create?

Suppose that God creates people on two planets in the universe: our Earth and Planet X. His creative will allows him to construct two admirable but different systems. We have some idea of how things work on Earth. On Planet X God created humanoids—beings like us but who have exometallic skeletons and limbs that replace themselves like our fingernails do, and who reproduce by spontaneously cloning their cells rather than by sexual intercourse. In fact beings on X are never tempted to fornicate or commit adultery (though disloyalty is a problem). Likewise, because they feel very little pain, torture is not a possibility (though suffering is).

On both Earth and X there are rules that are designed to ameliorate suffering and promote the survival and flourishing of rational beings. We have many rules in common—for example, rules prescribing truth-telling and beneficence and those proscribing disloyalty and the killing of innocents. But X does not have a rule against adultery or torture or dismembering humanoids.

God, who loves variety, could have created us like the beings on X, but he didn't. Had he done so, we would have some different moral rules than we in fact do. Instead, he chose to make us the way we are, so that certain rules of conduct are necessary for our survival and well-being. These rules are necessary, for even God can't change them now that he has made us the way we are. Moral right and wrong are solid facts, just as solid as those of arithmetic or logic or chemistry.

If this is correct, then morality has an independent rationale. It may indirectly depend on God, assuming he exists, in that he could have created us with a different nature; but once God creates rational beings like us, the moral law takes on a life of its own that even God must respect.

Of course, the question that takes precedence here is whether there is a God and whether he or she is totally benevolent, but this takes us into metaphysics and philosophy of religion, subjects outside the scope of this work.

We turn now to our second question.

ARE RELIGIOUS ETHICS ESSENTIALLY DIFFERENT FROM SECULAR ETHICS?

The second problem related to the matter of religion and morality has to do with the relationship between religion and secular morality. Are they essentially compatible or incompatible? We can divide this question into two subquestions: Does religion actually do moral harm and detract from deep morality? and Does religion provide, and do secular systems fail to provide, ethics with the necessary motivation to be deeply moral?

According to Immanuel Kant (1724–1804), who held to the autonomy thesis, there could be no difference between valid religious ethics and valid philosophical ethics—God and humanity both have to obey the same rational principles, and reason is sufficient to guide us to these principles:

[Christianity] has enriched philosophy with far more definite and purer concepts than it had been able to furnish before; but which, once they are there, are freely assented to by Reason and are assumed as concepts to which it could well have come of itself and

which it could and should have introduced. . . . Even the Holy One
of the Gospels must first be compared with our ideal of moral
perfection, before we can recognize him as such.[5]

Kant's system exalts ethics to an intrinsic good; indeed, doing one's
duty for no other reason but that it is one's duty is the highest good there
is. As such it is related to religion; it is as our duty to God. God loves the
virtuous and finally will reward the virtuous with happiness in proportion
to their virtue. In fact, God and immortality are necessary postulates of
ethics. Immortality is necessary in this way: According to Kant, we are
commanded by the moral law to be morally perfect. Since 'ought' implies
'can', we must be *able* to reach moral perfection. But we cannot attain
perfection in this life, for the task is an infinite one. So there must be an
afterlife in which we continue to make progress toward this ideal.

God is a necessary postulate in that there must be someone to enforce
the moral law; that is, in order for the moral law to be completely justified
there must finally result a just recompense of happiness in accordance to
virtue. The good must be rewarded by happiness in proportion to their
virtue and the evil punished in proportion to their vice. This harmonious
correlation of virtue and happiness does not happen in this life, so it must
happen in the next life. So there must be a God, acting as judge and
enforcer of the moral law, without which the moral law would be unjustified.

Kant is not saying that we can *prove* that God exists or that we ought to
be moral *in order* to be happy; rather, the idea of God serves as a completion
of our ordinary ideas of ethics. Is Kant right about this?

Is Religion Irrelevant or Even Inimical to Morality?

Many secularists, including Bertrand Russell and Kai Nielsen, have
argued that morality has no need of God: One can be moral and, within
the limits of thoughtful stoic resignation, even happy without God. The
world may well be a product of blind evolutionary striving—ultimately
absurd—but this doesn't remove our duty to fill our lives with meaning
and goodness. As Russell put it, "Nature, omnipotent but blind, in the
revolutions of her secular hurryings through the abysses of space, has
brought forth at last a child, subject still to her power, but gifted with sight,
with knowledge of good and evil, with the capacity of judging all the works
of his unthinking Mother."[6] It is this conscious power of moral evaluation
that makes the child superior to his omnipotent Mother. He is free to think,
to evaluate, to create, and to live committed to ideals. So in spite of
suffering, despair, and death, humans are free; life has the meaning that we
give it, and morality will be part of any meaningful life.

But theists may counter that secularists like Russell are "whistling in the dark." George Mavrodes has criticized Russell's secular view as puzzling.[7] If there is no God, then doesn't secular ethics suffer from a certain inadequacy? Mavrodes argues that the Russellian world of secular morality can't satisfactorily answer the question, "Why should I be moral?" For, on its account, the common goods, which morality in general aims at, are often just those that we sacrifice in carrying out our moral obligations. Why should we sacrifice our welfare for our moral duty?

The second oddity about secular ethics, according to Mavrodes, is that it is superficial—is not deeply rooted; it seems to lack that metaphysical basis that a Platonic or Judeo-Christian worldview affords:

> Values and obligations cannot be deep in such a [secular] world. What is deep in a Russellian world must be such things as matter and energy, or perhaps natural law, chance, or chaos. If it really were a fact that one had obligations in a Russellian world, then something would be laid upon man that might cost a man everything but that went no further than man. And that difference from a Platonic world seems to make all the difference.[8]

Of course, the secularist will continue the debate. If what I have argued in the previous chapter is correct, then secular morality based on a notion of the good life is inspiring in itself, for it promotes human flourishing and can be shown to be in all of our interests, whether or not a God exists. It may not need a metaphysical base to serve the needs that many of us believe it should serve.

Some secularists—call them antireligious—go even further than Russell and Nielsen. They claim that it is not the case that religious and secular morality are similar, but that religious morality is an inferior brand of morality that actually prevents deep moral development. Both P. H. Nowell-Smith and James Rachels have argued that religion is (or gives rise to) an inferior morality.[9] Both base their contention on the notion of autonomy. Nowell-Smith's argument is based on child psychologist Jean Piaget's research in child development. Very small children have to be taught to value rules. When they do, they tend to hold tenaciously to those rules, even when games or activities would seem to call for a suspension of the rules. For example, suppose there are ten children and a rectangular lot that is not large enough to contain on complete baseball field. Some children might object to playing baseball with only five on a side and no right field because it violates the official rules. Religious morality, in being deontologically rule-governed, is analogous to those children, who have not understood the wider purposes of the rules of games; it is an infantile morality.

Rachels's argument alleges that believers give up their autonomy in worship and so are immoral. He writes:

1. If any being is God, he must be a fitting object of worship.
2. No being could possibly be a fitting of worship, since worship requires the abandonment of one's role as an autonomous moral agent.
3. Therefore, there cannot be any being who is God.

Are these sound arguments? They seem to have problems. Take Nowell-Smith's contention that religious morality is infantile: Perhaps some religious people and some secularists as well are rigidly and unreasonably rule-bound, but not all religious people are. Indeed, Jesus himself broke the rule for the Sabbath day in order to heal and do good, saying, "the Sabbath was made for man, not man for the Sabbath." Does not the strong love-motif in New Testament religious morality indicate that the rules are seen as serving a purpose—the human good?

In Rachels's argument, isn't premise 2 false? In worshipping God, a person need not give up one's reason. Doesn't a rational believer need to use reason to distinguish the good from the bad, the holy from what is not holy? A mature believer does not (or need not) sacrifice his or her reason or autonomy in worship, but rather these traits are part and parcel of what worship entails. The command to love God is for one to love him with one's whole *mind* as well as one's heart and strength. If there is a God, he must surely want us to be intelligent and discriminating and sensitive in all of our deliberations. Being a religious worshipper in no way entails or condones intellectual suicide.

Of course, a believer may submit his or her judgment to God's, when there is good evidence that God has given a judgment. If this is sacrificing one's autonomy, then it only shows that autonomy is not an absolute value, but rather a significant prima facie value. If I am working in the physics laboratory with Albert Einstein, whom I have learned to trust as a competent authority, and he advises me to do something different from what my amateurish calculations dictate, I am likely to defer to his authority. But I don't thereby give up my autonomy: I freely and rationally give up my judgment because in these matters Einstein simply is a better judge and I may not be able to understand the complex mathematics needed to explain his reasons. One could say, "I autonomously give up my first-order autonomy." Likewise, the believer may submit to God whenever he or she judges God's authority to override one's own finite judgment; it seems eminently rational to give up that kind of autonomy. To do otherwise would make autonomy into foolhearty recalcitrance.

Does Religion Enhance the Moral Life?

Contrary to the contentions of philosophers like Nowell-Smith and Rachels (and even Russell and Nielsen), there may be some morally relevant advantages to theism. Theists argue that there are at least five ways in which morality may be enriched by religion. Let me briefly describe them for your reflection.

1. If there is a God, good will win out over evil. We're not fighting alone—God is on our side in the battle. Neither are we fighting in vain—we'll win eventually. This thought of the ultimate victory of goodness gives us confidence to go on in the fight against injustice and cruelty when others calculate that the odds against righteousness are too great to oppose.

2. If theism is true, there is a God who loves and cares for us—his love compels us (II Corinthians 5:7) so that we have a deeper motive for morally good actions, including high altruism. We live deeply moral lives because of deep gratitude to One who loves us and whom we love. Secularism lacks this sense of cosmic love. Whether or not human love is adequate to inspire the same type of high altruism is an interesting question, but human history has not given an affirmative answer. Perhaps the future will be different, but most of those whom we consider moral saints are also religious ones—Moses, Jesus, St. Francis, Gandhi, Martin Luther King, Jr., and Mother Teresa. You need special love to leave a world of comfort in order to go to a desolate island to minister to lepers, as Father Damian did.

3. If God exists, cosmic justice reigns in the universe. The scales are perfectly balanced so that everyone will get what he or she deserves according to his or her moral merit. There is no moral luck (unless you interpret the grace that will finally prevail as a type of 'luck'), but rather each will be judged according to how one has used one's talents (Matthew 25). This also gives an unambiguous answer to the question (discussed in the previous chapter), "Why be moral?" "Because it has an eternal and exact payoff" is the unequivocal answer.

4. If there is a God who created us in his image, then all persons are of equal worth because it is claimed by theism that God values us all equally. If we are all his children, then we are all brothers and sisters; we are family and ought to treat each other benevolently, as we would family members of equal worth. Indeed, modern secular moral and political systems often assume this equal worth of the individual without justifying it. But without

the parenthood of God, it makes no sense to say that all persons are innately of equal value. From a perspective of intelligence and utility, Aristotle and Nietzsche seem to be right; there are enormous inequalities, and why shouldn't the superior persons use the baser types to their advantage? In this regard, secularism, in rejecting inegalitarianism, seems to be "living off of the interest of a religious capital" that it has relinquished.

5. If God exists and is benevolent and all-powerful, then, according to most forms of theism, he will not allow us to rot. Death is not the end of our existence, but we shall live on, recognizing each other in a better world. We have eternity in our souls and are destined for a higher existence (of course, hell is a problem here that may cause difficulties with this sort of reasoning, but that doctrine may be defensible on reflection, or it may turn out at last that everyone is saved, as the second-century theologians Origen, Frederick Maurice, and Karl Barth maintained). So if theism is true, the world is a friendly home in which we are all related as siblings in one family, destined to live forever in cosmic bliss in a reality in which good defeats evil.

In sum, if theism is false, then it may be doubtful whether all humans have equal worth, or any worth at all, and it may be more difficult to provide an unequivocal response to the question "Why be moral, even when it is not in my best interest?" If there is no sense of harmony and objective purpose in the universe, many of us will conclude that we are sadder and poorer because of it.

Add to this the fact that theism doesn't deprive us of any autonomy that we have in nontheistic systems. If we are equally free to choose the good or the evil whether or not God exists (assuming that the notions of good and evil make sense in a nontheistic universe), then it seems plausible to assert that in some ways the world of the theist is better and more satisfying than one in which God does not exist. It could also be the case that through revelation the theist has access to deeper moral truths that are not available to the secularist.

Of course, two important points may be made on the other side. First, a lot of evil has been done by religious people in the name of religion; we need only look at our own sordid history of heresy hunts and religious wars, some of which are still being fought. Religion may be used as a powerful weapon with which to harm others. Second, we don't know for sure whether there is a benevolent deity who is the creator of the universe and who created us in his image. Furthermore, we don't have the kind of irrefutable evidence needed to prove that our interpretation of God's will and ways is the right one. Religion is based largely on faith, not hard evidence, so that it behooves believers to be modest about their policies. It would seem that most of us are more certain about the core of our morality than about the central doctrines of theology. So it might be inappropriate to require society to give up a morality based on reason for some injunctions based on revelation. Sometimes religious authority claims to put forth a command that conflicts with our best rational judgments and gives rise to the kind of a confrontation that can rip society apart. An example of this possibility is Iran's Ayatollah Khomeini's command to kill author Salman Rushdie for writing his allegedly blasphemous book, *Satanic Verses*. The late Ayatollah's views on the immoralty of blasphemy and what such blasphemy deserves conflicted with our notions of free speech and tolerance. People were killed in riots and bookstores were bombed as a result of this conflict. This is the kind of thing that deeply worries the secularist who sees religion as a threat to society. It is a legitimate concern that may take all of our ingenuity to solve in the years ahead.

Our hope in solving such problems rests in working out an adequate morality on which theists and nontheists alike can agree. If there is, as I have argued elsewhere, an ethics of belief, then we can apply rational scrutiny to our religious beliefs, as well as to all our other beliefs, and work toward a better understanding of the status of our belief systems.[10] It is a challenge that should inspire the best minds, for it may turn out that it is not science or technology, but rather deep, comprehensive ethical theory and moral living, that will not only save our world, but solve its perennial problems and produce a state of flourishing.[11]

Notes

1. Plato, *Euthyphro,* trans. William Jowett (Charles Scribner's Sons, 1889).

2. Carl F. H. Henry, *Christian Personal Ethics* (Eerdmans, 1957), p. 210f.

3. Quoted in *Divine Command Morality*, ed. J. M. Idziak (Mellon, 1979).

4. Robert M. Adams, "A Modified Divine Command Theory of Ethical Wrongness," in *Religion and Morality: A Collection of Essays*, eds. Gene Outka and John P. Reeder (Anchor, 1973). I have not been able to respond to all of the richness of this challenging article. The major portion of this essay is reprinted in my anthology, *Philosophy of Religion* (Wadsworth, 1987), pp. 525–537). For convenience, the page numbers cited in this text refer to that anthology. Adams's "Divine Command Metaethics Modified Again" is in the *Journal of Religious Ethics* (1979). Philip Quinn's *Divine Commands and Moral Requirements* (Oxford University Press, 1978) is a closely argued defense of a position very similar to Adams's.

5. Immanuel Kant, *Critique of Judgment*, trans. J. Bernard (Haefner, 1951), p. 410, and *Fundamental Principles of the Metaphysics of Ethics*, trans. T. K. Abbott (Longmans, Green, 1898).

6. Bertrand Russell, "A Free Man's Worship" in Louis Pojman, *Ethical Theory* (Wadsworth, 1989), pp. 528–532. Consider also the comment of my student, Laura Burrell (University of Mississippi):

> God is like a cosmic gardener—he tends and protects individual morality, he nourishes it and helps it bloom. Some people, like a hothouse orchid or a rancy rose, do seem to need religion for their morality to have a purpose or justification. Others are like the Queen Anne's Lace (qal)—able to withstand almost anything on their own. And many are borderline qal, who need just that extra bit of fertilizer to break into bloom—and God provides it. But mankind could do as well. The relationship between God and morality is as simple as that—God is a parent, gardener, etc. He strengthens and cushions individual morality, he gives motivation (in the form of the outcomes: heaven or hell) and justice and order in a sometimes extremely chaotic world. But morality exists apart from God, and as hard as it is for some to accept it, could survive and even flourish in a world without God.

7. George Mavrodes, "Religion and the Queerness of Morality," in Pojman, *Ethical Theory*, pp. 532–540.

8. Mavrodes, "Religion and the Queerness of Morality," p. 539.

9. P. H. Nowell-Smith, "Morality: Religious and Secular," in Pojman, *Philosophy of Religion*, pp.497–507; James Rachels, "God and Human Attitudes," in *Religious Studies* (1971); reprinted with a reply by Philip Quinn in Paul Helm, ed., *Divine Commands and Morality* (Oxford, 1979).

10. See Louis Pojman, *Religious Belief and the Will* (Routlege & Kegan Paul, 1986), Chapter XIV.

11. I am indebted to Michael Beaty and an anonymous reviewer for criticisms of an earlier draft of this chapter.

For Further Reflection

1. Imagine that a superior being appears to you and says, "I am God and I am good; therefore, obey me when I tell you to torture your mother." How would a proponent of the divine command theory deal with this problem? How would a proponent of the modified command theory deal with it?

2. Recall Leo Tolstoy's statement quoted at the beginning of this chapter:

"The attempts to found a morality apart from religion are like the attempts of children who, wishing to transplant a flower that pleases them, pluck it from the roots that seem to them unpleasing and superfluous, and stick it rootless into the ground. Without religion there can be no real, sincere morality, just as without roots there can be no real flower ["Religion and Morality," in *Leo Tolstoy: Selected Essays*, trans. Aylmer Maude (Random House, 1964), p. 31f].

Evaluate this statement.

3. In your judgement, how important is religion for a meaningful life? How would a secularist respond to the five claims made in favor of religion's ability to procure added meaning in life? Do you think that religion really does provide added meaning to life?

4. Karl Marx said that religion was the opium of the people (today, the metaphor might better be changed to "cocaine" or "crack"): It deludes them into thinking that all will be well with the world, leading to passive acceptance of evil and injustice. Is there some truth in Marx's dictum? How would a theist respond to this?

5. Discuss the matter of the problems connected with religious revelation and rational morality. What if one's religion prohibits certain types of speech and requires the death penalty for them, such as was the case when the Ayatollah Khomeini condemned the author Salman Rushdie to death for blasphemous words in the novel *Satanic Verses*? Some religious people believe that abortion or homosexual behavior is morally wrong based on religious authority. How should a secular ethicist who believes that these practices are not morally wrong argue with the believer? Can there be rational dialogue?

For Further Reading

Helm, Paul, ed. *The Divine Command Theory of Ethics*. Oxford University Press, 1979. Contains valuable articles by Frankena, Rachels, Quinn, Adams, and Young.

Kant, Immanuel. *Religion within the Bounds of Reason Alone*, tr. T. M. Greene and H. H. Hudson. Harper and Row, 1960.

Kierkegaard, Soren. *Fear and Trembling*, trans. Howard and Edna Hong. Princeton University Press, 1983.

Mitchell, Basil. *Morality: Religious and Secular*. Oxford University Press, 1980.

Nielsen, Kai. *Ethics without God*. Pemberton Books, 1973. A very accessible defense of secular morality.

Outka, Gene, and J. P. Reeder, eds. *Religion and Morality: A Collection of Essays*. Anchor Books, 1973. Contains important essays, especially Robert M. Adams's "A Modified Divine Command Theory of Ethical Wrongness."

Pojman, Louis, ed. *Ethical Theory: Classical and Contemporary Readings*. Wadsworth, 1989. Part XI contains important essays by Kant, Bertrand Russell, George Mavrodes, and Kai Nielsen.

Quinn, Philip. *Divine Commands and Moral Requirements*. Clarendon Press, 1978.

Robinson, Richard. *An Atheist's Values*. Clarendon Press, 1964.

Ward, Keith. *Ethics and Christianity*. George Allen & Unwin, 1970.

GLOSSARY

Absolute   A moral absolute is a principle that is universally binding; it applies to all people at all times and it can never be overridden by another principle. Utilitarianism is a type of system that has only one absolute principle, 'Do that action which maximizes utility.' Kant's system has several absolutes, whereas other deontological systems may have only a few broad absolutes, such as 'Never cause unnecessary harm.'

Absolutism or **Ethical Absolutism**   Refers to the notion that there is only one correct answer to every moral problem. A completely absolutist ethic is one made up of absolute principles that provide an answer for every possible situation in life regardless of culture. Diametrically opposed to ethical absolutism is *ethical relativism*, which says that the validity of ethical principles is dependent on social acceptance. In between these polar opposites is *ethical objectivism*. See **Objectivism**; **Relativism**.

Agapism   (from the Greek *agape*, altrustic love) An ethical theory based on the principle of love. Sometimes this is based in the New Testament injunctions to love (Matt 22:37–40; I Corinthians 13). *Act-agapism* holds that one ought always do whatever is the most loving thing to do; this has been called "situational ethics." *Rule-agapism* holds that we ought to follow the most love-embodying set of rules.

Altruism   Unselfish regard or concern for others; disinterested, other-regarding action. See Chapter 3; see also **Egoism**.

Aretaic Ethics   (from the Greek *arete*, virtue) The theory, first presented by Aristotle, that the basis of ethical assessment is character. Rather than seeing the heart of ethics in actions or duties, it focuses on the character and dispositions of the agent. Whereas *deontological* and *teleological* ethical systems emphasize *doing*, aretaic or virtue ethics emphasizes *being*—being a certain type of person who will no doubt manifest his or her being in appropriate actions. See Chapter 7.

Autonomy   (from the Greek for "self-rule") Self-directed freedom. The autonomous individual arrives at his or her moral judgments through reason, rather than simply accepting authority. The autonomy thesis states that ethical truths can be known and justified on the basis of human reason without the need for divine revelation. See Chapters 6 and 10; see also **Heteronomy**.

Categorical Imperative   The categorical imperative commands actions that are necessary of themselves without reference to other ends. This is contrasted with **Hypothetical Imperatives**, which command actions not for their own sakes but for some other good. For Kant, moral duties command categorically; they represent the injunctions of reason, which endows them with universal validity and objective necessity. See Chapter 6; see also **Hypothetical Imperative**.

199

Cognitivism   The theory that claims that moral judgments have truth-value. That is, such statements as 'lying is morally wrong' are not simply an expression of negative feelings toward lying but express an objective truth about lying, namely that it has a wrong-making quality (for example, it is bad). Such judgments are made true or false by reference to properties, either natural (for example, an object of desire or pleasure) or nonnatural (for example, Moore's simple unanalyzable property discovered by intuition). If the right property is present, the judgment is true; if it isn't, the judgment is false. See Chapter 8; see also **Noncognitivism**.

Cultural Relativism   The theory that different cultures have different moral rules. It makes no judgment on the validity of those rules, and, as such, is neutral between **Ethical Objectivism** and **Ethical Relativism**. Sometimes the moral systems of a culture are referred to as *positive morality*: any existing moral code as distinguished from an adequate or justified moral code. For example, Nazi morality is a moral code, but most objectivists would deny that it is an adequate or justified moral code. It contains invalid principles such as 'Always kill Jews and gypsies and Poles.' See Chapter 2; see also **Objectivism** and **Ethical Relativism**.

Deontic   (from the Greek *deon*, duty or obligation)   Refers to action-based ethical systems, such as deontological and teleological systems, and the type of judgment (that is, evaluations of actions) that proceed from these systems, as opposed to judgments of motivation and character that flow from aretaic systems. See Chapter 7; see also **Aretaic Ethics**.

Deontological Ethics   (from the Greek *deon,* duty or obligation)   Ethical systems that consider certain features in the moral act itself to have intrinsic value. These are contrasted with **Teleological Ethics** (below), which hold that the ultimate criterion of morality lies in some nonmoral value that results from actions. For example, for the deontologist, there is something right about truth-telling, even when it may cause pain or harm, and there is something wrong about lying even when it may produce good consequences. See Chapters 5 and 6.

Divine Command Theory   The theory that holds that moral terms are defined in terms of God's commands or that moral duties are logically dependent on God's commands. See Chapter 10.

Egoism   *Psychological egoism* is a *descriptive* theory about human motivation that holds that people always act to satisfy their perceived best interests. *Ethical egoism* is a *prescriptive* or normative theory about how people *ought* to act; they ought to act according to their perceived best interests. See Chapter 3.

Emotivism   A version of **Noncognitivism** that holds that moral judgments do not have truth-values but are expressions of our attitudes; they express our feelings and serve as a mechanism for persuasion of others to act as we desire. A. J. Ayer, a prominent emotivist, held that the moral judgment that murder is wrong reduces to the emotional expression "Murder—Boo!" See Chapter 8.

Ethical Relativism   Holds that the validity of moral judgments depends on cultural acceptance. It is opposed to **Objectivism** (below) and **Absolutism** (above). See Chapter 2.

Euthyphro Dilemma   Refers to the puzzle set forth in Plato's dialogue, the **Euthyphro**, in which Socrates asks whether God loves the pious because it is pious or whether what is pious is pious because God loves it. It is associated with the

Divine Command Theory (above) and the **Autonomy Thesis**. See Chapter 10.

Hedon (from the Greek *hedone*, pleasure) Possessing pleasurable or painful quality. Sometimes 'hedon' is used to stand for a quantity of pleasure.

Hedonism *Psychological hedonism* is the theory that motivation is to be explained exclusively in terms of desire for pleasure and aversion from pain. *Ethical hedonism* is the theory that pleasure is the only intrinsic positive value and that pain or "unpleasant consciousness" the only thing that has negative intrinsic value (or intrinsic disvalue). All other values are derived from these two. See Chapter 4.

Heteronomy Kant's term for the determination of the will on nonrational grounds. It is contrasted with **Autonomy of the Will** in which the will is guided by reason.

Hypothetical Imperative Hypothetical imperatives are commands that enjoin actions because they are useful for the attainment of some end that one desires to obtain. Ethicists who regard moral duties as dependent on consequences would view moral principles as hypothetical imperatives. They have the form: 'If you want X, do action A' (for example, 'If you want to live in peace, do all in your power to prevent violence'). This is contrasted with the **Categorical Imperative** (above). See Chapter 6.

Intuitionism The ethical theory that the good or the right thing to do can be known directly via the intuition. G. E. Moore (Chapter 8) and W. D. Ross (Chapter 6) hold different versions of this view. Moore is an intuitionist about the good, defining it as a simple, unanalyzable property; Ross is an intuitionist about what is right.

Metaethics The theoretical study that inquires into semantic, logical, and epistemological issues in ethics. It investigates the meaning of ethical terms, the nature of value judgments, and the matter of how ethical theories and judgments can be justified. A central metaethical issue is the relation of facts to values (see Chapter 8). Metaethics is contrasted with *normative ethics*, which constructs ethical theories and makes moral judgments from within various theoretical frameworks.

Naturalism The theory that ethical terms are defined through factual terms, in that ethical terms refer to natural properties. *Ethical hedonism* is one version of ethical naturalism, for it states that the Good, which is at the basis of all ethical judgment, refers to the experience of pleasure. Naturalists such as Geoffrey Warnock speak of the content of morality in terms of promoting human flourishing or ameliorating the human predicament. See Chapter 8.

Noncognitivism The theory that ethical judgments have no truth-value but rather express attitudes or prescriptions. See **Cognitivism; Emotivism; Prescriptivism**; see also Chapter 8.

Objectivism (or **Ethical Objectivism**) The view that moral principles have objective validity whether or not people recognize them as such; that is, moral rightness or wrongness does not depend on social approval, but on such independent considerations as whether the act or principle promotes human flourishing or ameliorates human suffering. Objectivism differs from **Absolutism** (above) in that it allows that all or many of our principles are overridable in given situations. See Chapter 2; see also **Ethical Relativism; Absolutism**.

Paradox of Hedonism   This is the apparent contradiction that arises between two hedonistic theses: that pleasure is the only thing worth seeking and that whenever one seeks pleasure, it is not found; pleasure normally arises as an accompaniment of satisfaction of desire whenever one reaches one's goal. See Chapter 4.

Prescriptivism   The noncognitivist theory, set forth by R. M. Hare (Chapter 8) that claims that although moral judgments do not have truth values, they are more than mere expressions of attitudes; moral judgments are universal prescriptions. For example, the judgment that Mary should have an abortion implies that *anyone* in circumstances relevantly similar to Mary's should have an abortion.

Prima Facie   The Latin word that means "at first glance." It signifies an initial status of an idea or principle. In ethics, beginning with W. D. Ross, it stands for a duty that has a presumption in its favor but may be overridden by another duty. *Prima facie* duties are contrasted with *actual duties* or *all-things-considered-duties*.

Relativism   Cultural Relativism (above) is the descriptive thesis that states that there is enormous variety of moral beliefs across cultures; it is neutral concerning whether this is the way things ought to be. **Ethical Relativism** (above), on the other hand, is an evaluative thesis that holds that the truth of a moral judgment depends on whether or not a culture recognizes the principle in question. See Chapter 2.

Skepticism   The view that we can have no knowledge. *Universal skepticism* holds that we cannot know anything at all, whereas *local* or *particular skepticism* holds that there are important realms in which we are ignorant (for example, Hume regarding metaphysics). *Moral skepticism* is the view that we cannot know whether there is any moral truth.

Slippery Slope Fallacy   The fallacy of objecting to a proposition on the erroneous grounds that the prososition, if accepted, will lead to a chain of other propositions that will eventually result in an absurdity. For example, I might object to the statement that some people are rich in the following manner: You will agree that owning only one cent does not make one rich and that adding one cent to whatever we own will not in itself make anyone rich. So imagine that I have only one cent and then imagine giving me an additional penny. I still am not rich. You can give me as many pennies as you like but at no point will you change my status from being poor to being rich. Even though I might eventually end up with a million dollars' worth of pennies, there is no point where the transition from poverty to wealth takes place. Therefore neither I nor anyone else can be rich. This, of course, is false.

Solipsism   The view that only I exist (asserted by the speaker); everyone else merely exists in my mind. *Moral solipsism* is the view that only I am worthy of moral consideration; it is an extreme form of egoism. See Chapter 3.

Supererogatory   (from the Latin *supererogatus*, beyond the call of duty) A supererogatory act is one that is not required by moral principles but contains enormous value; it is "beyond the call of duty," such as risking one's life to save a stranger. Although most moral systems allow for the possibility of supererogatory acts, some theories (most versions of classical utilitarianism) deny that there can be such acts.

Teleological Ethics   Teleological ethical theories place the ultimate criterion of morality in some nonmoral value (for example, happiness or welfare) that results from acts. Whereas **Deontological Ethics** (above) ascribe intrinsic value to features of the acts themselves, teleological theories see only instrumental value in the acts, but intrinsic value in the consequences of those acts. Both **Ethical Egoism** (above) and **Utilitarianism** (below) are teleological theories. See Chapters 3 and 5.

Universalizability   The principle, found explicitly in Kant's and R. M. Hare's philosophy and implicitly in most ethicists' work, that states that if some act is right (or wrong) for one person in a situation, then it is right (or wrong) for any relevantly similar person in that kind of a situation. It is a principle of consistency that aims to eliminate irrelevant considerations from ethical assessment. See Chapter 8 and **Prescriptivism**.

Utilitarianism   The theory that the right action is that which maximizes utility. Sometimes 'utility' is defined in terms of *pleasure* (Jeremy Bentham), *happiness* (J. S. Mill), *ideals* (G. E. Moore and H. Rashdall), or *interests* (R. B. Perry). Its motto, which characterizes one version of utilitarianism, is "The Greatest Happiness for the Greatest Number." Utilitarians further divide into *Act-* and *Rule-Utilitarians*. Act-utilitarians hold that the right act in a situation is that which results (or is most likely to result) in the best consequences, whereas Rule-utilitarians hold that the right act is that which conforms to the set of rules that in turn will result in the best consequences (relative to other sets of rules). See Chapter 5.